LOS

MANCHESTER

TOURIN' AMERICA

Dalia

Rock N Roll Never Dies!

N. C...

N.J. CARTNER

ISBN: 978-1-915147-39-4 (Paperback)
ISBN: 978-1-915147-41-7 (Ebook)

Book Design by HMDpublishing

To My Parents - Thank you for the music

For Sheridana – Reasons for Seasons

*For every band or artist that deserved more
than this industry gave them*

THE FIVE MANTRAS FOR LIFE BY 'THE PEOPLE'S POET', RIK MAYALL

Equality – *All men are equal, therefore no one can ever be your genuine superior.*

Opportunity – *It is your future. It is yours to create. Your future is as bright as you make it.*

Wisdom – *Change is a constant in life. You must never ever lose your wisdom.*

Freedom – *If you want to live a full and complete human life you have to be free. Freedom is paramount.*

Love – *Love is* the answer

LOST IN MANCHESTER, TOURIN' AMERICA PROLOGUE

I was back in America with the endless open road stretching ahead of me. An adventure simmered on the horizon as I barrelled down the dusty highway that pierced the desolate lands of the West. The brutal desert cauldron loomed ahead, and a transcendent echo consumed the metallic red Chevy Malibu. It was the seductive opening guitar work to 'The Chain' by Fleetwood Mac, a fitting song for such a journey.

The incandescent sun hung overhead and battered the sweltering tarmac, creating a mirage effect in the eye-straining distance. I plunged further into the unknown wilderness, hypnotised by its mysteries, curious to discover the secretive and spectacular kingdom.

The first part of the song ended and gave way to the unmistakable bassline made famous by Formula One Racing. As it kicked into gear, I became overwhelmed by an irresistible urge to see how much faster I could go. My foot slammed down like I was powering my way to victory at Monaco. The hairs on the back of my neck tingled, and I repeatedly beat the steering wheel as the song climaxed. I was perilously close to topping 100mph and risking an encounter with a rookie cop out to make a name for himself. But right then, worry over such threats was non-existent. An inner rebellion and sense of pushing boundaries prevailed over conformity.

The warped energy that had momentarily devoured me started to wane as the song faded into the background. I eased my foot off the 'gas' and waited for the next offering on a carefully thought-out *America Road Trip* playlist.

'Heart of Gold' by Neil Young began, and the calming nature of the track caused my mind to drift. I recollected how I found myself on a once in a lifetime endeavour that was too unbelievable to imagine only twenty-four hours earlier.

I had taken off from my home city, Manchester, and landed in San Francisco with vastly different intentions. After a brief phone conversation upon landing, I found myself boarding another flight to the dazzling city of Las Vegas for one night only. Then I was instructed to drive the long road to Tucson, Arizona. The reason? I, Ricky Lever, had been given the opportunity to tour with one of the most promising rock bands in the UK. The band, Cutthroat Shambles, also hailed from Manchester, and they were causing quite a stir with their fiery blend of rock music. In a self-profiting twist of fate, I found myself being the man invited to document and blog the whole journey for the music fanzine I wrote for, Sonic Bandwagon.

The events that led me on this enlightened path began months earlier. The split from my ex-girlfriend, Mandy, had left me questioning my existence and purpose. I realised that life had passed me by. My soul and spirit were crushed beyond belief, assisted by my dire, meaningless work situation - customer services for an insurance company. I was just another pawn on the chessboard, cannon fodder to society, hampered by a career I despised where I was meant to be thankful for the opportunity to exist like an amoeba. The only perk of the day was looking forward to the next caffeine hit from a stale cup of coffee. It wasn't a life.

The catalyst for change came in the form of a six-night adventure in Las Vegas with three of my best friends. I daringly vowed to return from that trip a new man with all the answers to the riddles that plagued my mind. The intensity of the euphoric highs and emotive lows culminated in a hazardous, soul-searching mission into the desert to find my true purpose.

It wasn't just the surreal desert experience, a hallucinogenic encounter with a lizard, or even everything that Vegas offered which contributed to altering my mindset. It was meeting my Puerto Rican rose, Eva Espinoza, that perhaps had the biggest impact. She had seduced me on the first night with her striking beauty, intoxicating character, and spiritual enlightenment. She was instrumental in helping me return from Vegas with a renewed vigour to make drastic life changes.

Shortly after returning home, my ambition to work in the music industry came to fruition. I became a part-time writer and reviewer for Sonic Bandwagon. They were building quite a reputation in the underground/ alternative scene as *the* go-to music magazine, featuring all the best up-and-coming bands and artists. I steadily learnt my craft and was still a little raw and inexperienced, but showed potential, according to the Chief Editor, Jamie Stacks.

I continued to work full-time at the insurance company, but I worked on another plan whilst gaining invaluable writing experience. That plan was to scrimp and save for nine months solid, so I could live my ultimate bucket list adventure - travelling across the enthralling lands of America. I could still contribute to the fanzine and write album reviews, which would give me extra pocket money for the trip.

When the time came, and I'd saved enough money, I plucked up the courage to quit my full-time job. Soon after, I was off on my travels. The only plan I had was to spend a few days in San Francisco to soak up the city's spirit and channel my inner hippie vibe. Then I was going to slowly make my way south to meet Eva at her home in San Diego, about 500 miles away.

We had remained in contact since Vegas, talking regularly online, but long-distance relationships rarely have a habit of surviving, so we weren't an exclusive couple. Besides, we'd never discussed it - but she had become a vital part of my life, and I ached to see her again.

Life has a funny way of suddenly changing direction, and upon arrival in San Francisco, it had twisted once again. Jamie from Sonic Bandwagon called me. He told me that the magazine had been invited to tag along with Cutthroat Shambles on their US tour. The aim was to provide regular blog updates about life on the road with a rock band. It was a project Jamie and his good friend and Cutthroat Shambles manager, Ozzie Joyce, had discussed for some time.

They wanted the magazine to develop a sixties/seventies Rolling Stone-type article for modern times. The hope was that it would help the band to be signed and enhance Sonic Bandwagon's reputation.

The original journalist given the task, Tommy Ashcroft, had built up a relationship with the band, but he had been having some personal issues with his wife and couldn't make the trip. Because of that, and with all other options fruitless, the only alternative was to ask me to pick up the baton due to the timing of my landing in San Francisco. My inexperience and lack of knowledge of the band weren't an issue. There was no other option but to send me on the campaign trail. I jumped at the chance, which scuppered my initial plans to meet with Eva at some point. When I explained the change in circumstances to her, she completely understood and told me that I would be stupid not to go.

As a side note, Jamie gave me a further warning about the lead singer, Dee Darrell, who had not taken the news about the last-minute switch of journalist too well. Still reeling from being presented with the task, I didn't fully take in the warning. I was too excited to be part of a plan that could help shape something special in music and culture.

CHAPTER 1

Dusk was setting in on our descent to Vegas, and the mesmeric lights on the tantalizing Strip stared back at me. It felt like I was returning to some sort of definition of home as I recalled how the place had shaped me nine months earlier.

I glided through the familiar corridors at McCarran Airport straight to baggage claim, flooded with nostalgia and ghosts from the past. Amazing how different my emotions and circumstances were on this occasion. The man who confidently strode to the taxi rank was completely unrecognisable to the downtrodden man who arrived months earlier.

There wasn't any air of desperation about this brief Vegas stay, nor any pressure to milk the city for all its worth by bingeing on booze and gambling and throwing myself balls deep into the hedonistic, wild nightlife. It wasn't an important part of my visit, simply a mere pimple of insignificance compared to the bigger picture ahead.

Sonic Bandwagon had booked me a cheap room at Hooters Casino & Hotel, situated off Las Vegas Blvd. Hooters had quite the reputation back home as being a bit sleazy, but in Vegas, sleaze and depravity were rife and welcomed underneath the false facade of the glitz and glamour.

The familiar sense of hope, fear, and decadence gripped the air as I drifted through the hotel lobby after check-in. Punters were relentless and robotic in their desultory quest for *that* big gambling win at the tables or slot machines. The subtle smell of cigarettes, pine, and polished wood brought back the memory of a Las Vegas casino, making me feel a contorted sense of security and cosiness.

The fifth-floor room was decent, certainly a step up from a Premier Inn or Travel Lodge, but not as plush as Planet Hollywood, where I'd stayed on my first round in Vegas.

I switched to professional mode, took out my laptop, logged onto the Wi-Fi, and downloaded the information Jamie had sent me about Cutthroat Shambles, or the Cutthroats, as they were known.

The tour was to last two weeks - Jamie must've got his wires crossed when he mentioned three weeks to me on the phone outside the airport.

On the trip, there was the band: lead singer, Dee Darrell; lead guitarist, Kyle Levitt; bassist, Will Thorley; and drummer, Josh 'Quince' Quincy. Then their manager, Ozzie Joyce, who had orchestrated the tour.

They had been in the States for three days already and had played a gig in Charlotte, North Carolina. They were due to play the following night in Tucson in a venue called Sky. We were staying at the residence of Bobby and Tien Brooks, but I was unsure as to their connection to the band.

I had heard of Cutthroat Shambles, but I hadn't had a chance to listen to any of their tracks. With so many bands in the scene, it was hard to keep track of all the ones that had a bit of buzz about them, especially when my focus was always on the next writing assignment.

I listened intently to each track and immersed myself in their world. I was impressed and recognised why they were held in such high esteem, which would make my job much easier. They had a commercial appeal but they were raw enough to not be pigeonholed into the current 'pop' scene. They suited the American market, fitting well with the dynamic Sunset Strip sound - innate riffs and a piercing vocal that could shatter glass.

It seemed strange they hadn't already been snapped up by a label. A few had shown interest, but Jamie revealed that a label based in Los Angeles, Lynwood Music, showed the most promise. It was rumoured that they would be monitoring the string of upcoming gigs. I guessed a lot was riding on each show as the band strove to demonstrate their worth.

Jamie had mentioned that the lead singer, Dee Darrell, was quite the volatile character. I was surprised to learn she was Bermudian and had moved to Manchester a few years earlier searching for her musical dream. The promo images of her were mainly onstage in full throttle. She looked like a true rock 'n' roller. Despite her diminutive stature, she appeared larger-than-life when thrust into the limelight. She had thick, jet-black, wavy hair that stretched down to the small of her back. Sometimes, it was stylishly tied up or even covered with a cowboy hat or bandana (that she mainly wore in posed promo shots away from the stage).

She wasn't blessed with soft facial features, but she oozed sex appeal in the form of high cheekbones, naturally plump, devilish lips, and penetrating eyes doused in hauntingly dark eye make-up. Tattoos plastered both her arms and shoulders, which completed her image as an eye-catching, edgy frontwoman.

Her singing style was described as powerful with a tremendous range. There was a comparison to Cher's prowess in her eighties rock heyday, but with the grit of Janis Joplin when required. The band were compared to a softer Metallica, with riffs and rhythm that rivalled AC/DC and poignant undertones like some of Led Zeppelin's more touching ballads.

There was less information about the rest of the band. Kyle Levitt was the lead guitarist, and from his photo, I knew he was someone who would get pulses racing in the female fan base. He was the quintessential image of a good-looking rock star, blessed with the fountain of youth and flirtatious eyes. He was clean-shaven with messy, long, dark brown hair, the kind that fell into place with minimal effort in the morning. A chic dress sense on a lean frame helped him look the part. His weapon of choice was a mahogany Parker Nitefly Guitar, which hung effortlessly from his shoulder like an extension to his arm. He was every wayward teenager's dream crush, with a too cool for school, rebel without a cause, glow about him.

Will Thorley, the bassist, posed with a red Fender Jazz Bass guitar. He was also a good-looking guy, with eyes as blue as the midday sky. Will was of average build with a rugged, stubbly face that contrasted with the freshness of Kyle and the devilishness of Dee. His hair covered his ears, thinned out with a bit of length to keep that musician demeanour about him.

Josh 'Quince' Quincy was the drummer and a beast of a man, as drummers tend to be. His arms were bulky, and his blonde hair was shaved at the sides with a long top style that he slicked back. A short goatee beard completed the intimidating Viking look. He looked like he could double up as the band's security if necessary - someone who could put a few beers away with one hand whilst bench pressing my body weight with the other.

As I let the band's music play in the background, I scoped the rest of the bio and itinerary. I was elated when I saw the places I was about to visit. Vegas to Tucson was thrilling enough from a road trip perspective without considering the rest of the tour. From Tucson, we would head east to El Paso, then back West to Phoenix, onto Flagstaff, Palm Springs, and finally Los Angeles to play at the famous Whisky a Go Go, earmarked as the main gig. I couldn't believe I would get to step inside such an iconic venue, so strongly connected to rock 'n' roll's history.

I had absorbed enough of the band's music, so I closed my laptop. I thought about going out for a beer, but considering how the place hooked me into its claws last time, I played it safe and decided an early night was the better option. *Great start to a rock 'n' roll adventure*, I thought. I felt ashamed, like I was doing a disservice to all that was sacred in that crazy city, but the trip wasn't about one night in Vegas. There was plenty of time for partying in the coming days. With a laborious drive to contend with the following day, coupled with having already travelled several hours on two planes, I let sense prevail and conserved my energy.

It was impossible to be in Vegas and not think of Eva and the time we shared. The reminiscing got the better of me, so I pulled out my phone, found her number in my recent logs, and hit 'Call'. She answered on the third ring.

'Hey there, Mr Englishman.'

Her soft Hispanic accent always melted me.

'Hey yourself. I hope I didn't wake you?'

'No. I was just lying on my bed thinking of you, and then my cell rings, and here you are. You must be psychic. Did you land safely?'

'Yeah, I'm in the hotel. It doesn't feel the same as last time.'

'Oh. Why's that?'

'I'm missing my mates, of course, and the crazy times we had,' I joked… with an element of truth.

'Ha. I'm sure you are missing them. Those guys were fun to hang with.'

'I'm missing you more.'

'Don't try and creep up to me now.'

We both laughed.

'It feels weird to be back here so soon, especially on my own,' I said.

'You must be excited?'

'I am, but I don't think it's properly sunk in yet. Only this morning, I thought I'd be in San Francisco for a few days before making my way down to see you. But here I am in Vegas, about to drive down to Tucson and hook up with a rock band that I have to write about.'

'This is your moment, cariño. I am so happy for you.'

'I'm a bit scared. Am I a good enough writer for something this big? I'm not sure I have the right experience for this.'

'Oh, we are having a dark night of the soul, aren't we?'

'Just me getting in the way of myself again.'

'You lack faith in yourself. You're talented. Write how you write, don't try and change. You've been given this opportunity for a reason.'

'Only because no one else could do it, and I was already here.'

'I'm sure they would've cancelled the idea if they thought you couldn't do it or flown someone over with more experience.'

'Perhaps. I don't know. I guess I'm just a bit anxious that the band will hate me given how I ended up here and that I'll fuck the blogs up.'

'Will you stop? Embrace this opportunity. It will be the making of you. I can feel it. Stop being afraid of what could go wrong and start being excited about what could go right. You've worked hard for this break, just reach out and grab it with both hands.'

'You always have a way of making me see things differently. You're a star.'

'Don't you forget it, cariño. When you're a rich and famous writer, I'll demand a commission off you.'

'You keep throwing pearls of wisdom at me, and we'll talk.'

'You're on. You should get some rest and be ready for that long drive tomorrow.'

'Ok. I wish you were here with me.'

'If I were there with you, you wouldn't be resting, believe me.'

'Don't put dirty thoughts in my head. Not now.'

'I'm just playing with you.'

'What did I just say?'

She laughed.

'Are you working tomorrow?' I asked.

'Sure am. I'll check-in with you if I get time. Be good, and don't forget what I told you. Enjoy and embrace this opportunity.'

'I will. Thanks…again…as usual.'

We said bye to each other.

I slumped onto the bed, where the smell of fresh sheets wrapped itself around me. After a few minutes of my mind wandering between Eva, the band, my writing, and the enormity of the task at hand, I fell into a deep slumber.

I woke up as sprightly as a Cocker Spaniel with two dicks, a juicy bone, a lamppost to piss on, and someone else's garden to shit in. My decision to not have a few beers or a late night felt justified. The familiar blast of the air con in a Las Vegas casino probably had something to do with the rekindled enthusiasm. It was like smelling salts filtered through from the ducts.

I picked my phone up to see two messages waiting for me. The first was from Eva: *'Life begins where fear ends.'* The inspirational quote from Osho gave me a shot of courage to start the day.

The other message was from Ozzie, the Cutthroats' manager: *'Looking forward to meeting you later Ricky. Any problems give me a shout. Heading to the gig at around 6pm. Not sure if you're aware but when you cross into Arizona the time will jump an hour so set off earlier if you didn't already know. Safe journey down pal. Cheers Ozzie.'*

It was something I did *not* already know and had not factored into my journey, so I was already an hour behind schedule. The first 'biffle' of the trip had been made. The term, biffle, was a phrase coined amongst my friendship group to describe a self-made error that caused a degree of embarrassment, inconvenience, anger, or discomfort.

I replied, telling him of my error, and he responded sharpish: *'Sorry I should've told you yesterday. No worries. Meet us at the venue if you're gonna be a bit late. I'll stick your name on the guest list. Come and find me once you're in. I'll send you the venue address shortly.'*

It wasn't ideal to have to meet everyone at the venue. I'd rather have met them at Bobby and Tien's house and jumped in the car with another designated driver, so I could have a couple of beers. Although, having the decision not to drink made for me, and have a clearer head to be at my most observant for the gig, was probably the better option.

I initially planned on skipping breakfast and stopping off somewhere along the way for a bite to eat and break up the driving, but considering I was an hour behind schedule, I knew I had to get a shift on. I ordered a Philly cheesesteak to go. It was a good job that the Americans weren't shy with their portion sizes because it was my food ration for most of the day.

I checked out of the hotel, threw on my orange-tinted aviators, and hopped into a taxi to the airport car rental lot.

I picked up the Chevy Malibu and made another biffle. I approached the car from the right-hand side and opened the door, finding the steering wheel on the left. I rolled my eyes as the valet let out a snigger at my blunder.

Once I climbed into the car, a sudden spate of stomach twinges made me feel nauseous. I became acutely aware that it would be my first time driving on the right-hand side of the road. It was a good job the Chevy was automatic because changing gears with my right hand was far too weird at that stage. I set up the Sat Nav and directed it to the gig venue as per Ozzie's text. The journey would take six hours and thirty minutes. Factoring in traffic, I guessed it would take longer, but I was confident of making it before the show.

I took a deep breath and plucked up the courage to pull away and slowly exit the parking lot with all the concentration of someone carrying an ice cube tray full of water from the sink to the freezer.

I managed to negotiate my way through two left turns at traffic lights until I hit the freeway, where I hugged the right-hand lane for dear life. I gripped the wheel with hands at ten to two and held on too tight like Cougar from 'Top Gun', about to blow it and turn in my wings at any moment.

I eventually grew in confidence and settled into a steady speed. The number of cars on the road began to dissolve after I escaped Vegas and rounded the edge of Lake Mead. I trekked deeper into the arid wasteland, and the relentless size of the desert made its presence felt. The capacious territory was filled with delirious imagery and succulent backdrops as civilisation surrendered to the natural world. I felt alone and at peace as the true nature of the journey hit me, just as 'The Chain', by Fleetwood Mac was about to begin.

CHAPTER 2

The sense of freedom from the drive was palpable, heightened by the rampage of terrific music that emerged from the illustrious *America Road Trip* playlist. The Doors, Creedence Clearwater Revival, Tom Petty, Eagles, The Rolling Stones, America, Jimi Hendrix, Mamas & Papas, Neil Young, and Led Zeppelin were just a few of the iconic bands featured, as well as songs from various films, like 'Easy Rider'. They all epitomised the aura of the open American roads. Listening to those same mood-enhancing tunes whilst driving over Barton Bridge in Manchester, with the smell of raw sewage lingering in the damp air, didn't have the same effect.

I felt like I was in another world, basking in breathtaking surroundings that made my soul dance to the tune of nature's drum. The odd trailer and caravan appeared out of nowhere, making me wonder whether some 'Breaking Bad' 'cooking' shenanigans were occurring. Small trailer parks surfaced every so often, along with solitary rundown bars that had no business being where they were. I felt like stopping for an ice-cold, frosty beer in one of them, but the thought of the American version of 'The League of Gentleman' stopped me in my tracks. I feared being skinned alive and buggered by a band of hillbillies who'd have liked nothing better than to add the scalp of a Brit to their dilapidated bedpost.

Four hours were obliterated in the blink of an eye as I spent the entire time admiring the colourful landscapes. I passed through Sun City on the outskirts of Phoenix, the first proper town I'd seen in hours. Dusk descended in minutes and consumed the daylight in one hefty mouthful. The sudden shift to darkness mirrored my predicament on the road. Frustratingly, I joined the arse end of a traffic jam at rush hour, hitting Phoenix's answer to the M62/M60 interchange where I played Dodgeball with several cars. I frantically lane hopped to navigate my way to the correct exit that led to Tucson. It was a good job I had the Sat Nav or else I'd be having a Dumb and Dumber moment: *"You drove halfway across the country in the wrong direction!"* and probably end up in the bowels of somewhere like Tijuana.

The traffic calmed after skirting around Phoenix, and I was back on track. Ozzie messaged, telling me the band were on in an hour or so. The Sat Nav said I was fifty-four minutes away, so I smashed my foot down and started to get cocky about overtaking cars to make good time. The roads cleared, and with 'Born to Run' by Bruce Springsteen for company, I embraced the anthem and all it stood for, using it as fuel to edge closer to Tucson.

Back on quieter country roads, I was submerged into a creepy blackness. The only illumination came from my headlights, and the reflectors of the few cars in the distance. But what disappeared from the land was gained in the sky as the unpolluted, smog-free night was punctured by clusters of sparkly, silver diamonds glistening as far as the eye could see.

Society crept back into view after I exited the freeway, and a montage of images swept by that resonated with films and shows set in that part of the world. Streetlights glowed to irradiate the multi-coloured buildings scattered across the profusion of land. They were painted in orange, pink, and blue, colours that highlighted the cultural aspect of the region. I wasn't too far from the border of Mexico, which became more apparent when I hit the town centre. Most folk that congregated on the streets looked like their heritage originated south of the border. The abundance of spiritual and holistic shops showed the level of faith the natives held dear to their hearts, rooted more in America's history that predated the migration influx from Europe.

Tucson was a lively place, brimming with a carnival, party-like atmosphere associated with the Hispanic culture. My head swivelled at every crossroad to eyeball the action on most street corners. The most noteworthy was a Mariachi Band. Three guys were dressed in sparkly sombreros, black glittery waistcoats and trousers, and oversized red bow ties. They played high-tempo acoustic guitars to a buoyant crowd that danced with gusto on the sidewalk.

High-octane, intricate guitar music with a tinge of romantic darkness and melancholy continued to shriek from every orifice on the main drag, sounding reminiscent of a Tarantino film.

I arrived at Sky. Judging by the number of punters smoking outside, having their final nicotine fixes, it looked like I had just made it in time. I turned into the car park, found a space, exited the car to stretch my seized-up limbs, and made my way back towards the main road where the entrance was. I messaged Ozzie to let him know I'd arrived.

The Latino beat rumbled through the air, making me think of Eva and the way she danced the first night we met in Vegas. Those snake-like seductive hips that could enchant the most celibate of men were etched into my mind.

My name was on the list at the door as Ozzie had promised. As a reviewer, it's surprising how often the name *isn't* listed despite numerous confirmations beforehand. The attendee gave me a laminated lanyard with the word 'Press' printed across it and stamped my hand.

As soon as I entered the venue, I was hit by a gust of heat and the stench of sweat, made worse by the low-rise ceiling. 'Down in Mexico' by The Coasters reverberated through the PA, a track not usually played just before a band was about to take to the stage, but this was a different arena to those I was used to.

The place was rammed, looking like it exceeded its four-hundred-person capacity. There was no chance of getting any further forward than the few feet in front.

My phone buzzed. I uncomfortably managed to dig my hand into my shorts pocket to see a message from Ozzie: *'Meet me after the show. I'll be at the merch stand.'*

I could see the stand on the opposite side of the room near the stage. I struggled to reply, impeded by the burly shoulders on either side of me that boxed my arms in, but I managed to type: *'See you after the show. I'm stuck at the back anyway and can't move.'*

I was stranded in a sweat pit amongst a crowd whose impatience led to a chorus of feverish, repetitive chants of *We want the band! We want the band!*

I laboured to break out my small notepad and pen, choosing to take notes the old-school way.

Suddenly, the lights dimmed, plunging the venue into a shadow. A buzz that seemed infused with the intense electricity of the fans rushed through me as the Cutthroats entrance was a whisker away. The background music ended, and a roar echoed around the room as three silhouettes appeared from the side of the stage. I could make out the outline of their haircuts and swaggering Mancunian walks as they took their places.

An American accent hollered from the speakers, 'Ladies and Gentlemen... from Man-che-ster, En-ger-land... please welcome, Cutthroat Shambles!' As the voice trailed off, the lighting kicked in with spotlights and special effects shooting all over the stage. Cheers intensified as the band hit the first notes to one of their well-known songs, 'Rock N Roll Heaven', one I'd connected with back in the hotel room in Vegas. The opening instrumental hurtled into gear as we awaited the arrival of the esteemed frontwoman.

The three guys were dressed casually. Kyle, the lead guitarist, wore a white, deep V-necked t-shirt and navy-blue slim jeans. Will opted for a plain black t-shirt and black jeans, with the big man at the back wearing a taut black vest that enhanced his vast frame and muscular arms.

Kyle appeared nonchalant and completely unfazed by the countless ladies at the front reaching out to him. A well-aimed smouldering smile served to tease them more. After the swashbuckling opening riff finished, Dee Darrell strutted into view with all the confidence of a seasoned assassin about to complete a routine kill. Another loud cheer boomed at the sight of her. Despite her petite frame and size, she had an unfathomable presence and was drenched in attitude. She was dressed to kill in a stylish black vest top, which revealed her abundance of tattoos and accentuated her sizeable breasts. Tight, denim blue shorts, on top of black tights, worked with black mid-calf boots that added a couple of more inches to her stature. She completed the look with a burgundy-coloured cowboy hat that looked like it was stolen from a nearby saloon bar. She looked the epitome of rock 'n' roll as she glided up to the mic stand that was draped in a burgundy-coloured silk scarf to match her headwear.

'How y'all doin' out there?' she hollered.

Screams bellowed back at her.

I forgot that she was Bermudian. Before that, I had no clue what a Bermudian accent sounded like, but to me, it sounded American.

She launched into the opening lyrics, *'See me in the sun, rocking just for fun, got our Ray-Bans on, like we're the only ones.'* Wow! What a live vocal. I was blown away and desperately began making notes as the words fell out of me.

The chorus hit, *'Take me to Rock N Roll Heaven, throw your hands in the air, let's do a little living, take me, oh take me there, higher and higher.'*

The audience were hooked and were unable to divert their eyes from Dee. The way she paraded with such fluid force and commanding power reminded me of Freddie Mercury. There was something special about her.

People were pushed to the front of the barrier as hedonism charged the souls of the mob when the next blistering song, 'Oblivion', began. It was just as pulsating as the opener and raised the energy level.

Thumping songs continued to bombard the senses and kept the spectators effervescing. The chemistry between all four band members was highly profound, with musicianship that was multi-talented and multi-layered. Kyle continued to play up to the adulation. He wasn't over the top, just flashing enough flamboyance to keep the girls wanting more.

It wasn't just their ability to rock out that was captivating. They were just as enthralling when they toned it down a couple of decibels. The quieter 'Two Million Heart Beats' was a power ballad that showed a different dynamic, but what struck me more was the grace and charm in the delivery of 'Curious Morality'. I was swept up by the song's emotion, to the point that I nearly shed a tear in the middle of a sweltering cesspit. Dee tempered her vivacious stage antics and took a much softer stance, singing gently from the heart to deliver a song of substance. Kyle leant back and closed his eyes, riffing the chords, letting the lifeblood of the tune drown him. The mosh-pit behaviour waned and was replaced by a still appreciation for poetic harmonies. Phones were held aloft to capture the moment.

The emotional level didn't last long as Kyle launched into the face-melting opening riff of 'Enter Sandman' by Metallica. It created mayhem as the fans belted out the words to a giant of a track. Dee discarded the cowboy hat and rocked out. Her hair stuck to her face due to the sweat that poured profusely from her head. She pranced around the stage, swinging the stand, and screamed down the mic to bring a new slant to the famous tune.

The band finished and left the stage, but they were urged to reappear for an encore. They returned and began a two-song finale that ended with one of their better-known tracks, 'Lifetime Sunshine'.

Dee explained the meaning behind the lyrics before it started. 'This song is about why I went to Manchester from Bermuda. I got fed up with the sunshine and I needed a little bit of rain, babe. That's just how it goes sometimes in life, you know.'

The song merged soulful charm with a superlative rock riff and rhythm. It was that potent combination that made them such a highly sought-after band. The song reached its crescendo, and the musicians showed off with an impromptu jam that ended in a blaze of fury. Cymbals were bashed, and guitars strummed ferociously, leading to yells and rapturous applause from the crowd.

Dee shouted over the chaos, 'We've been Cutthroat Shambles. You've been fuckin' amazing, Tucson! Hope to see you again real soon!'

She left the stage and blew a kiss. After a few seconds, the band trickled off with hand gestures of peace and love.

I fought my way to the merch stand, where many people queued up for one of the band's three five-track CDs, t-shirts, badges, friendship bands, signed pictures, lighters, and other merch being sold to help fund the tour.

I approached the man who stood behind the desk. 'You must be Ozzie?'

'Yeah, Ricky, I presume?'

We shook hands, and he said, 'Glad you made it.'

He was a true Manc with an accent that made me feel right at home.

'Just in the nick of time, thankfully,' I answered.

'What did you think of the show?'

'Absolutely brilliant. They were class. I can see why they're so popular.'

'They weren't bad tonight, I have to say. Glad you enjoyed it. That should give you something to write about.'

'I've got pages of notes here to sort through. I wish I could get started now.'

'There's plenty of time for that. You've got to meet them first.'

I felt sick at the thought but tried to remember Eva's motivational words to reduce my anxiety.

He offered me a beer, and I accepted. I thought I could stretch to a couple but didn't want to chance any more than that for fear of being locked up in cells overnight due to the stringent DUI laws.

He reached for a bottle of Budweiser from the nearby crate stashed under the table and handed it to me. He then took a heavy swig of his own. The sweat glistened on his forehead as he tilted his head back.

Ozzie was in his early fifties and a cool-looking bloke with silver hair and stubble. His hair was shaved more at one side and coiffed over on the other. He wore a black, Deep Purple t-shirt, with '1972 Highway Star' emblazoned across the front, and slack khaki cargo shorts.

'Let them come down a bit after the show, and we'll head back there. Hopefully, things will have calmed down from before they went on.'

'Why? What was going on?' I asked.

'The support band, "The Shirelights", have a bit of an entourage with them, and it was getting a little… rowdy, let's say. Can't be helped in this industry unless you're like fuckin' Coldplay.' He winked.

Apprehension and excitement overcame me. My short time in music had seen me backstage with some bands, but there was always a conservative element to most of them, so it didn't end up being rowdy. I couldn't discount that my role as a journalist made bands a little warier about fully being themselves. The fear of bad press may have swayed that, but that wasn't my style or why I wanted to write in the industry. My mission was all about promoting the music. Given the circumstances, I was a little torn on what I should include when witnessing the antics beyond the stage.

With the queue building and Ozzie managing alone, I offered to help.

He was appreciative. 'That'd be great, pal. Here's a price list. Most people will want CDs which are all seven dollars each. T-shirts have been selling OK. They are twenty dollars. Just do your best to keep the queue moving, and I'll start to replenish some of the stock.'

I sold a t-shirt straight away, and when the fan held it up proudly, I could see how striking the band logo was. The black t-shirt had the logo plastered dead centre in white to make it stand out. The font was large and smooth. The letter 'S' at the end of 'Shambles' continued to swoop underneath and morphed into a samurai sword that underlined the whole band name, acting like it was cutting the name's throat. Very clever.

I assumed the gig was over and readied myself to venture backstage, but another act began setting up.

'How come another band are playing? Weren't Cutthroat Shambles the headline?' I asked Ozzie.

'This is how a lot of American gigs are structured. Cutthroat Shambles *were* the headline, but a closing act finishes the night off.'

It had escaped me that it was still relatively early as gig times go in the UK. I liked the idea of an early finish. There was an option to enjoy the rest of the night elsewhere after the main band had played if you wanted to.

Plenty of people *did* stay for the end, suggesting it was worth sticking around. A girl with wild, funky red hair took to the stage along with three male musicians. She introduced herself as Jess Kemp. I watched on from behind the stand. Her voice was unique, switching between a bluesy and soulful snarl to something silkier and gracious. The songs were catchy and sat more on the pop side of the fence, which was a welcomed change after the Cutthroats' boisterous showing.

During Jess Kemp's inspired offering, where the song, 'Camden' really caught my ear, the queues at the merch stand eased up, so Ozzie said he'd take me backstage while one of the bar staff took over.

Jamie's comments about me replacing Tommy Ashcroft made me edgy again. I feared I was about to be ambushed by a wall of hostility. After all, I was considered the 'enemy' in the band's eyes, if the film 'Almost Famous' was to be believed. Tommy built his rapport with the band over time, which was a luxury I didn't have.

I voiced my fears, 'Ozzie, there's something that's been on my mind.'

'What's up?'

'I know plans changed quite dramatically, and the change in situation isn't ideal, but are you sure I'm OK being here?'

'Dead right you are. I checked out some of your work before approving this. I like the idea of a rookie writing it as I think the blogs won't be as typical as a pro writing them and will say something different. I'm looking forward to seeing what you can do.'

'Rookie? So, you know my experience level? Jamie made out no one did.'

'Jamie's a good mate of mine, so he told me everything about you, but let's keep that quiet from the band for now, especially *her*.'

He rolled his eyes, suggesting something had already been said before my arrival.

He continued, 'Look, all anyone can ask is for you to do your best. Between you and me, I was never a fan of Tommy, so the fact he's not here suits me. He's a good writer, but he's a bit of a know-it-all and has a habit of pissing people off eventually, so inevitably he would've got on my tits. Jamie told me you're sound, and because you're a lot younger than Tommy, I think you might develop a better connection with the band.

They aren't as crazy as they've been made out to be. We've staged a lot of it for show.'

'Staged?' I asked.

'Tricks of the trade, man. You'll learn as you go along, I'm sure. Just enjoy the experience,' he reassured me.

CHAPTER 3

Walking down a narrow corridor, I could hear chatter becoming ever louder from the room to the left at the top.

Ozzie opened the door, and the music amplified. It was 'Hot Legs' by Rod Stewart, a real stomping track, and what went with it was the sweet smell of marijuana. The room was basic and shrouded in a light shade of grey fog, the sort of ambience expected behind the scenes at a rock gig. The open window had little effect in subduing the haze. I had no idea what the smoking laws were, but it seemed like no one gave a shit.

The right-hand side of the room acted as a lounge area, where most people congregated. It was a party-like atmosphere with young folks dancing and laughing, an extension of the festivities occurring on the streets of Tucson.

'Are all these with the Cutthroats?' I asked Ozzie.

'Not quite. This is The Shirelights' doing, who I told you about earlier. I think their whole college emptied to see them tonight, which is why we got such an energetic crowd.'

My presence as an unknown bystander made me feel even more nervous. There were roughly thirty to forty people in the room, an eclectic mix of attractive hipsters and quirky-looking individuals. One particular group dressed like the 4 Non Blondes had thrown up on them, and they swarmed around The Shirelights, an all-girl group. I guessed from their clothing, tattoos, hairstyles, and piercings that they were a punk-orientated band.

The other side of the room was more like a kitchen, and where I recognised the guys from the Cutthroats, placed strategically next to a crate of beer. A joint was being passed between them as they riffed with a few girls.

Ozzie grabbed their attention. 'Guys, I want to introduce you to Ricky from Sonic Bandwagon, our tour blogger.'

Simultaneously, the guys nodded, 'Alright, Ricky,' in different, moody Mancunian tones. The girls were a little giddier and childlike with their high-pitched staccato, 'Hey Ricky from Sonic Bandwagon.'

The mocking delivery of their greeting didn't help matters. I held my hand up and managed an uncomfortable grin in conjunction with a flick of the eyebrows and a muted Karl Pilkington-like response of, 'Alright.'

Ozzie asked, 'Where's Dee?'

Quince spoke up, 'Fuck knows. You know what she's like. Who can keep tabs on her?'

'You haven't pissed her off again, have you?'

'No. Don't worry, it's not like the Liverpool gig.'

Ozzie rolled his eyes and ushered me around to the three male members of the band as I wondered what the hell happened in Liverpool.

He introduced me to Kyle first. It was better for my ego that I didn't stand directly next to him so the girls couldn't compare us, like choosing between prime rib steak and spam in a can.

We'd not even got past the introductory phase of the greetings when the door swung open and in stepped two girls. One I instantly recognised as the talented vocalist I'd seen rock the stage earlier. She stood with a commanding poise, hand on her hip, and an intense expression on her face. Her eyes searched the room, and her glare landed on me. I broke eye contact as if not to be seen. I could see her continue to stare at me from my peripheral vision. I felt awkward and stiff, paralysed by dread.

Ozzie shouted over, 'Dee. I want you to come and meet somebody.'

Dee strutted towards her bandmates with her sexy compadre. Ignoring Ozzie's request, she plucked the joint from Kyle's hand like candy from a baby without saying a word. She sat on a stool, leant back and folded her legs one over the other. For some reason, my eyes locked on her again like a magnet, but I shifted them when she clocked me.

'What the fuck are you looking at?' Her prominent Bermudian accent turned menacing.

Lost for words, I just about muttered, 'Nothing. Sorry.'

'If it's nothing, then why are you sorry?' she snapped.

I felt like I was shrinking into myself.

'Cut it out, Dee.' Ozzie said.

She carried on staring at me malevolently without saying a word, getting off on making me feel uncomfortable. I wasn't even looking at her, but I could feel her icy stare pierce my throbbing skull.

Ozzie shouted over to me to break the tension, 'Ricky? What did you think of the gig?'

It provided me with an opportunity to score some brownie points.

'Incredible show. That's the first time I've seen you play. Completely blown away by it.'

Big mistake.

'You've never seen us play before?' Dee shot back.

'I hadn't. Sorry.'

'Again, what you sorry for?'

Her coarse tone cut me to shreds. She took another toot and blew smoke rings in my direction to taunt me in some way.

'I'd listened to your music before, and I was already impressed. You sounded awesome.'

I was desperately trying to salvage the situation, but I inadvertently dug myself further into the mire.

Dee rose from the stool and grabbed the attention of her bandmates. 'Hear this, guys? Hot Shot Writer here is impressed because he heard us a few fuckin' times, probably through a Facebook group for nobodies. Aren't we fuckin' privileged?'

Dee's sarcasm caused the lads to snicker, but Quince did at least appreciate my arse-licking words.

'Thanks, man. Glad you liked our vibe.'

'Brown nose,' Dee muttered.

Ozzie repeated his stern tone, 'Dee.'

She brushed off his warning with a dismissive exhale of the joint.

Rather than remain quiet, I continued to try to endear myself to the rest of the band.

'I heard the gig in North Carolina was great. Was it in Charlotte?'

Ozzie elaborated, 'Yeah, it was top. An unexpected place to play, a bit of a strange gig really. Quince's Uncle knows a guy out there who offered to put them on and guaranteed them a great reception and a decent payday. We didn't advertise it because this mate of Quince's Uncle, Leo, pretty much had a ready-made audience. We used it as a warm-up show.'

Quince jumped in. 'That place was weird, man. It was a gated community in the middle of nowhere surrounded by woodland and country parks that went on for miles. Leo's gaff was fuckin' massive, and he let us stay there. It had a lake on it and everything. Fuckin' freezing though when we jumped in it.'

Will piped up after overhearing the story and turned to face us, leaving Kyle alone with the girls.

'Yeah, I think my balls shrivelled up into my stomach it was that cold.'

Quince joked, 'Your dick's already like a shrivelled prune.'

Flicking the V's at Quince, Will continued, 'The youngest person there was about sixty. I think the whole community emptied, so we had a mint crowd. All these old biddies doing the mum dance to our bangin' tunes. Weird as fuck. We were lucky to get outta there alive. They probably hadn't seen anyone younger than retirement age in years. Even Ozzie could've got laid in there.'

'Nah, they weren't that desperate,' Quince teased.

'Funny fuckers, aren't you?' Ozzie responded.

Dee was stony-faced and disrupted the merriments. 'Well, you boneheads better up your game. Good job it was a warm-up to get the shit out of your system before it gets serious out here. You were only passable tonight while we're at it.'

I found that hard to believe as I thought they were outstanding.

'Dee, we were ace in Charlotte,' Quince argued.

'You fuckin' weren't. Will was out of time, Kyle was sulking cos there was no pussy to play up to, and don't get me started on your fuckin' rhythm Quince. There was more rhythm in a Zimmer frame.'

Kyle's head popped up when he heard Dee's harsh words. 'And what the fuck was wrong with tonight, Dee?'

Ozzie stepped in to calm it down. 'Look. You were good tonight, and you were good in Charlotte, but you *can,* and you *will* be better, so let's leave it there shall we before we have another episode.'

The word 'another' didn't fill me with confidence. What had I walked into?

Dee's moroseness soured the atmosphere on our side of the room, but the party was still going strong on the other side.

Ozzie leant into me to talk business and change the subject. 'Is there anything you want to do regards these blogs? I've got some ideas to throw your way. Has Jamie given you any direction?'

I was about to answer when Dee abruptly interrupted our conversation. 'How long have *you* been a writer?'

I turned to face her. 'What?'

'It's not a hard question. How long have *you* been a writer?'

'Erm…about four years.'

The little white lie concocted between Jamie, Ozzie, and I had me on edge.

'You seem unsure of that. I've never heard of you, and I know anyone worth knowing in this game around Manchester.'

'I've been working behind the scenes a lot.'

'Behind what scene? Local pantomime?' she berated before adding, 'So you fancy yourself as a bit of a player in this game? Never has a punk been so lucky to land a gig. Do you even know who the fuck we are? You've never even seen us play before tonight.'

I began to feel hot and sweaty and couldn't think straight, and I shrunk faster than a post-climactic penis.

Dee answered for me, 'No, I didn't think so.'

'I know a lot about the scene,' I threw back at her.

'Fuck the scene. We *are* the fuckin' scene. Who the fuck is this joker, Ozzie?'

'Calm down, Dee. You're like a pissin' Rottweiler. Ricky can handle what's required. Leave off him.'

'I don't like it, and I don't like him. Tell me, Hot Shot Writer, who are you into? What bands do you like? What genre? Who've you reviewed or interviewed who's worth talking about?'

It was a whole new level of bitchiness I hadn't encountered before. She didn't give me a chance to answer before exclaiming, 'Just stay the fuck out of my way. You fuck us over, and I'll *end* you. You'll be lucky to write carp of the month articles for a fuckin' fishing magazine, you hear?'

Quince spoke up. 'Yo Dee, take it easy on the journo. At least give him a day to settle in before you chop his balls off.'

Dee stood up and stormed towards the door, and the girl she came in with, who had not said a word apart from giggle at Dee's quips, followed her like a well-trained puppy.

Quince turned to me. 'Don't worry mate, she'll come around. She's just playing to the gallery, making a scene.'

I felt awful, and my worst fears were confirmed. I felt like I'd made a big mistake accepting the job. I was warned Dee might be difficult, but I didn't expect a performance *that* neurotic. I was shell-shocked, reduced to pieces, and all I wanted at that moment was to fuck off, drive to Eva, and curl up in a ball.

The browbeaten look on my face showed my disappointment. Quince took pity and passed over the joint.

'Looks like you could do with a blast of this, mate.'

I'd not smoked weed in years as I usually pulled a whitey. But after an emasculating interrogation, I took it without thinking. I inhaled deeply, coughed a little, and felt the hit of tranquillity caress my body.

'Trust us, Ricky. This is the only way to take the edge off her. We never smoked weed before she joined us,' Quince joked.

The lads giggled a stoner's giggle. I took another hit, lolled my head back, and let my eyes roll inwards as the potency instilled calmness.

Perhaps it was the new-found spell I was under, but the atmosphere seemed to perk up after Dee's exit. Jess Kemp and her band had arrived too, much to the delight of The Shirelights and their gang. Their presence signified an elevation in the amusements as the joys spilt over into the kitchen, and more intermingling went on. While I was a little daunted by it all, the band took it blissfully in their stride.

It wasn't surprising that Kyle had attracted the attention of one of the best-looking girls in the room. She was perched on a stool next to him and hardly played it coy. Her constant physical contact of hand and leg touching was unmistakable. I was sure it wouldn't be too long before lips were used, but Kyle was unperturbed by her blatant interest. He casually noodled on his acoustic guitar to mesmerise her – the musician's magical weapon.

Quince and Will weren't exempt from the groupie worshipping either as more girls camped around their vicinity.

Ozzie chatted with the venue owner outside, but he popped his head around the door and said, 'I'm gonna load the car back up. It's not really my scene anymore all this backstage nonsense. I've seen enough in the past, and I'm too old to cramp their style. You stay though and get to know the lads a bit better.'

'That's easier said than done when they're overrun by women, Ozzie. I don't think they're interested in a chinwag with me right now. You sure you don't want any help?'

'Nah, man, I'll be fine. Only take a couple of trips, plus I need to speak to the promoter and sort out the cash. You want to be the muscle in case things go south?'

'Is that a possibility?'

'Only kidding. This gig will be fine. The promoter's sound, but it has been known to happen where things don't go so swimmingly.'

'Well, if that happens on this trip, let me know, and I'll tag along and look intimidating.'

'I think I'll stick with Dee, thanks,' he jested.

'I don't blame you.'

Ozzie left, and I cut an uneasy figure, rooted to the spot like a spare prick at a wedding that no one cared to notice or give a shit about. I was just an amateur journalist and didn't have the same status as being 'in the band'.

Despite my willingness to help Ozzie, something pulled at me to *not* be the guy who left the backstage area at an American rock concert without at least seeing how the evening unfolded. I was unsure whether to watch as a journalist, a fan of rock 'n' roll, or as a curious human being. It was a unique situation to be privy to, and although a bit out of my comfort zone, I had to get used to it. That was the reason I was there after all.

Will yelled, 'Hey Ricky, what happens on tour stays on tour, yeah? Whatever you see here stays out of the blogs.'

That put me in a predicament between my professionalism as a journalist and my loyalty to a band. I signalled that my lips would be sealed. Will slapped his arm around me and handed me a joint. I took two small puffs to try and control its effects.

It wasn't too long after I'd passed it onto Quince that one of the girls pulled out a small cellophane bag from her tiny, glittery pink purse. She emptied the contents onto the glass table in front of her. White powder mounded like a mini volcano. She began cutting it with an American Express card and joked, 'Don't leave home without it.'

With beer, weed, coke, rock bands, and music making up the offstage cocktail, I expected the Quaaludes to be brought out next.

I'd never taken cocaine. It was a pointless drug in my eyes. I never quite grasped why people had to have that heightened ephemeral feeling of invincibility. Ultimately, it resulted in arrogance and was a facilitator of violence. I couldn't understand why it was rife everywhere. Why couldn't people have a good time without it? But in the world of rock 'n' roll, coke had found a natural habitat and flourished amongst the delicate egos of the artistes and their followers.

The dollar bills were brought out and rolled up as the attention diverted towards the powder glinting on the table. Snorting sounds rippled through the air as many took turns to shove the shit up their snouts, including the three Cutthroat lads. Sharp recoils and cries of 'FUCK!' rebounded as the room turned into a den that was even further removed from my comfort zone.

I was offered a bump but respectfully declined without judgement, much to the dismay of a couple of partakers. I continued to bear the brunt of minor peer pressure, being accused of being a 'Narcotics Agent' as crisp bills were thrust at me. I made the excuse that I was working, so I was happy with the tiny bit of weed to chill me out. I didn't think it was the time or place to bark out my true feelings on the matter and lecture the ensemble on the perils of drug use.

One of The Shirelights' entourage, buoyed by the shot of coke, made her way over to me. She was good-looking with glowing blonde hair and icy blue eyes, the token American sweetheart who pulled the wool over Mummy and Daddy's eyes with a false portrayal of innocent sweetness. That was until the dead of the night when she hit the drug-addled lair of a rock gig. Little did they know the alternative life she led. Her heaving breasts made her white, sparkly top tighten, revealing her bronzed, shapely abdomen and shiny belly button ring. Her jaw swung beneath an assured smile. She said, 'So, are you like in the band then?'

Trying hard to keep my head straight and upright, I felt like Chevy Chase in National Lampoon's Christmas Vacation. I hoped a boob-related word wouldn't inadvertently leave my tongue before I had a chance to cast a rod to haul it back. It was a good job it wasn't nippy outside if the topic of the weather came up. Instead, it turned extremely hot, and a bead of sweat broke from the furrow of my brow.

I finally found the use of speech. 'I'm not in the band. I'm their... personal writer.'

'So, you're like the guy that tells the world what's happening here tonight?'

'Yep, that's me.'

I think I underestimated my tolerance level for weed. Even after a few small puffs, it seized me as I desperately tried to keep a degree of coolness.

'I really love your accent. Where are you guys from?' she asked.

'Where do you think I'm from?'

Natural flirtation mode engaged.

'I guess you're from Scotland or Australia?'

Some things hadn't changed since my first visit to the States.

'Close. I'm from England. Manchester, to be precise.'

'England? Is that near London?'

I felt like planting my palm into my face with an almighty slap. I contained my laughter.

'Erm, no. London is the capital of England, and Manchester is a couple of hundred miles north of there.'

'Oh, sorry. My bad.'

I brushed it off. 'It's OK. You're not the first to think that, and you won't be the last, I'm sure.'

'So, as you're a writer, will you like, write about me?'

'That depends on whether, you *like*, do anything worth writing about?'

I couldn't resist an accent mock.

'Maybe I could think of something. Might not be PG13, if you like, know what I mean?'

Before I had a chance to think about what she meant, I was clasped firmly by the pernicious drug, not helped by Velvet Underground's, 'Venus in Furs' playing in the background to add a further layer of paranoia. Looking around the room, I could feel eyes on me. My skin flushed and itched, and I was sure the band were talking about me, but I couldn't be sure through the illusion. My eyes became fuzzy, and my head span right round like a record, baby. The girl noticed the change in my demeanour and asked, 'Are you OK? You look a little pale.'

'Sorry... I need to get some air.'

The layers of smoke made the room stuffy and claustrophobic, so I quickly escaped. In the corridor, I looked left, then right. The venue was to the right, and a door further down on the left displayed the word 'EXIT'. I made a break for it, desperate for fresh air to level me out.

The door was slightly ajar, wedged open by a brick. I pushed it open with the little strength I had and placed the brick back into place.

I took a few steps forward and found I was at the side of the venue in an open alley. The secluded path was murky and eerie. The only light to stop me from being plunged into complete obscurity came from the moonlight and street lighting beyond the metal fence in front. I shut my eyes and took a few deep cleansing breaths to settle down and sober up. The clean air filled my lungs and imparted a sweet serenity, and a swift breeze built up and wrapped around my flesh to cool me down.

Thoughts of Eva flooded my mind. I felt the need to call her, which probably wasn't the best idea given the spell I was under. Anything she said could've been misinterpreted, but it still didn't deter me. I took out my phone and searched my recent logs, but I stopped short when a banging sound to my right startled me. For some reason, I decided to investigate, which is basically how horror movies start - some idiot going solo. But I was drawn into finding out what the bang was.

I tip-toed down the alley to get a clearer view, seeing a couple of large dumpsters resting against the wall. The noise changed to more of a moan and heavy breathing. Rather than bail, I took a few extra steps forward and saw two silhouettes. I stepped on a discarded bin bag which rustled and diverted the attention onto me. The shock on my face was evident as I took in the scene. A woman was pressed up against the corner of the dumpster with her panties resting around her ankles. The head of another woman was visible at waist height. I couldn't see faces, but I knew exactly what was going on, and when one saw the whites of my eyes, a shout boomed out, 'What the fuck are you looking at?' I was horrified to identify Dee staring back at me.

The woman on her knees was the one Dee had left with earlier. She swivelled her head, equally as unfazed as Dee at being caught with her pants down, literally. She smiled and turned back to what she was doing that had made Dee moan in the first place. I was far more embarrassed than those two. The saving grace was there was nothing like seeing the female lead singer of a rock band being treated to oral sex to shock you into a sober state.

I fled the alley and headed back to where the band were. I fought my way through the mist towards the bathroom to splash some water on my face. Everyone was too high to warn me as I burst through the door and straight into Kyle. His jeans were around his ankles in a compromising position with the girl who broke out the cocaine earlier.

'What the fuck?' I exclaimed as AC'DC's 'Givin' the Dog a Bone' ripped through the speakers to fittingly soundtrack the debauched incident. Why I stood and gawked without averting my eyes was a mystery. I couldn't seem to pull myself away from the pornographic image.

Kyle shouted, 'Get the fuck out, Ricky!'

He scrambled to slam the door shut, tripping over his own jeans in the process, falling into the door as I left.

I turned to Quince, Will, and a few girls, who were in fits of belly laughter.

'Thanks for the heads up,' I cried.

'What do you expect when you come barging in here like Jack Bauer,' Will argued.

Through sheer humiliation, I left, thinking it was best to get back to the main stage and stick with some element of normality, but my escape was thwarted. Dee and her promiscuous companion marched toward me as soon as I closed the door.

'Hey! You!' she yelled.

I froze, and my head and shoulders slumped as I knew what was coming.

She came right up to my nose, jabbed her finger in my face and snarled, 'If you breathe a fuckin' word of what you saw in your precious little blog, I'll personally cut your balls off and throw them into the crowd at our next gig. You understand me, Hot Shot Writer?'

I was twisted up and nodded out of panic. I quietly apologised and inexplicably added, 'I didn't know you were a lesbian.'

'What the hell does it have to do with you? Are you jealous or something? You want to get in on this? I like both men and women, you know,' she teased.

She sidled further up to me as if trying to entice me into a false sense of security.

'No? I didn't think so,' she sneered.

Thankfully, Ozzie approached. Seeing that I was a little flustered, he asked, 'You OK, Ricky?'

'Yeah. I just needed some air.'

'Yeah, Ozzie. He just needed some air,' Dee repeated, before going back into the room to join her bandmates.

'I'm ready to go if you want to leave,' Ozzie said.

I didn't even have to mull it over. After the long drive and Dee's evident dislike for me, I was in favour of leaving quickly.

'I'll come back with you. I've got the Sat Nav, so you don't have to hang around for me to follow. I'll get there OK.'

'Cool. You'll love Bobby and Tien. They're old friends of mine from back in the day. I doubt they'll be up when we get in, so you can meet them tomorrow. They would've come tonight, but they had some community do already booked in.'

'That's OK. I think I need to get to bed anyway. It's been a long day.'

Ozzie grabbed the lads' attention. 'Okay, boys. Van all packed, money in tow. I'm ready to go when you are.'

'Think we might hang around, Ozzie. See what Tucson has to offer,' Will shouted.

'Well, you can be fucked if I'm hanging around with you. If you want a lift, you come with me. If not, you'll have to get a cab, but just remember we're staying at Bobby and Tien's tonight, so let's try and respect the place and not have another episode like we did in Hull, shall we?' He warned, as if this was common practice.

I quietly asked Ozzie, 'What happened in Hull?'

'Let's just say they abused the digs, and guess who got billed for the damages?'

'That bad?'

'Horrendous, best you don't know. Top gig, though. Probably the best I've seen them. I know they seem like they argue all the time, but that's down to artistic temperaments, especially from Dee. They're not bad kids. They all love each other really.'

'I'm sure most bands are like that,' I concurred.

'Yeah, to some extent. Dee is a little more demanding than most. Anyway, let's get out of here. I'm knackered.'

Shortly after 1am, I found myself in a cul-de-sac with about six large houses dotted around the crescent. Ozzie was waiting outside the first one on the right. I pulled up behind his Dodge and got out of the car. The only sound to break the stillness was the orchestra of chirping crickets.

I took note of the size of Bobby and Tien's abode before walking up the pathway. There were many sections, shapes and sizes that went far beyond the spheres of my eyesight.

Ozzie showed me to the guesthouse I was staying in and handed me the key. It was attached to the front of the main house to the right, accompanied by a small garden, table, and chairs. The single, sizeable room was elegant, complete with a double bed, mini kitchen, and a walk-in wardrobe. Was this the luxury afforded by travelling with a rock band?

As if he read my mind, Ozzie quickly kyboshed that thought. 'Don't get too used to digs this good. It's because I know Bobby and Tien that we're here. Helps save a bit of money. It'll be cheap Airbnb's and motels afterwards.'

He left to retire to his guesthouse. I was beat and needed rest. I stripped down to my boxers and fell face-first onto the bed. I hoped to wake up a little more refreshed. I thought about what I'd witnessed in the couple of hours spent with the band and how the life of rock 'n' roll debauchery was different from my own. I underestimated my ability to ease into the situation. If I was going to survive and do my job effectively, I was going to have to embrace it… and quickly.

CHAPTER 4

Jetlag had me by the balls. Around 4.30am, I was sat upright in bed, wide awake and shrouded in darkness after about three hours of sleep. There was no way of nodding back off, so I got up and decided to make myself a brew. I searched the kitchen for a kettle but realised that the sparkling silver contraption in the corner was actually a coffee maker. It looked like it had fallen off the Starship Enterprise with its various knobs, buttons, and levers sprouting from every cavity. I fumbled about with it and concluded that I hadn't a clue how to work it. Making a monumental balls of it, I inadvertently poured coffee beans all over the surface, which added to my frustration. I nearly launched it out of the window as my agitation brewed. Something the coffee wasn't doing.

I gave up, searched the cupboards, and almost released a little sex wee when I eyed a jar of instant coffee. I took a deep, cleansing sniff as I opened the lid and almost dissolved at the smell of the fresh Colombian granules - one of the finest aromas ever.

With no kettle in sight, I placed the cup in the microwave to heat the bastard in an unorthodox fashion. I was fixated on the mug twirling around in the microwave, checking it every twenty seconds or so. It was taking an age to heat up, so I left it in for two minutes to get it going. It pinged and steam fired out when I opened the door. Too preoccupied with the thought of a fresh, hot coffee to start the day, I stupidly picked up the cup and almost dropped it immediately due to the scalding heat. I yelped through gritted teeth to stifle the sharp burn and almost kicked the table in anger. I refrained when I thought a broken toe would only add to my woes. Composing myself, I ran my hand under the cold tap, retrieved a nearby tea towel from the side, and used it to lift the cup from the microwave.

Whilst waiting for the coffee and my temper to cool down, I carefully unlocked the guesthouse door and stepped outside. There was a quaint freshness in the air, a strange sensation given that it was merged with a surreptitious warmth. I walked barefoot to the end of the terracotta-coloured tiled path and looked east. The transcendent spectacle of an Arizonian sunrise was moments away from blossoming.

I trotted back to my room, grabbed my coffee via the tea towel, scampered back outside, and rested against the hood of my car. The cul-de-sac was still cloaked in darkness, apart from a ray of sapphire blue light that bloomed in the distance like a flourishing flower on the first day of spring. Scenes of such magnitude were lost amidst the pollution on a typically bitter Manchester morning, but out in the remote desert, it was a sea of lustrous tranquillity when the sun began to peer over the horizon.

'Quite something, innit?' A voice behind me said.

'Jesus fuckin' Christ!' I squealed. A bit of coffee spilt to the floor.

'Shhh. You'll wake everyone up,' Ozzie said mid-guffaw.

'You scared the shit out of me.'

'Sorry, mate. I couldn't resist.'

He chuckled and lit up a cigarette.

'What are you doing creeping about at this time?' I asked.

'Same as you in all likelihood. No chance of getting any sleep with this jetlag.'

'Yeah, me too.'

'I had to get up anyway to sort some business out back in the UK. Phone never stops.'

'What about the band? Are they not up?'

'Up? They're not even back.'

'What? Really? Are you worried?'

'Nah. This is quite common for them. I don't know half the shit they get up to, and sometimes it's best not to know, but they'll be back. Probably found some house party somewhere.'

There was a pause before I asked, 'Hey, do you know how to work that coffee machine?'

He laughed and said, 'In all the time I've spent in America, it's still something I haven't quite mastered. Pain in the arse, aren't they?'

'I know, right? How complicated do they make it? I'd have brought a travel kettle if I'd known it was this difficult.'

Pointing at the mug full of coffee, he asked, 'Microwave?'

'Yep.'

'First time doing it that way?'

'Yep.'

'Burn your fingers?'

'Did you not hear me scream?'

'I did actually. Something told me it was to do with brewing up when I heard the microwave pinging.'

The coffee dilemma was swiftly forgotten as the sun inched higher to brighten up the background behind the cul-de-sac. I made out just how big the houses were on the patch. It looked like Ramsey Street in 'Neighbours', complete with a token basketball stand and hoop, set up at the top end of the crescent at the foot of someone's driveway. I was waiting for Lou Carpenter or Harold Bishop to appear and give Bouncer his morning walk.

The sunrise continued to astonish as the cobalt blue gave way to the amber dawn, which uncovered the reddish-brown, monolithic sandstone ridges in the distance. It looked like a portal to another world. I tried to take a mental picture as we stood in silent appreciation, rooted to the spot until the sun took its place high in the sky. There weren't going to be too many times in life that I got to savour a sunrise in the Arizona desert. It was everything I imagined it to be.

Ozzie broke the silence. 'You know I've seen this a few times, and it never gets old.'

'The closest I've seen to anything like this is the Grand Canyon,' I recollected.

'You've been to the Canyon?'

'Yeah. In a helicopter too.'

'Wow. I've never done that. How did that come about?'

'Long story. Vegas last year on a six-night trip.'

'Love Vegas, but not been for years. What did you make of it?'

I smirked as the memories flashed through my mind. 'It was incredible. Loved it.'

'Sounds like you have a tale to tell judging by that shit-eating grin.'

I laughed as he stubbed out his cig in a nearby ashtray on the floor.

I turned to marvel at the house we were in and its enormity. Changing the subject, I said, 'This place is huge. How do you know Bobby and Tien?'

'I've known them for years. Bobby was active in the music scene, but he doesn't do much anymore. They've both been good friends to me, hence why we're here. Like I said last night, don't get too used to houses this big.'

'I don't mind where we stay. I'm just happy to be here and can't wait to get out on the road.'

'Careful what you wish for. These tours are gruelling and take their toll, especially with this lot and what's at stake.'

'That much pressure, then?'

'We've taken a gamble, but I'm hopeful it'll pay off.'

Thinking about my writing assignment, I had a brainwave. 'Ozzie, I have an idea. Would it be OK to interview you for the blogs? Maybe find out more about your history and how the business side works? I think it'll make an interesting piece to use at some point mid-tour. We don't have to do it now, but we can record it when we get time.'

'Not a problem. Let me scan through it before you send it to Jamie. I don't want to come across as being *too* honest if you know what I mean? There needs to be an element of being tactful.'

'Of course. I won't send it without your approval.'

'There's no time like the present. We can do a bit now if you want?'

'Ok. I'll record bits throughout the tour and throw it all together.'

'Sounds good to me, kid.'

I went back to the room and retrieved the dictaphone. He plucked out another cigarette and lit it with a Rolling Stones Licks Zippo.

'Do you like Hunter S Thompson?' he asked.

'Who doesn't?'

'Well… you wanna know about the music industry, I'll begin with a quote of his.'

I pressed the red circle on the dictaphone.

'To quote the great man himself, "*The music business is a cruel and shallow money trench, a long plastic hallway where thieves and pimps run free, and good men die like dogs. There's also a negative side.*" That statement is as true now as it was back then. Doesn't life seem better when narrated by Hunter S Thompson?'

'Haha. It does.' It was impossible not to hear the quote in Thompson's unique tone of voice.

Ozzie continued, 'Anyway, I've been in this business a long time, and it's a proper back-scratching game. This industry will beat you into submission, and when you think you've had enough, it'll beat you some more.'

'Is it really that ruthless?' I asked.

'You bet your arse it is.'

'Why do you still work in it if it's so thankless?'

'What else am I gonna do? Become a fuckin' recruitment agent? It's who I am, and it's all I know. But things are different since I set up on my own. As Sinatra said, I do things *my* way. I've been in this industry for thirty-plus years, one way or another. I've been a roadie, promoter, event manager, band manager, tour manager, and worked for record labels - the works - but mainly for someone else. I've been part of some amazing bands who never made it for whatever reason, and I've been part of some average bands that *have* made it. But I've been fucked over countless times by the machine from both sides of that coin. I got sick of working for others and with pricks, so I set up on my own a few years ago. I know who the sharks are, and I won't do business with those tossers if it can be helped.'

'How many bands do you look after?'

'I have seven bands on the roster at different levels, but most won't do anything too special. They'll keep the underground venues ticking over but won't get crowds beyond a thousand or so. It's like throwing money on several numbers on the roulette wheel and hoping the ball lands on the number you heavily backed. But none of the bands on the roster are as promising as the Cutthroats.'

'Do you just look after bands, or do you get involved in anything else?'

'I get involved with a few events and festivals from time to time. I get asked to look after the bar, negotiate with bands, or look after backstage. Things like that. Sometimes it's not music-related, which can be a welcome change at times.'

'How did you get involved with that?'

'I know a lot of people, and I always get asked to provide some sort of assistance when it comes to big events cos I know what to do, who to talk to, and how to put people together. It helps keep me ticking along financially, but the ultimate aim is to take a band to the top, which is why this trip is important.'

'Take me back to the beginning. What was it like when you first started in music?'

'It was great in the nineties. I was lucky enough to experience it, but it was a different time. The smaller labels could make shit loads of cash back then. Selling millions of CDs at £13 each was like printing money, but the quality of the music spoke for itself. The way people worked was so different. We basically only worked two days a week and were at gigs and parties the rest of the time. Crazy times man, crazy times.'

'I just missed out on the nineties as an adult, but I remember it well. Just before the internet transformed everything.'

'I can tell you a story about that. The owner of one of the labels I was working for at the time kicked a guy out of the office once for talking about this new sensation that was going to revolutionise the industry. Most of us didn't believe him, and we couldn't imagine what he meant. Turns out this guy was from Yahoo and was talking about the internet. Everything changed after that. We had the opportunity to get in on the ground floor and blew it. But most companies were like that at the time, too blinkered to see past the next day.'

'You'd have made a killing if you'd invested then.'

'I bet some of the label bosses are kicking themselves now.'

'What's the biggest change the internet has brought since the nineties?'

'Well, albums used to make up 80% of a band's income. But now, because of streaming, they need to go back out on the road to make money. Live music is alive and well, especially with the increase in festivals, which helps bands reach new fans and establish reputations. It's easier for artists to get their music heard these days, but not in a mass way like it used to be with radio. People generally invest in tracks, not artists now.'

'How did you cope with the shift in mentality when the internet and social media boomed?'

'Training and learning mostly. I can't afford to stand still and not know how the technology works. Luckily, I've enlisted the help of a social media business to help on that front. What they do through various analytic programs and algorithms blows my mind. It's the new form of A&R. They find where interest and opportunities lie in entertainment, media, or live gigs. It's more about building campaigns, having relationships with influencers, and creating blogs and vlogs. It's a minefield, but I'm glad I have the help of this young enterprise company because I can't understand this generation's way of thinking for shit.'

'Me too. I couldn't imagine going to school in the age of social media. It'd be hell.'

'I shudder at the thought.'

'Coming back to the tour. Why America as opposed to keeping the Cutthroats in England?'

'As you know from hearing them last night, they have a distinct sound that removes them from the typical British indie rock scene. Britain is a fuckin' sewer, and the industry is full of nobs. Don't get me wrong, there are nobs here too, but I can tolerate them more. There's so much uninspiring, samey drivel with no soul that somehow gets heavily promoted. Labels don't take any risks anymore. The bands all look the fuckin' same too. I can't tell one from the other. You've seen how the Cutthroats differ. America embraces their style more, so that's where we're pushing them.'

'Were there any offers from British labels?'

'Yeah, I've had offers to do business with a few UK labels but rejected them for one reason or another. Mainly it's because I don't trust certain people from experience. They'll stick the Cutthroats on the back burner and won't progress them.'

'They were doing OK in the UK, surely? There's been a buzz about them.'

'UK has been decent, to be fair. I'm just not convinced they'll take off fully back home. We released a few EPs in quick succession, which sold alright, and gigs have been modest in size at some good venues up and down the country. There's been a lot of fans raving about them, claiming they're rock's next big thing, but not enough for my liking. I'm not prepared to risk it, even though this tour is an equally big risk. If it takes off here, then maybe the UK market takes care of itself.'

'Could they get a lucrative deal out here?'

'Who knows, but even lucrative deals aren't as lucrative as people think. All bands want to get signed, but they rarely know what that means. They see a certain up-front figure and get excited but fail to factor in the costs of studios, lawyers, managers, and labels. Oh, and tax, of course. That all gets deducted from the top line. After all that, there's not much left, especially when you split it between four members.'

'I've heard that Lynwood Music are interested. Is there an offer from them?'

'Nothing concrete, but they are interested. They're based out in Los Angeles and have a decent enough reputation. There are some risk factors with them, but they have a respectable track record and are growing. They've sorted the Whisky a Go Go gig, so they've come in handy and at least put some sort of statement of intent down. Some good bands have done alright with them. Who knows? I've been in touch with loads of labels, so hopefully, they'll send the A&R guys down to gigs to take a look. But this shit isn't a given. I've had a band before who I thought were a dead cert to be signed, but the American labels passed on them. They weren't half as good as the Cutthroats, and we never put on a tour for them either to tickle their fancy.'

'What happens if no one offers them a deal?'

'Then we're fucked. Not like I've got much of an alternative regards a different career path, but I'm getting sick of this industry. If the Cutthroats can't make it, then I don't have anyone else on my books that can, and I'm getting tired of the game and the search for that *one* band who have the potential to achieve global success. Time is of the essence, and time's running out.'

'And what about my involvement? How has that come about?'

'I've known your editor, Jamie, for years now. We've always had this idea to use a journalist to document a band tour to drum up interest. It started as a bit of drunken talk, but it began to creep into more sober conversations, especially more recently when I took on the Cutthroats. By giving constant updates of the tour, we think it'll raise the profile of the band and the mag. Sonic Bandwagon has been progressing well too. So, when the America tour came up, we started to put the idea into practice. Good for all parties. That's if you're writing lives up to the hype.'

'Well, if I didn't feel pressure beforehand, I do now.'

'Pressure sorts the men from the boys. Important eyes will be reading, I'm betting.'

I took a moment to let that sink in, and in my mind screamed *FUCK!*

'Why didn't Jamie do it himself?'

'Too afraid to fly, luckily for you. He's not been on a plane since a Dublin-bound flight in 1998.'

'I didn't know that. What happened on that flight?'

'Emergency landing. The poor sod has holidayed in the UK ever since, getting piss wet through every year on a campsite in Nefyn.'

Shifting his attention to me, he asked, 'What about you anyway? Jamie said you were already in San Francisco. What were you doing there?'

'I was about to go on a trip down the West Coast and eventually meet a girl.'

'A girl? Long way to come for a shag,' he joked.

'Not quite like that. I did want to travel first and then meet up later, but this girl's special. I met her in Vegas last year.'

'So, it suddenly becomes clear why you had that shit-eating grin when you mentioned Vegas.'

'Well...she was one reason, amongst others. I'll tell you about it at some point.'

'Time is all we have when we're on the road.'

'And stress, given what's at stake.'

'You're not kidding. Aside from the business side, I have to deal with those clowns and keep them out of trouble, which is an impossible task.'

Our chat lasted ages, but I was pleased with how forthcoming Ozzie was and how I could incorporate it into the blogs further down the line. It was about 6.30 in the morning, and Ozzie's story motivated me to crack on with the first piece. I let him know my plan, and he said he had calls to make to keep on top of his UK operation.

Back in the guesthouse, I pulled out my laptop and used the quiet time to write about the gig and why the Cutthroats were in the States. I remained tight-lipped when reporting what happened backstage. I didn't feel comfortable ratting the band out and revealing that drugs were plentiful, loose women were everywhere, and people were being banged in toilets and against dumpsters. I played it safe, which also didn't sit right. I convinced myself that I was setting the scene, hoping that the gig review would be enough to open the blog without delving into the nitty-gritty of the night. I sent it off with little confidence and awaited Jamie's response.

Twenty minutes later, while I lay on the bed mid-doze, I was interrupted by the buzz of my phone. I was surprised to see it was a call from Jamie, given it had passed midnight back home. I nervously answered. After an initial exchange of pleasantries, he told me that while it was a decent effort, he was editing parts to sharpen it up and removing some of the needless points. He also quizzed me on why there wasn't much about being behind the scenes at the gig. I lied and said I wasn't backstage for long because I was helping at the merch stand. He stated that I needed to be with the band as much as possible going forward as that was the hook to the story. He didn't want a series of gig reviews. He wanted more about what occurred offstage on tour and about life on the road in modern times. I was a little disheartened by his feedback but took his points on board.

CHAPTER 5

I opened the door to the guesthouse, and the heat blast was like I'd just opened the oven. The morning had landed in all its untainted glory. I made my way up the short, stoned path to the main house. The door was slightly ajar, so I tentatively entered and shouted, 'Hello.'

'Come through,' a female voice answered.

The place was immaculate and spacious. I walked down a glossy brown, natural stone floor to an expansive living area, where I was greeted by a couple in their late sixties. Both stood up from their chairs when they saw me wander in. The woman moved to hug me. 'You must be Ricky?'

'I am.'

'Welcome to our home. I'm Tien, and this is my husband, Bobby.'

She was affable and welcoming. Bobby extended his hand from behind Tien and drawled in a thick American accent, 'Welcome, my friend.'

I took his hand and nearly stumbled forward from the force with which he clutched and shook it. He didn't mean it as a sign of aggression. It was because he was a brute of a man with the grip of a seasoned marine.

Tien was of oriental descent and was short with a slender frame. Her hair was charcoal-black and cropped, falling just below her ears. She wore rounded, red spectacles that complemented her rosy red cheeks. She was well presented with make-up applied to perfection and dressed casually in a green vest top and black leggings. She hadn't stopped smiling since we met, and it was such an infectious, heart-warming smile that I couldn't help but reciprocate.

Bobby was tall and stocky, with a great head of mopped greying hair. His rugged face was complete with a bushy, hippie-style moustache, and his hulking arms and chest muscles were prominent underneath a psychedelic-coloured Grateful Dead t-shirt. If I'd still been a bit stoned from the night before, fixating on it for too long would've messed me up further.

Tien shifted into mothering mode, asking whether I'd eaten and if I wanted a drink. She reeled off a selection of choices, ranging from water to Jack Daniels. I gasped for another coffee and took the opportunity to ask about the coffee maker.

She giggled. 'You British. You're useless.' She showed me how it worked. Even as I watched, it was lost on me.

She offered to make me breakfast. Her first suggestion of scrambled eggs on toast was welcomed. I'd not eaten since the Philly cheesesteak, and I was starving. Tien kept a pristine and wholesome home. Several exotic plants flourished in the living room, and large paintings bordered by gold emblazoned frames hung on every wall. Pictures of Bobby and Tien with various family members were placed on top of the rich, mahogany furniture.

I took up a seat on a wooden rocking chair when Tien brought me the scrambled eggs and toast on a tray. I thought it would keep me full for most of the day as she must've used about five eggs and given me four slices of thick, wholemeal toast, professionally presented to circle the eggs.

'Jeez, I don't get this much food at an all you can eat buffet,' I exclaimed.

'Tien loves to cook. That's why I have this here.'

Bobby slapped his belly.

'I never hear you complain,' Tien laughed.

'I'm not. I'm just saying it's why I have this stomach bulge.'

I wasn't surprised, given the size of the portion placed in front of me.

Bobby spoke. 'Ozzie told us you came back with him last night and didn't stay out with those crazies.'

'I was too tired from the drive. Judging by the fact they haven't returned yet, I'm glad I didn't stay out.'

'Man, they'll be having a great time. I'm jealous.' Bobby added.

'Like you could keep up now,' Tien joked.

Ozzie joined us and overheard us talking about the band as he walked into the room.

'I'm proper sorry, you two. They shouldn't be staying out like this while they're staying at yours. It's bang out of order.'

Bobby answered, 'Don't think nothing of it, Oz. Kids will be kids. We've all been there. It's good to see that the traditions carry on. I could tell you a lot worse... especially from my time with the Eagles.'

If there was ever a moment that stopped me right in my tracks, that was it.

Fork primed next to my mouth, I leant forward, just as a bit of egg fell back to the plate.

'Whoa! Whoa! Whoa! The Eagles?' I cried.

'Yes. The Eagles.'

'The proper Eagles? As in Glenn Frey and Don Henley?'

'Yes, I believe they were in the band if memory serves. All a bit hazy now, you see.' He winked.

'You can't be so blasé saying, "my time with the Eagles". How did you...? When did you...? What...?' I genuinely fumbled to express the right words and questions.

'It's no big deal. Don't forget, that was my time. If this band of yours are all they're cracked up to be and make it, you'll get a similar reaction when you tell some kid that you toured with Cutthroat Shambles.'

'I get your point, and no disrespect to Cutthroat Shambles, but the Eagles are poles apart. Never mind that. You need to tell me about them.'

He chuckled. 'I was new to the music scene back then. This was before I worked at Tower Records. Probably in my early twenties, and the Eagles weren't who they ended up being at the time.'

'Whoa! Back up. You worked at Tower Records?'

'Yeah, but that's a different story.'

Bobby told me that he hung around with the Eagles in the early days of their first tour before they moved on to bigger and better things. He spoke about smoking weed with Glenn Frey like it was an everyday occurrence. I felt humbled to be in the presence of someone who had such a compelling story to tell of sixties America.

Speaking of his stint at Tower Records, he revealed he had been a good friend of the legendary founder, Russell Solomon. He had subsequently worked himself up to store manager in San Francisco. He moved about to different stores across the West Coast of America before getting involved in the more hands-on side of music. He had worked for big labels and in various divisions, including A&R, promoting, and managing. He reeled off legendary acts he'd met and worked with over the years. It was an impressive list, including most of the top sixties and seventies bands from that side of America.

I asked if he'd met the Doors (my favourite band). He said he'd never had any dealings with them as Morrison had died before he started to find his feet in the industry, but he had seen them live once when he was a teenager. That sparked a barrage of questions he couldn't answer all at once.

Bobby talked about his favourite band, the Grateful Dead. He said he moved to San Francisco to be closer to them, so he could see them in their hometown rather than travel from Los Angeles. He claimed he'd seen them over three hundred times throughout his life and had toured with them.

I was tongue-tied and absorbed his stories like a sponge. I was being schooled in a way the education system couldn't provide. He was open about his experimentations with acid and how crazy and liberating that time was in San Fran. I told him about my experience with peyote nine months earlier. He described his own first time, which was, of course, on tour with the Eagles. He said he had an hour-long conversation with a seven-hundred-year-old Medicine Man claiming to be part of a reincarnation line that was currently Bob Dylan. Trippy.

He talked more about Tower Records and how it was structured and managed. It seemed like the perfect business model for rock 'n' rollers back in the day, but perhaps not for your average modern-day company in a capitalist society.

He revealed how they'd partied all night, but they were always in work the following morning, regardless of how bad they felt. To feel a bit hungover was referred to as 'cocktail flu', which 'wasn't an illness but a lifestyle.' He talked avidly about the parties thrown in the back office on a Tuesday during open hours, and the drugs, oh so many drugs. It was mainly marijuana and cocaine that flooded the stock rooms, to the point that they even added it to the stock inventory, disguised as 'hand truck fuel'. It sounded insane.

There was a glint in his eye when he spoke of those cherished days. 'Working at Tower wasn't a job. It was a way of life. You were part of a family.'

Bobby had been somewhat of a drifter most of his life because of his role in music. He only settled down about ten years ago when he married Tien, although they'd been together fifteen years. They looked and acted like they'd been soul mates since being teenagers, which was refreshing to see in their advanced years.

He was retired from the music field. Having made his money, he spent a lot of his time doing voluntary work at the local community centre with underprivileged children. His contacts in the industry ensured he kept a hand in on some level. He was happy to let his house be used for bands passing through, which led me to ask how Bobby and Ozzie met.

They had dealt with each other in the early 2000s when many English bands were earmarked for US tours. Their relationship progressed from there as Ozzie gained more influence and scope. He used Bobby as a key contact in the States for various dealings, describing him as one of the rarest, most genuine people in the industry he could trust.

Bobby asked about the gig the previous night and cited the 'damn community awards' as the reason for his absence. While filling him in on the details, Ozzie's phone buzzed. He stared blankly at the screen and said, 'It's a local number. Wonder who that could be?

I hope it's not the venue, and those clowns haven't trashed the place or anything.'

He answered, and all we could hear was one side of the conversation.

'Hello…Yeah, this is Ozzie…Yeah, they're my guys… You what? Is this a wind-up?'

He looked startled, bringing his hand to the back of his neck. It didn't take a rocket scientist to know something was wrong.

He continued, 'What did they do? Is this serious? Yeah, I can come down. OK, thanks for letting me know.'

He hung up, and we waited for the verdict.

'You'll never guess what those set of clowns have done? They've only got themselves arrested!'

Bobby rolled his eyes.

'Arrested? For what?' I asked.

'They went to a house party last night where there were a few underage drinkers. Then, they were giving mouth to the police when they came in to break it all up. The officers threw them in the cells for the night. I've got to go down and bail them out. Why do I bother putting myself through this shit?'

'Which station are they at?' Bobby asked.

'Tucson Rillito.'

'That's a stroke of luck. The chief was at the community awards last night. He's a close friend. He owes me a favour after I got him VIP tickets to Alice's gig a couple of months ago.'

'Alice?' I jumped in.

'Cooper. He's an old friend.'

I just turned away and laughed. Was there no end to the surprises this guy threw out?

Bobby continued, 'I'll come with, in case they're looking to take it further. I'll get it quashed, don't you worry.'

'Cheers, Bobby. You're a lifesaver.'

'No sweat. C'mon, let's go.'

'You want me to come with you?' I asked.

'No, it's OK.'

Bobby added, 'The station isn't far. We shouldn't be long.'

I'd barely been with the band for twelve hours, and I'd already witnessed them rock the shit out of a packed venue, take class A drugs, been scarred for life by seeing two of the members having sex, and heard they'd been arrested. That was quite the impression to make in a short space of time. Rock 'n' roll was very much alive.

'Bobby will take care of it. Drunk and disorderly isn't such a big crime here,' Tien assured me.

'I hope so. It wouldn't be good if they can't cross State lines because of it.'

She giggled and said, 'You watch too many movies.'

I warmed to Tien. She had an eloquent charm and a soothing tone that imposed calmness. Her hospitality and kindness to a bunch of people she'd never met before was astounding. I certainly wouldn't let a mischievous band loose in my house, but I got the impression that even the most notorious rock band would behave themselves in her presence.

Having been enamoured by Bobby's story, I hadn't realised that Tien would have a similarly enigmatic past. I learnt she was quite the character herself. She was nineteen years old when she moved to the States from Vietnam, having been involved in the Vietnam War in a nursing capacity. Moving over to the US at that age was one of the bravest things I had ever heard. She moved away from nursing and had worked as a make-up artist for the past thirty years.

She invited me to a separate part of the house, which doubled as her private make-up studio where clients came to visit. Once there, my eyes shifted to the walls where pictures of celebrities decorated the entire room. I assumed it was a gimmick for the studio, but then Tien remarked, 'These are some of the people I've worked for. I like to have a signed photo of them on the walls in the studio.' She was just as blasé as Bobby was about his band tales.

Motionless and in utter shock, my mouth fell open. The pictures weren't just of any celebs, like the false ones you get nowadays. These were real Hollywood A-listers who'd done something other than being famous for being orange, having a six-pack, or posing on Instagram with Botox-filled duck lips.

'You two are a right pair of dark horses, aren't you? How the hell are these your clients? They're globally famous.'

'I used to work for a big movie studio. When I started to freelance, a lot of the actors and musicians stayed loyal to me.'

'Who the hell are you two? Where have I landed?'

This couple were extraordinary. I could've easily abandoned the tour and stayed with them for months.

Sometime later, during a barrage of questions I threw at Tien, I heard a car pull up outside, so I went to investigate. Bobby and Ozzie were in the front seats of the Dodge. Seconds later, the doors opened, and the band rolled out of the back. Will plummeted straight to the tarmac as he exited, met with jack-knife laughter from Quince and Kyle. They were clearly still wasted. Will picked himself up in stages and staggered around like Eddie from 'Bottom'.

Ozzie was visibly pissed off as he stomped towards the house. He muttered, 'Lucky fucks they are. It's a good job Bobby came with me.'

'What happened?'

'Turns out they were at a house party where there was quite a bit of underage drinking. Don't forget the legal age is twenty-one out here. They would've been fine getting away with that because they're well over the age limit, but Dee opened that gob of hers and tore one of the cops a new one.'

'I can imagine,' I joked.

'She called him a fascist piece of shit.'

I smiled at the thought.

'The cop she insulted wanted to do them all proper and have them in front of a judge tomorrow, but Bobby got it thrown out.'

'That's good then.'

'They're like cats. Worse actually. They've had way more than nine lives.'

My journalistic mind worked in overdrive.

'Should this little episode be mentioned in the blogs? I know it might be a sensitive subject but rock bands being arrested is always good publicity, especially in this instance.'

'I like your thinking but hold fire with that. Let me think about it.'

'No problem. Your call.'

The band wobbled over as Ozzie and Bobby went inside.

'Ricckkkyyyyy...our journalist...where were you, man? You missed out,' Will slurred while putting his arm around me.

His breath stunk of stale beer. I flinched and wafted my hand in front of my nose.

'Jesus, Will. That smells like dog shit. Here, have a mint.'

I handed him a piece of chewing gum.

'Where did you go?' I quizzed.

Kyle explained, 'It turns out Tucson is a pretty awesome party town. We went back to one of the girls' houses from that band, The... what were they called... Shitlights?'

'Shirelights,' I corrected.

'That's the one. Yeah, we went back to their gaff to practice our lines, if you know what I mean,' he said, tapping his nose.

'Cops didn't find any of that in the house,' Quince said.

'I saw some fucker flush it before they came in. When someone said, "The Police are here", I thought Sting and that had turned up,' Will joked.

Quince laughed, adding, 'I thought that copper was gonna cry when Dee laid into him. Funny as fuck.'

Dee still looked stunning despite spending the night on the piss and the morning in cells. Cool as a cucumber, she remarked, 'Yeah, the arrogant fucker deserved it, didn't he? I could see him perving at my ass. That's why he wanted to charge me so he could try and bribe me with sex. Fuckin' power abuser.'

She went into the house as me and the guys stood talking.

'What did Dee say to the cop?' I asked.

Will answered, 'Called him a fascist at first. Then she went more political, calling him a slave to society, a robot, power-hungry cock sucker... what else...?'

Kyle carried on, 'She got creative from there and called him, another prick in the wall, a small dicked jabroni who can't get it up without a truncheon, a twat faced bellend, a woman-hating bag of dildos. It was piss funny.'

'I'm surprised the charges got dropped.'

'Me too,' Will agreed, adding, 'that Bobby dude is sound, man. Sorted it all out for us. I don't know about the others.'

'Others?'

'Yeah, there were about twelve of us in those cells. I'm sure they'll be alright. I don't think they were serious about taking it further. They just got caught up in the melee.'

Kyle spoke up. 'I'm gutted. I was banging that girl again when the police came in. Seemed to be a theme of the night, not being able to get any alone time without being interrupted.'

He glared at me, and the lads sniggered at the obvious connotation. I felt uncomfortable and tried to justify myself. 'No one told me what you were doing in there. Believe me, that's the last thing I wanted to see.'

'That'll be an image you can keep for this trip and whack off to whenever you want,' Kyle mocked.

I recoiled. 'You're sick.'

'You should've stayed out with us, then you would've seen worse than that. You missed out, man,' Kyle reiterated.

'I think I saw more than enough.'

'Oh yeah, you saw Dee too, didn't you?'

'She told you then?'

'Of course.'

'What did she say?'

'Exactly what you saw. It's not like Dee's gonna be arsed about anything like that.'

I turned to Quince and Will. 'And what about you two? Were you two just as bad as Kyle?'

Kyle butted in. 'Will can't cos he's got an STD.'

Will turned red and said, 'Fuck off telling people that, Kyle.'

'Well, it's true, isn't it? You're riddled.'

'But journalists don't need to know about it.'

'Don't worry, I'm not gonna expose that to the world,' I assured him.

'I've only got a week left with this cream before it clears up.'

'He's got warts,' Kyle blurted out. Will punched his arm in response, but Kyle continued to mock his bandmate's plight, causing Will to scuffle with him and drag him to the floor.

Once they wore themselves out, we entered the house together. Dee had gone straight to bed, and Bobby, Ozzie and Tien were standing in the kitchen.

'Don't you think you should apologise?' Ozzie advised the lads.

They all apologised.

Tien responded, 'They don't have to apologise. They're little rebels. Let them enjoy it. I think you better get to bed, though. And before you come back down, have a shower, you dirty, smelly boys.'

'Yeah, get to bed.' Ozzie scowled at them.

Tien decided she was cooking us a traditional Vietnamese buffet for dinner, ready for when everyone woke up. While she prepped everything, Bobby continued to tell stories from his past. He was a priceless relic from rock 'n' roll's heyday, a fountain of knowledge. I could imagine sitting on rocking chairs with him for days and looking out into nowhere, sipping moonshine as he described his experiences from an important time in culture.

Later, the band filtered downstairs. The three boys looked worse for wear with dishevelled hair and exhausted eyes. Dee still looked untroubled by the heavy night, tiptoeing about in a vest, shorts, and no make-up.

The outside terrace was a zen-like terracotta-coloured sun trap, brimming with exotic plants and a gorgeous stone water feature in the corner that filled a small pond.

A smorgasbord of food engulfed the table as three enormous platters awaited. Cellophane covered the feast and was being begged to be ripped off so we could plough into it. To top it off, Bobby had placed bottled beers in nearby coolers. The band delved into them, despite not being up long. Bobby disclosed that he didn't drink anymore, and he'd 'spilled more beer in my life than you've drunk.' I didn't doubt it.

Tien explained what was customary when eating Vietnamese cuisine. We had to wash our hands in the bowls provided and pick the food with our fingers. She showed us how to roll traditional rice paper and how to add the food contents in the correct order. It started by soaking the rice paper and then adding lettuce, cucumber, carrot, mint leaves, sweet onion, and herbs. Prawn and/or chicken with noodles was placed on top, and then came the hard part, rolling the damn thing. My attempt was abysmal, but the lads handled the challenge with ease. I suspected that the experience of rolling joints gave them an advantage. Tien's secret homemade sweet chilli sauce was the piquant ingredient to dip into.

If we weren't stuffed enough from the main course, Tien brought out a sizeable bowl of fruit salad and rice biscuits, followed by cherry chocolate ice cream. Belt buckles well and truly loosened afterwards. For a trip on a budget, the overindulgence was a welcomed and rare treat.

After the meal, Ozzie turned to me. 'I read your first piece this morning.'

I felt nervous as I asked, 'What did you think?'

'It was good. I see you left out what happened after the gig. I'm sure the band will be pleased about that.'

'I thought it'd be best at this stage.'

'You're probably right. I'm sure they'll appreciate what you said about their show.'

'I was being truthful. I've got to admit, Jamie has edited a bit of the piece.'

'Don't worry about it. That's his job, and this is new to you. You'll find your rhythm, I'm sure. Just stick at it.'

'What about revealing that they got arrested on the next blog?'

'Fuck it, use it. Be vague as to why. I'll say it was my decision to include it if there's any backlash.'

I was glad he agreed. It would certainly spice up the blogs and appease Jamie.

'I was thinking about writing a piece on Bobby and Tien too? What do you think? Do you think they'll be OK with it?'

'Yeah, that's a good idea. Just ask them first, but they'll be cool.'

The beer steadily flowed, and Bobby's music choice had been exemplary for the mood. The Greatest Hits of Buffalo Springfield had lurked pleasantly in the background during our meal, followed by a series of 'Golden Nuggets' from the San Francisco sixties psych scene. Most of it was new to me, but I was engrossed with it and could hear the acid dripping out of most tracks.

I asked Bobby and Tien if I could write about them for the blogs. They were more than happy for me to include them. Their story was far too remarkable to leave out.

Dee had spent most of the evening in deep conversation with Tien away from the rest of us and had ignored me all night. I was thankful she had so that I wasn't on the receiving end of another tongue lashing. However, I was concerned that the piece for Sonic Bandwagon would lack something if she refused to be forthcoming with me. An interview with her was expected at some point.

The rest of the evening played out without incident. It turned out to be a great elbow bending session. Just a set of music lovers shooting the shit. Bobby was the focal point with his endless yarns and anecdotes. The band had been on their best behaviour all evening, but I got the impression that the politeness was a prelude to the excess and controversy that waited on the rest of the tour.

CHAPTER 6

5am, wide awake again thanks to the relentless jet-lag. After an hour or so spent tossing and turning, I was up, fully packed and in the kitchen waiting for everyone else to surface, microwaved coffee in tow.

I checked the social media interaction of my first blog post. The hits, comments and shares dwarfed most of my previous reviews. It was testament to the band's popularity and how the tour had been spun back home by both Sonic Bandwagon and Ozzie's management. I was told when I began writing reviews that if the readers focused on the author's writing, it took attention away from the band. My first piece for the Cutthroats succeeded in keeping the attention on the band's performance and the build up around it.

I was productive in the quiet period, knowing that time was a precious commodity with everything that could happen on tour. I wrote about Bobby and Tien and transcribed what Ozzie had told me about his past as prep for future submissions and to reduce the chances of a rushed job.

We'd planned to get away as soon as possible, so it wasn't long before everyone was up. Bobby offered to take us out to a breakfast bar called Bobos, which he referred to as the 'Best Breakfast in Tucson'. We brought everything with us so we could head straight onto the interstate for El Paso, where the band were due to play DesertFest in the early evening.

Bobos was a single-storey, stand-alone, small yellow prefab by the side of the carriageway. The area consisted of numerous small buildings and strip malls with massive car parks, quite a different set-up to back home.

The queue for Bobos stretched outside, and it hadn't even passed 8.30am. We were given a number and told to wait to be seated. Maybe Bobby's assessment of being the 'Best Breakfast in Tucson' was correct.

When we were called, the waiter greeted Bobby, clearly knowing him as a regular. We had to split into two tables of four. I stuck with Bobby, Tien and Ozzie, and the band sat together on the other side of the café. Bobos was only small and resembled a UK greasy spoon, indicating that it was delicious from a home-cooked point of view. I ordered a Californian Omelette, and the rest ordered different variations of the pancakes on offer. When they arrived, they looked nothing like our Shrove Tuesday pancakes. They were huge, thick, and packed to the rafters, resembling a flying saucer. The amount of sugar layered on top made my teeth sore just looking at it. There was enough on there to kill off a diabetic.

After breakfast, Bobby insisted on handling the bill, despite Ozzie's protest that he'd already done enough. His concerns fell on deaf ears.

We congregated outside. Tien had a tear in her eye when she said her goodbyes.

Bobby joked, 'Here she goes again. Always with the drama. She gets emotional when saying goodbye to guests she likes.'

She hugged each of us and said, 'Stay safe and good luck with the rest of the tour. I hope we see you again. You're welcome anytime.' Her final parting words were, 'You all have a home and a family in Tucson.' That sentiment summed up our hosts.

Once they disappeared in their car up the carriageway, we sorted out the route to El Paso. Will attempted to wind Ozzie up about the tour logistics.

'Ozzie, this planning is shocking. We've come to Tucson to go east to El Paso, and then we come all the way back again, bypassing Tucson, and then off to Phoenix.'

'Well done, Will. I'm surprised you can read a map, what with your failure to even attend your GCSE Geography exam.'

'How do you know about that?'

'Your mother told me.'

'Oh, he's done you there,' Kyle teased.

'It had to be this way because of the festival in El Paso, which I've pulled several strings for you to play, and at a decent time slot. We could only get the good venues in Phoenix and Tucson on the days I've booked, so stop your whinging, appreciate what I've done for you, and enjoy the drive. You never know, you might expand your brain cells to at least three by travelling in this part of the world.'

Will was silenced as Kyle and Quince laughed.

I was happy when Ozzie said he'd ride with me to keep me company. Quince drove the others in the Dodge and had gone on ahead as I had to make an early pit stop to 'gas' up before the long journey commenced.

Ozzie wandered off to make a call while I filled up. I was left alone at the pump and became confused about what to do, so I had to embarrassingly go to the kiosk and ask the assistant for help. The cashier was a plump lady with straggly brown hair, and she loudly chewed gum.

She said, 'You have to pay first. How much do you wanna put in, honey?'

'I don't know. Thirty dollars?'

She looked surprised and responded, 'Thirty bucks? Are you sure?'

I nodded as I tentatively handed over my card.

'Ok, I'm sure it'll be much less than thirty bucks.'

I was nearly on empty, so how could it not be over thirty bucks?

Back at the pump, the tank took a while to fill. The cost crept up slowly to the point where I assumed there was a blockage somewhere. Then, it stopped at eighteen dollars. I kept pressing the trigger, and it wouldn't go any further. When I got back in the car, the tank was full. I was shocked. That was about fifteen quid. If I filled up a car that size back home, I'd have had to have sold a limb. Just another example of how we get screwed in the UK.

I couldn't hide my giddiness from Ozzie at my discovery.

He joked, 'It doesn't take a lot to excite you, does it? Let's hope I don't see you when you're about to get laid.'

El Paso was four hours away, but we had plenty of time to get there. We settled in for the trek, prepping the car with some music to ease the passing. 'Green River' by Credence Clearwater Revival was what the 'shuffle' function brought up next on the playlist.

We quickly got onto the subject of Dee. Ozzie described her as a closed book and that there was something deep-rooted that made her tick the way she did. Whatever it was consistently manifested itself in sporadic spurts of aggression, anger, and the need to push the limits - especially when things didn't go her way.

My presence fell into that category. On the flip side, it made her an extraordinary performer who gave everything onstage.

We got back into the groove of the conversation we'd been having the previous day about Ozzie's history and current role. Again, I let the dictaphone record the conversation and asked him, 'How did you find the Cutthroats?'

'I discovered them quite early in their career. I think they'd only been together a month or two before I saw them at The Deaf Institute supporting another band I was there to see. Off the back of that performance, I had a frank conversation with them, offered my services, and the rest is history.'

'When did you have the idea about the US tour?'

'That night.'

'Seriously? The night you saw them?'

'Yep. I knew right then where their destiny lay. I couldn't get them over here immediately, of course. We had work to do, but the America gig was always the plan.'

'Are you funding the tour yourself?'

'All the upfront costs, yeah.'

'You're mad. It must cost you a fortune?'

'It's not too bad, but don't forget we're getting paid decent money for some of the gigs, so that'll put a dent into it. The people in Charlotte had a whip-round after the show. You wouldn't believe how much was in the pot at the end.'

'How much?'

'Just over five hundred dollars and that was just tips. That's given us more than enough breathing space.'

'Did it cost a lot to ship over all the gear?'

'Not really with just the guitars, merch and luggage. Luckily, we've agreed with all the venues we're playing to use the drumkit of another band, so we didn't have the added cost and ball ache of shipping one over. I've not even taken up the offer at some venues to pay for someone to watch the merch stand throughout the show. I'll do it myself, and you can help too.'

'Not a problem.'

'I'll pull a fast one anyway and just draft one of the bar staff to look after it every so often when needed. I'm not shelling out fifty bucks a gig just for that.'

'I get that. What exactly have you fronted?'

'I've paid for flights, car rental, accommodation, and give them a bit of food allowance. But the lads especially aren't too fussy foodwise, and Dee is always wary of remaining slim, so she doesn't eat much. I can take them to Maccies. They'll be happy sharing a fuckin' gherkin between them.'

'And what about their booze allowance?'

'That comes from them, but a lot of booze comes from riders so it's not going to cost them too much.'

'Some might think that the tour is too short, considering the cost factors. Did you not think of extending it?'

'I did, but money is a huge factor if we extended it for a month or so. Ultimately, we are losing money, but we hope to recuperate it in the long run. The fact we got the Whisky gig in Los Angeles is a massive coup, so that alone was worth coming over for. I have a couple of irons in the fire that I'm not going to share just yet that might prolong it.'

'Have the band made similar sacrifices to you?'

'More, I'd say. I encourage a band to be all or nothing, and the Cutthroats didn't hesitate to adopt that approach. They've gone all in and made sacrifices regards their jobs. That's how much we believe in this thing.'

'I know that feeling,' I added before he carried on.

'Also, don't tell Jamie I told you this, but he's a right tight arse at times. He didn't want to shell out the costs for you, the journalist, and I had to tell him it was his duty. He relented at travel and accommodation costs, but the rest is on you, I'm afraid.'

'Fine by me. Travel and accommodation are more than enough.'

'I'll shout you a beer from time to time, as long as you don't drink like the Cutthroats.'

'I've had my moments getting blitzed in the past, but something tells me I won't be quite as bad when I'm technically working.'

I paused before firing the next question at him. 'What is it about them that has you so invested?'

Ozzie thought for a moment. 'First of all, if you can't perform live with a great dynamic, then forget about it. Singing is one thing, performing is another, and the two together can be a rarity. Dee has both in abundance. There is the sex appeal aspect too that's the icing on the cake. You can have a good song, but if you don't look right, the song might die. You can have a semi-decent song, look good and probably do OK. But if the look is good, and the song is good, then there's a great chance it could blast off. They have it all: tunes, looks, talent, and that edge and attitude.'

'I never really thought of it like that. I guess I've just liked or disliked a song or band, and not really thought about the mechanics behind it.'

'Don't underestimate the fickleness of the average listener. It can be a nightmare when piecing everything together behind the scenes. It goes beyond just having a good song nowadays.'

'Are the band always as crazy as they were in Tucson? Things were getting a bit wild backstage at Sky.'

'What can I say? They're young, good-looking, free and single, and in a rock band.'

'I almost don't like standing next to them. I probably look like a gremlin in comparison.'

He laughed.

'How do you think I feel being an old geezer and watching all that shit happen around me? But hey, I'm used to it. You feeling a little left out? Did you not get any action because the boys took all the girls from you?' His tone turned sarcastic.

'Not quite. I could've done if I wanted to. I was kind of propositioned.'

'So why didn't you? You're on tour with a band. It's what you're meant to do.'

I shrugged my shoulders, but he saw right through me.

'Ah, I see. This have anything to do with the girl you were meant to be meeting up with?'

'Partially.'

'What's she called?'

'Eva. She's Puerto Rican.'

'Nice. So, come on then. Time is all we have on the road. Tell me about her.'

I retold the story about how Eva and I met and how she helped transform me into the person I'd become. I rambled on like some lovesick teenager about how and why I was in Vegas nine months earlier and the revelations I had in the desert when I was there. I spilt everything from my ex-girlfriend to my shit job to how I ended up writing for a music magazine.

I surmised, 'I might not be here if it wasn't for Eva. So, here was my dilemma after the gig last night. I'm backstage with a rock band, with a bunch of girls hanging around. I could've been like every other dog with a dick and got my rocks off, and probably feel shit about it because I'm kind of with someone that lives thousands of miles away with no real future in it.'

'And the other option?'

'I can be the guy who went on tour with a rock band and didn't get his rocks off because he was kind of with someone that lives thousands of miles away with no real future in it. It'd be easier if I were just like any other lad and not give a shit, wouldn't it?'

'Sounds like this girl is pretty special. You've got a lot of thinking to do.'

'Typical. Another quest for answers. That's not like me at all,' I quipped.

'Do we ever stop looking for the answers to our riddles, Ricky? I'm still fuckin' searching, and I'm a bit longer in the tooth than you.'

He was right. Do we ever stop searching for answers?

As silence descended upon us, the music became a welcomed buffer to the conversation. Thunderclap Newman's, 'Something in the Air' played, and again I acknowledged the importance of music being played on the road. The synergy between the road and music was substantial and defined the whole desert driving experience. Each song's core and connotation seemed to intensify and somehow managed to find an easier route to my soul than in any other setting.

We had fled the desert. Slowly, luscious backdrops and greener pastures inched into the terrain, with farms becoming more of a roadside feature on the lengthy I-10 Highway. I noticed just how big everyone's car was as they passed us. No one had a Punto or a Mini. Everything in America had to be big and overpowering, and the 've-hi-cles' were no different. Top of the range, shiny pickup trucks swarmed the freeways, and they looked like they'd never seen a building site.

Four hours raced by, aided by the heavenly surroundings and onslaught of classic tunes that prompted periods of quiet reflection. Much like my journey down to Tucson, we'd crossed another time zone and jumped forward another hour.

After turning off the I-10, we hit a litany of secluded streets that led to our modest abode. The landscape was flat but harsh, and foliage grew sporadically by the sides of the dusty roads. The amount of space between each building and house was vast. Despite not being in the most affluent of areas, each house was detached with a long driveway, garage, and front and backyards that covered a sprawling square footage. To own a similar size plot in England would be a pricey affair. In parts of the States, they could be picked up for peanuts.

The band had arrived about fifteen minutes before us. They had found the key in the lockbox provided by the Airbnb host, who wasn't around to greet us. Airbnb has many perks for travellers. To stay in cheap houses or apartments in the middle of conventional neighbourhoods was welcomed. It was certainly a more fun way to travel. We could immerse ourselves into the culture of a town and not just a tourist version of it, cooped up inside a hotel, having same experience as everyone else.

The place wasn't too bad for the cost. It was basic and unembellished, with enough essential furniture, amenities, and space to not be considered sub-standard. There were three bedrooms so we could at least spread out and not have to sleep together in the same room. Dee took the biggest room with a double bed. There was one room with three single beds, which the lads took, and the other room was left to me. Ozzie didn't mind taking the sofa bed in the living room.

He pointed out. 'We only need a place to get our heads down for the night. I'm not looking for anything like the Radisson on this trip. Besides, slumming it keeps you grounded and is kind of the point of a tour with an unsigned band.'

He was, of course, right.

CHAPTER 7

We were a good twenty minutes away from the heart of the festival. Standing outside the house, I felt just how hot and sticky El Paso was. We were in the cavern of a late afternoon heat spurt, which intensified as we piled into the Dodge. Dee demanded Ozzie switch the air con to full blast for the drive to Desert-Fest.

The three-day festival promised to be a busy, action-packed affair, given the coverage and the event's reputation. It prided itself on showcasing a cornucopia of the best in unsigned rock in its rawest form, with the additional better-known band headlining as an added draw. The festival's layout spread across various locations in the downtown area through pop-up stages and utilising the many local music venues.

DesertFest was also heralded as a networking haven for managers, promoters, and labels alike, which was why Ozzie was champing at the bit. It was a chance for him to promote, create opportunities, and attempt to get as many people as possible to attend the Cutthroats' slot.

He'd spoken to Jamie earlier, and the message to me was that I had to be part of the networking game and meet the big dicks to help promote Sonic Bandwagon. I hadn't even considered it until that point, but given what Jamie had done for me, I knew I had to make the effort, despite networking being a far cry from my persona. I wanted to enjoy the festival without trying to do the whole fake shake, what can I do for you, what can you do for me, I'll scratch your back if you scratch my bollocks, bollocks.

We hit the busy drag leading into the heart of El Paso. Traffic was unsurprisingly heavy given the town's merriments, meaning we crawled at a snail's pace. The streets were flooded with rockers of all stereotypes, from cowboy to biker, spilling out of bars and venues that elevated the festival's buzz.

The early rumbling of 'Sweet Emotion', by Aerosmith, came on the radio and served as our entrance song.

'Crank this up, Ozzie,' Kyle demanded. Ozzie complied, and the tune blasted out of the windows, drowning out any nearby music.

We barely managed to hit above ten miles per hour for the rest of the way, but we finally made it to the car park reserved for artists and staff at the Mohawk Stage. The venue was in the middle of a small park on the edge of the central area. It was the second biggest of the four pop up stages and was reserved for rock and blues acts.

Before unpacking the Dodge, Ozzie found one of the stage organisers. After briefly talking to him, he brought him over and introduced all of us one by one.

'Hi, dudes. I'm Martin.'

'Centre Partin' Martin, wahey,' Kyle mocked. I was forced to turn and walk away for fear of bursting in front of poor Martin, especially as he did have a nasty parting.

Martin smiled awkwardly. He was a gangly man in his late thirties, and he looked out of his depth in rock 'n' roll.

He began arse-licking the band. 'It's a pleasure to have you guys here. I know you're going to rock out, you dig?'

Kyle double-thumbed up and overenthusiastically said, 'We dig, Martin, we dig indeedy-roo.'

Again, I fought to compose myself as Martin turned his attention to Dee.

'I'm a huge fan of your work, Ms Darrell. I've seen you perform on YouTube many times, so I'm stoked to have you here tonight playing on our fabulous Mohawk Stage.'

Martin's attention turned to Ozzie as they discussed timings and set-up details.

Dee turned to Kyle and said, 'I've had my ego stroked before, but this guy's having a serious full-on fuck sesh with it. What a joker.'

Being an unknown journalist, no arse-kissing came my way when I eventually introduced myself. Nothing more than a handshake and nod was presented to me. Dee clocked the disregard, shot me a look and whispered, 'Told you you're a fuckin' nobody.'

I laughed back to humour her.

The band were whisked off to fulfil a quick interview with the festival organisers for their website. Ozzie and I were ushered to a different area under an enormous canopy. It was busy, but not as much as out front, where the wind carried the crisp and smooth sound of an amplified Fender guitar in full flow, placing it gently into my ears.

Ozzie and I worked the circuit. He was more proactive than me and at least had business cards to give out. I had nothing.

I met a few fellow journalists and photographers, who I stuck with, which I didn't think was what Jamie had in mind when he asked me to network. From my point of view, it was terrific meeting different people in the same field. Most had far more experience than me, and given that the band didn't know my level, I had to be prudent not to give the game away. Some of them worked for big magazines I'd heard of, either printed or online. They were there to cover the whole festival, which was enviable, but when they found out I was solely covering a band on a US tour, they were astounded. Some questioned whether that type of coverage happened anymore, but they were inspired and intrigued by the concept. Maybe what we were doing with the blogs was to be the start of a trend. The intention didn't need to be about researching a world-renowned band for a book or global-wide magazine. The idea was more innovative, set in different times about a band who still hadn't 'made it', whatever that meant in today's scene. Being published by an emerging magazine gave an added impetus and beauty to the whole idea.

After an hour or so, Ozzie came over to me.

'How's it going? Been eaten alive yet? It's full of some right bullshitters this place. I know I can blag with the best of them, but I can at least back it up. I know America is the best place for the Cutthroats, but fuck me I've had to listen to some right pricks who are full of shit.'

He pointed to a man in his fifties with a crew cut and big chin. 'That fuckin' sack of shit over there is a right arrogant bastard. He's an A&R guy but a fuckin' snake, a right know-it-all. Trying to give me advice and tell me where I'm apparently going wrong. Had to walk away before I chinned him.'

'What's he called?'

'Fuck knows. Can't remember. The "Oracle" for all I know.'

'Have you seen anyone from Lynwood here?'

'I've spoken to a rep associated with them.'

'Are you gonna tell the band?'

'Nah. They don't need any more motivation. How about you? Who've you been chatting to?'

'Just been talking to a few journos and togs really, hearing their stories. I've told them to watch the Cutthroats later and said who I write for and what I'm doing here. A few raised an eyebrow at the tour being covered like this, especially for an unsigned band.'

'I guess that's what we're trying to do. Create a new slant for a band not as well-known as some. Bring some reality to the story rather than the lavish side.'

The band entered the canopy after their interview. Dee had also changed into performance attire. She looked stunning, wearing a stylish black and silver catsuit, which had all the flamboyance and sparkle of a seventies glam rock star. Her hair was different too. The wavy black locks had been tampered with and styled funkier, with hairspray giving it an extra bounce. She sauntered over to the drinks table, poured herself a glass of white wine and downed it in one.

Soon after, the band were called to get ready as they were due onstage. Dee gathered her bandmates.

'Ok, bring it in, you fuckers.'

The band huddled together, and bowed heads against each other. Dee started harmonising, The Beatles', 'With a Little Help from My Friends'.

I muttered to Ozzie, 'What's the reason behind this?'

'I don't know. They've never told me, but it's a ritual done before every gig.'

A few spectators nearby clapped as the spontaneous harmonising came to an end. Dee remained impassive. Instead, she fitted her burgundy cowboy hat before telling the band, 'I want a better performance than Tucson.'

Her strive for perfection was a sign of a true star who wouldn't accept anything less than absolute excellence.

Ozzie and I moved into a small press pen outside at the foot of the stage. Six hundred or so rockers looked our way, which was a bit daunting, but at the same time, kind of a rush. We hovered by the complimentary drinks table, and I poured myself a glass of cava - so sophisticated. A few of the togs and journos I'd met earlier acknowledged me and revealed they were looking forward to the show. It seemed my plugging had worked.

Martin took to the stage and strode to the microphone nervously. He engaged the devotees of blues rock for a few seconds before announcing, 'Our next band are from England. Let's give a warm welcome to Cutthroat Shambles!' Modest applause and whistles rang out as the three lads took their positions. They blazed out of the blocks with the fiery, 'Rock N Roll Heaven', the same opener from Tucson. Dee appeared after the short instrumental and hit the crowd with her sonorous vocals.

The songs continued to dazzle as they blitzed through another three pulsating, blood-pumping tracks: 'On Your Knees', 'Even', and 'Oblivion'. With lips puckered and confidence oozing, Dee heavily rocked her head and body back and forth to every power thrust from Kyle's cutting guitar licks.

The impact made on the audience, the suits, the photographers, and the journalists was evident. The Mohawk Stage became a hub of electricity. Maybe Dee was right, and the Tucson gig wasn't up to standard because there seemed to be a noticeable step up in class, sounding crisper and tighter. They took a breather after four rousing tracks in a row, and Dee used the interlude to riff with the festivalgoers while the guys tuned up for the next onslaught.

'How y'all doin' out there, El Paso?' she bellowed.

Moderately loud cheers fired back.

'No, no, no. That's no good. I said, how y'all doin' out there, El Paso?' in a louder tone that brought about a rowdier response.

'That's what I'm talking about. Y'all meant to be rockin' 'n' rollin' out there.'

Another loud cry rang out. Dee just smiled, oblivious to the reverence.

She brought the mic back up to her mouth.

'We're so happy to be here. This next one is dedicated to all the weird and wonderful rockers out there. Hold your beers up in the air and take a drink for me!'

The spectators obeyed her command.

'Al-right!' she shot back before nodding to Kyle. He launched into the opening of a re-imagined version of 'Gold Dust Woman' by Fleetwood Mac. I was a big fan of the song beforehand, but something in the way Dee performed it took it to an even more haunting dimension if that was possible. It was one thing to even attempt to cover Stevie Nicks, but to rival her took a whole new level of talent I'd never encountered before. I was gobsmacked and besotted. It was *that* good and one of the best cover songs I'd ever witnessed. Despite the tension between us away from the stage, I started to adore Dee on it. She really was two personalities.

The forty-five-minute show mesmerised the crowd. They showed their adoration with a boisterous ovation that left Ozzie with a satisfied smile on his face.

Shortly after they departed the stage, the band were mobbed by various industry types. The Oracle, who Ozzie mentioned earlier, sniffed around them.

Ozzie sprang into action. 'I'm gonna have to go over there and make sure that prick knows who's boss. I can just see him trying to undermine me.'

'You need any help?'

'Nah it's cool, man. I'll drop him like a small sherry if he says anything. You stay here and enjoy the next band.'

I hung around with a few of the togs and journos from earlier. They gushed over the Cutthroats' performance and reiterated how lucky I was to be on the trip.

The next band up were Twisted Wheel. They demonstrated why they were worthy of such a lofty slot at the festival with a swagger reminiscent of past idols. The onslaught of sharp lyrics about the everyday areas we lived in, and the quirky characters that inhabited them, merged with high-octane, adrenaline-fuelled punk/rock music. Those factors were a lethal combination that brought hedonism to their set, especially when 'You Stole the Sun' started, which sent their fan base berserk. It was a sight to behold and a fitting song to elevate the atmosphere as beer and plastic cups became airborne. The fans cried, 'Wheel! Wheel! Wheel!' throughout the show, and the energy never relented. They were a revelation and blew me away.

I wondered why bands blessed with immense talent weren't a commercial success and had escaped the clutches of managers and promoters to lift them to global icon status? Why did the drivel that swarmed the charts become mainstream? What had happened to a generation? Why was it lost? Why wasn't music of that calibre played on every radio station all over the world? The questions burned inside me as my third glass went down easy. Somehow, this generation had become brainwashed into making idols out of the current pop scene. A scene that now carried no depth or soul and required about thirty people to write and produce songs. The type of band music deemed pop when the youth culture exploded had now been driven underground. It made me angry to think that mainstream culture had changed so much.

Ozzie returned. 'Everything OK?' I asked.

'Yeah. I had to be subtle but firm with that prick. Didn't want to make a scene, but I think he got the message by the way I stared at him. He's fucked off to another stage now.'

'Ha. Don't fuck with a Mancunian.'

'Too right, man.'

Ozzie's attention turned to Twisted Wheel. 'This is where I need to get the Cutthroats to.'

'I don't think they're too far off. Tucson was pretty special, and the fans here loved them.'

'I reckon most of the crowd were probably already here for Twisted Wheel. I need to get a crowd this size purely for them and for everyone to be singing the lyrics back. They're not quite there yet.'

'It'll happen. I'm convinced of that.'

'Better had do, or else all this is a waste of time. I just had a brief word with the rep from Lynwood. He was impressed, so hopefully, he'll report good things back to his boss.'

I could sense the anxiety and strain Ozzie was under in his quest to push the band to where he thought they deserved to be. His aggressive and overprotective action to scare off the Oracle seemed out of character, even though I'd only known him a couple of days. Perhaps the Oracle deserved it, and I wasn't experienced enough to recognise the snakes in the industry like Ozzie was.

Referring to my earlier thoughts, I asked him, 'Why do you think bands like Twisted Wheel aren't proper global commercial successes anymore?'

'There are a few reasons. Money plays a big part. If you've got some private backing and are a bit marketing savvy, then it can go a long way. Unfortunately, there's not a great deal of money in the rock industry to go around. Do you think what you hear on mainstream radio is just the DJ's own choice? It may have been at one time, but not anymore. They play the music where the money comes from, and most of it comes from crap.'

'Is that why the pop scene does better? Because that's where the money is?'

'There was a time when rock 'n' roll *was* pop. It's just that the definition of pop has changed. It's become less about the actual music and more about appearances.'

'I can't argue with that. I wouldn't exactly say I was a fan of girl groups like the Spice Girls, but as a horny teenager, I was into them on a hormonal level.'

'Precisely. That's what the moguls do. They get a few people together who are fuckable and put them in front of a horny teenage audience, and bingo, you got yourself a money machine.'

'Just like those reality TV Shows.'

'Don't get me started on that bollocks. Culture really has undergone major cosmetic surgery. There's been a massive shift in attitude that evolves monthly. It's the work of the fuckin' devil. Look at those glorified TV karaoke shows and how they play games with the contestants' emotions. It's a modern-day blood sport. I've had the displeasure of dealing with one of the creators of those shite shows.'

'Which one?'

He raised his eyebrows. 'The main one.'

'Really?'

'Yep.'

'What's he like?'

'Do I need to explain?' he joked.

'Haha. No. I get it.'

The look on his face said it all.

'Those shite shows are one of the reasons for the death of rock 'n' roll in popular culture. Band music won't stand a real chance as long as that type of shit is on TV brainwashing people. I've been approached by them a few times regards one or two of my acts.'

'Really? What was your reaction?'

'Told them to fuck off. You wouldn't believe the level of manipulation that goes on behind the camera.'

'I can imagine all is not what it seems.'

'One of the show's researchers called us at least four times asking for this talented girl we had to go on the show. We declined every time, so do you know what they did then? Offered us a pass to the producer's audition...a fuckin' pass. What's talent got to do with it if you can sidestep every other fucker by persistently saying no to the researchers?'

I was becoming just as irate as Ozzie, who had gone into full rant mode.

He continued, 'I've always said that if they're gonna persist with a show like that, then why don't they use bands and artists who have done something apart from singing in the fuckin' shower? Use acts that currently have managers and that.'

'That's a good idea.'

'If it's about the music, the passion, the desire to let the world discover amazing talent, then why the fuck can't you go on the show if you're already signed? I'll tell you why. Because that then takes away control, and more importantly, takes money out of the machine. The big dicks hook some naïve artist, then shit them out the other end when they've had the cream of the deal and rinsed them for all their worth. I refuse to believe that the music I love, which has been a huge part of my life, is now second-rate to a shitshow that gets to decide who the planet's icons are. Fuck that and fuck them.'

Steam was coming out of his ears by the time he'd finished.

'I think we need another drink,' I advised.

'I think you're right. You've got me riled now. I'm coming in hot.'

We hung backstage while Ozzie continued to speak ardently and share his insights and opinions about the business.

The band were never far away from the booze, filling their plastic cups with whatever concoction they could get their hands on. They had such an aura about them, even in a setting full of charismatic rockers. Typically, a few women circulated around them, with Kyle being the focal point. He took it all in his stride but had allowed one black-haired temptress, wearing next to nothing, to latch onto him.

Dee sat on the couch, surrounded by admirers, suits, journalists and other band members. With her burgundy cowboy hat back on, she lit up the room and attracted everyone's attention. The lead singer of one of the performing blues rock bands strutted over to her, introduced himself and sat next to her on the sofa. He had that good-looking, lead singer look about him: long unwashed hair and heavy stubble. He wore leather trousers, biker boots and a brown unfastened, leather sleeveless vest that exposed his lean frame. He was completely covered in tattoos. Dee sat unperturbed, a pillar of coolness.

Like in Tucson, Ozzie wanted to call it a night around midnight and get back, stating that he wanted to be fresh for the long drive to Phoenix the following day. The band had other ideas when Ozzie revealed his intentions.

Will argued, 'Aw, come on, Ozzie. The party's just getting started. Stay for a bit longer and let your hair down. I'll get you a shag.'

'As much as I appreciate *and* rely on you to sort out my love life, I'm gonna have to decline.'

'Go on. I'll bet you I can find someone who'll have you.'

'You can't even find someone who will have *you*, Will. Well, no one with class anyway.' Everyone laughed.

Ozzie continued, 'Some mug has to chaperone you clowns around and organise shit, and we've got a long drive and gig tomorrow, so it's best you call it a night too.'

'You're a killjoy. You need to get laid,' Will replied.

'I thought you were riddled with STDs anyway.'

Kyle and Quince whooped.

'There's more to life than sex, Will. You're yet to discover that you little perverted one-track mind cretin,' Ozzie teased.

Kyle butted in, 'Will, you're wasting your time. You've got no chance with that girl. Give it up.'

'I bet I have,' he countered.

'She's making eyes at some other dude as we speak.' Quince cemented the argument.

'What? Some hillbilly, sweaty bastard? I can beat him.'

'It shouldn't be a competition,' Quince said.

'It's always a competition,' Will argued.

Seeing us talking, Dee came over, 'What's goin' on, dickbags?'

'I'm ready to go, but the lads want to stay,' Ozzie informed her.

Will spoke, 'What about you, Dee? I see you've been talking to the lead singer of Wild Grave and went out to watch their set too. Not like you.'

'They're a good band. They watched us perform so I thought it was right to return the favour. Unlike you three selfish, perverted pricks, I appreciate other people's music and respect it when someone has taken the time to watch us.'

'There you go. A professional way of thinking,' Ozzie chipped in.

'Ah fuck that. Dee's in love with a redneck. Careful, the journalist will write about it,' Will teased.

Dee punched him in the arm. 'Like fuck he will.'

She shot me one of those scary glares.

'I didn't say anything. Don't listen to him. Like I'd mention something as trivial as you talking to someone else,' I defended.

'You just keep it that way, yeah?'

Alcohol gave me the impetus to argue my case. 'I didn't mention your exploits the other night when you were with that girl. How about a little trust, yeah?'

'Trust? Trust is earned. I don't trust you at all.'

'Right, you two. Pack it in,' Ozzie demanded.

Kyle spoke for the band. 'We'll stay for a bit. Don't worry, we won't have a crazy one like Tucson. I'll make sure we get back at a reasonable hour.'

'Is 7am reasonable?' Will added.

Ozzie shot him a disapproving look. 'Ok, Dee. You're in charge. Ricky, why don't you stay and enjoy the night?'

'Yeah, Hot Shot Writer, I'll hook you up if you're man enough.' Dee's words were drenched in mockery.

'It's probably best that I come back with you, Ozzie.'

I panicked at being left without Ozzie to lean on, and I couldn't be arsed hanging around watching the lads trying to pull or having to endure Dee's torments.

As we readied to leave, Ozzie turned back to the band. 'Try not to take the piss. You've got a big gig tomorrow.'

Whether the band would take heed of Ozzie's advice was a lottery.

CHAPTER 8

A few minutes away from the house, Ozzie said, 'I think I saw a 7-Eleven near our digs. What do you say we buy a bottle and sit on the porch putting the world to rights? I could do with a proper drink.'

'Sounds like a plan. I thought you wanted to get an early one for the drive tomorrow?'

'Sod it. A few drinks away from the drama won't do us any harm.'

We returned to our abode with a small bottle of Jack Daniels, two bottles of diet coke, and two large bags of 'chips'. Sat on the rickety, wooden porch, Ozzie lit a candle and placed it on the table to give us just enough ambience for two men with a bottle of JD to sink.

Ozzie took out his iPad and put on a playlist of older British indie music that started with The Seahorses', 'Love is the Law.'

As the guitar work began, he commented, 'Fuckin' tune this. I was with the band when they released it. What a night that was.'

'I bet that was something.'

'Yeah, man. I was around a lot of the time with those bands that made it big. I was young, daft and partied way too hard back then.'

'Who else did you work with?'

'Done a bit of work with Ocean Colour Scene, Charlatans, The Verve, Puressence. Loads, really.'

'That must've been class.'

'Good times, man, good times. Never see the likes of those again. Like I was saying earlier, everything's changed now. It's a different world governed too much by money and power. Both mainstream media and music fall into those categories and are run the same.'

'What do you mean?'

'People don't choose what they want to listen to or believe in anymore. They think they're choosing, but the reality is that the choice is made for them. Because of that, all the best bands are mainly underground now, and what's famous is soulless and bland. But rock 'n' roll never dies. You just have to search a little harder to find it these days.'

I raised my glass to him.

He pulled out a delicious looking, chunky spliff and fired it up to heighten the mood. The sound of the rizla burning was soothing. I licked my lips in anticipation of it being passed my way. It was unusual for me to crave such vices, but, in that moment, it was the perfect accompaniment to a spectacular setting and a necessary antidote to the early pressures of the tour.

Taking a hefty puff, he said, 'Some of the shit I've seen over the years would make your eyes water.'

'You must have the patience of a saint. Even with the Cutthroats. Dee must be one of the most difficult people you've worked with.'

'She's had her moments, but nowhere near the worst.'

'Who was the craziest band?'

'Ah. That would be telling. I never reveal the secrets of a tour. That's your job.'

He passed me the joint.

'I think Dee will have my bollocks pickled on a plate if I print a word of what she does away from the stage. It might make a good memoir in future if I ever write a book. Have you ever thought about writing a memoir about your experiences in the industry?'

'Yeah, plenty of times. It's on the agenda.'

'If you need a ghostwriter, you know where to come.'

'You're getting sure of yourself, aren't you? Shittin' yourself about writing a tour blog a couple of days ago. Now you want to write my biography after one decent review?'

'Must be that joint, strong shit this. Not like the crap you get from the local dealer back home.'

'Haha. Well, we are in a better place to get the good stuff. I got given this backstage earlier, and this bag too.'

He pulled out a small bag of weed.

'Seriously?'

'This is the *mildest* stuff I was offered. A bag of pills and coke were thrown my way, but I just said no… like a Grange Hill advert. I'm not into the hard stuff anymore, but I can't say the same for the band.'

'No one offered me shit.'

'Cos you look like a narcotics agent,' he joked.

We both giggled.

After a few more tokes, he revealed, 'The lads read your review by the way and were made up with it.'

'Really? That means a lot.'

'Have you spoken to Jamie?' he asked.

'Yeah. He's relatively happy, but he wants more about behind the scenes, which puts me in a predicament. I can't betray the band's trust, especially whilst being stuck with them day and night, not that I would anyway. But it's obviously harder to reveal anything even a little juicy that might have repercussions and drop them in it.'

'Ah, the rock journalist conundrum. The old adage that you can't be a journalist and be friends with the band.'

'That's what they say. But times are changing. Why can't we be friends now?'

'There are no set rules to this game anymore. You just do what you think is right.'

'And what about them spending a night in the cells? Are you sure you want me to bring it up?'

'Definitely. You should lead with the arrest. It'll be a brilliant opener. Don't say it was Dee's fault though, be vague. Leave it to the reader's imagination.'

I made a few notes on my phone.

Out of the blue, Ozzie asked, 'So, you met a girl in Vegas?'

He took me by surprise.

'She sounds quite the girl, this Eva. When did you last speak to her?'

'I've not messaged her since I arrived in Tucson.'

The drug had made Ozzie almost horizontal in the chair, and his voice turned more Mancunian.

'You should message her now and let her know you're thinking about her whilst chilled and stoned as fuck,' he giggled.

'I should, really. I've just not had time to think.'

It wasn't too late, so I texted her: *'Hey. Sorry I've not been in touch. I've been so busy. Thinking of you... always! x'*

Ozzie slurred, 'Don't do what I did Ricky, if she's special.'

'What did you do?'

'Chose this life. Which isn't a bad thing, but I fucked up and completely neglected my version of Eva.'

'You sound regretful.'

'No point in having regrets.'

'Everything happens for a reason,' I countered.

'Precisely, brother. I'll drink to that.'

We clinked glasses before Ozzie lit up another joint he'd been building, which we passed between us in blissful silence. The night had a feel to it that I never wanted to end.

Sometime later, the headlights of a car approached in the distance. It was the band in a taxi.

Ozzie goaded them as they left the car. 'Here they are. And not too late. A minor miracle.'

Dee clocked our relaxed state. 'Are you two stoned?'

'Baked like a Mr Kipling cake,' I answered.

'Pass me some of that,' she insisted.

I leant over and passed her the spliff before collapsing off the chair in my intoxicated stupor. The gang belly laughed at my plight, and Dee sneered, 'You can't handle your shit. How are you ever going to survive this tour?'

My mind was completely mashed, and my response was nonsensical. 'We're all one in this universe and part of the same energy, so as long as your energy is high, my own will follow.'

She looked at me oddly and said, 'Jesus, you're fucked.'

'How was the night then?' Ozzie asked.

'Dee's got a boyfriend,' Will barked out.

'Like fuck I have,' she snapped as she stormed into the house without further explanation.

'So, what happened with her and that greasy lead singer?' Ozzie quizzed.

'Just winding her up. Nothing happened. I think he wanted her to come back to his trailer or something, but she was having none of it,' Will answered.

'What about you, "Petri Dish"?' Ozzie teased Will.

'Fuck off. No, I didn't. These warts are my downfall. Why did I have to get them now?'

'Do you know that wearing condoms makes no difference to spreading warts?' Ozzie informed.

'Stop lying. You'll say anything to wind me up and stop me getting laid.'

'Trust me, I'm not. You do what you want, but don't be surprised to get rejected and a battering from some girl if she sees them winking at her when you whip it out.'

Kyle pitched in, 'I'm surprised that's all you have considering some of the women you've been with.'

We spoke a little longer until the band and Ozzie trundled off to bed. I wanted to hit the sack too, but the herb had incapacitated me, and I could barely move. 'Everyday' by Slade began and chilled me out even further. With only a few drops of JD left, I decided to embrace the moment of sanctuary and polish the whole thing off. I was locked in the zone, connected with the mysteries of the world. The drug diverted my thoughts to the spiritual and ethereal. I stared at the cloudless, star-ridden sky that looked like a scene from Star Wars. My drug addlepated mind began to adopt a weird sense of profoundness about how the universe, planets, and humanity were connected. The stars hypnotised me and heightened my emotions, bringing strong feelings for Eva. I relived the nights with her, and then as if the universe had listened, my phone beeped as she responded to my earlier text: *'Hey. It's fine. I understand you're busy. I wanted to give you some space. I miss you too. Hope you're having a blast.'*

Reading it brought my heart to a standstill. I tried to decipher my feelings and where we were going in our unique long-term relationship that would be difficult to sustain living on opposite sides of the world. We'd never had a conversation about it. We were probably too frightened to bring it up for fear that one of us would see sense and suggest breaking contact so we could get on with our lives separately. But the thought of not speaking again made me nauseous. It wasn't an option.

Maybe being distracted by the tour and not heading straight to San Diego was a blessing in disguise. It hadn't escaped my thoughts that I could return to Manchester without seeing her after the tour. In a twisted way that may have been the more humane and self-protective option. If I spent a few days with her, how difficult would it be to leave? It would be worse than when I left her in Vegas nine months earlier. It wasn't the time to reason with myself over it, not with half a bottle of JD down my gullet and some of Howard Marks' finest in my system. I hauled myself up from the chair, overcame the momentary dizziness, and headed inside.

As I staggered into my room, another text came through: *'Hey. Are you still up? I can't sleep.'*

I replied: *'Yeah, I'm still up. Why can't you sleep?'*

'Too hot, and I'm thinking of you. I really am missing you. More than usual tonight.'

Strange that my own thoughts had swayed the same way. I decided to call her.

She picked up immediately, 'Hey.'

'Hey yourself. Are you OK?'

'Yes, I'm fine. It's so hot here. I'm struggling to sleep, but it's OK. It's good to hear your voice.'

'Yeah, yours too. I've been sat on the porch drinking Jack Daniels on my own.'

'I can tell by your voice that you've been drinking,' she laughed, asking, 'On your own? Where's the band?'

'They've all gone to bed now. Long story.'

'So, Mr Englishman. How's the big rock 'n' roll tour going?'

'Mixed bag. I'm struggling with the lead singer. She's making it obvious that she doesn't like me.'

'Oh. I'm sure she'll come around. Just use that English charm of yours. It worked on me.'

'Ha. I don't think that would work.'

She asked me how the tour had been so far. I relayed everything that had happened and prattled on about how incredible Bobby and Tien were.

'Wow! That's amazing. The perks of being a rock writer.'

'I guess. It's not the same without you here.'

'Aw. You're sweet, but you need to do this on your own.'

'Maybe. But you helped me get here by encouraging me to go after my dreams. I feel like you should share the experience somehow.'

'Knowing you're on the path you're meant to be on is enough for me.'

My heart sank. 'You're too good to me.'

'Better believe it, Cariño. I must admit, I am desperate to see you. It's been far too long, and I'm getting horny thinking of you. It must be the fact you're now a rock 'n' roll tour writer. Can't be anything else,' she joked.

'Yeah, yeah, yeah, cheeky arse.'

We paused before an idea popped into my head.

'So, you're horny, are you? What are you gonna do about it if I'm not there?'

On the same wavelength, she replied, 'I'm already doing it.'

Caught off guard, I blurted, 'What? Really?'

'Just listening to your accent is turning me on. I'm reaching down underneath my panties.'

'Fuck! What else?'

'Ah ah. You tell me first.'

Fuck it, I thought.

'I'm reaching inside my boxers, and I'm getting so hard just thinking of you and what you're doing right now.'

'I'm playing with myself, and it feels so awesome, Ricky. I'm imagining being back in Vegas with you, and you're on top of me. Are you there with me?'

'Oh, I'm with you. I'm thinking of you riding me, and it's so intense, Eva.'

She let out a spine-tingling moan. 'Tell me more.'

'I'm grabbing your arse and fuckin' you so hard. You're biting my ear, and it's so passionate. I can tell your close.'

'I am close. Are you?'

I yanked away at myself, and my mind was back in that Vegas hotel room.

'I am Eva. Just thinking of the two nights we had. I'm cl...'

A loud bang struck the now slightly ajar door to my room and startled the shit out of me.

'Don't stop, Ricky. I'm close too.' Kyle's voice boomed in.

My cock flopped immediately.

'What the fuck?' I yelled.

Eva cried out, 'What the hell?'

'You bastard! How long have you been there?' I shouted.

'Enough to know you shagged a girl called Eva in Vegas and that you're a dirty bastard. Payback for Tucson, fucker.'

'What the fuck? You followed me in here?' I shouted back.

Still in hysterics, he shouted, 'We only came by to shit you up, but seeing you molest yourself has made my life.'

'What's going on?' Eva asked.

'I've been caught by one of the band.'

'Oh my God!'

'I need to go.'

'I think you better.'

Eva was laughing as I hung up.

'You absolute bastards,' I shrieked.

I got out of bed and opened the door fully. Quince was with him and was on the floor in stitches.

'I can't believe you saw that!'

I was red with rage and embarrassment.

'That was fuckin' brilliant. Highlight of the tour so far,' Quince said through tears of laughter.

'I suppose it'd be too much to ask to keep this between us,' I pleaded.

'Not a chance. Stick this in one of your reviews, why don't you?' Quince joked.

Dee shouted from the other room, 'You fuckers better shut the fuck up out there.'

'Please don't say anything to anyone?' I implored.

'You know there are no secrets on this tour,' Quince teased.

'Pricks!' I was mortified and went back into the room as they scuttled off. I leapt back onto the bed, put my face into the pillow, and screamed loudly into it to release the anguish and shame.

CHAPTER 9

The next morning, I sheepishly crept downstairs and was greeted by Ozzie, who stood grinning like he had wind. I intuitively knew the reason.

'Good night last night?' he goaded as the smirk never left his face.

'Fuck off. I take it you know?'

'Oh, I do. Kyle couldn't contain himself this morning when he came downstairs. I hope you washed those sheets?'

My face went bright red, and I snapped, 'Well, I would've done if I'd finished, but I never got to that point, did I?'

'You must have blue balls then. No wonder you're tense this morning,' he quipped.

Will came in singing 'Teenage Kicks' by The Undertones in honour of my adolescent act. He couldn't stop laughing. Neither could Kyle and Quince when they came in to add to the tirade of piss-taking.

Will shook his head at me, mocking disappointment. 'Tugging yourself silly. Disgraceful behaviour.'

I growled, 'I wasn't tugging myself silly, I was merely playing wi...you know...it doesn't matter. Whatever I say, I'm not gonna make it sound better, am I?'

'Not a chance,' Quince confirmed.

Ozzie jumped in, 'It is embarrassing, but shit happens on tour. Trust me, I've seen worse, and I know this lot have done worse.'

'Like what?' I probed.

'Kyle once told me he caught Will washing his balls in the sink before he went off with a girl because, and I quote, "I've not showered for three days and my balls stink like a wet dog."'

I nearly spat out my mouthful of water.

Will's tone changed. 'Fuck off, Ozzie. Can't believe you told him that, Kyle.'

'Why would I not? It's a great story. Still gives me nightmares now, seeing your little cocker humping a tap. Best sight I've seen, until last night, of course.'

Even Dee got involved when she surfaced. Expressionless, she simply remarked, 'Always knew you were a wanker.'

I let out a sardonic chuckle.

She added, 'Shame I didn't see that. Tit for tat and all that, but I doubt I'd have seen anything worth shouting about.'

My shoulders slumped as the lad's laughed at her cutting words. It was going to take a while to live down. So far, the trip had been about catching each other in compromising situations, and I hoped we'd seen the last of it.

Once we'd packed up and loaded the cars, we were ready to head to Phoenix. Ozzie offered to drive the Chevy with me while the band followed in the Dodge.

'If I'm driving, I'm playing DJ,' he demanded.

'Fine by me.'

I slumped back in the seat.

'Right, I'm gonna play a couple of newer bands for you. Let me know what you think.'

He connected his phone to the stereo and scrolled through before landing on his choice. 'See what you think of this.'

An almighty riff recoiled through the car. It almost made me jump out of my skin thanks to the volume being on max. I instantly resonated with the song.

'Who. Is. This?' I asked.

'Rival Sons.'

'It's brilliant.'

'I know. This is "Pressure and Time".'

I was practically air-guitaring in my seat as he played a couple of other numbers from them.

'How have I not heard of these before?'

'They've been around for a few years. One of L.A.'s finest newer bands.'

I listened intently and absorbed every riff. He then played several tracks from various other artists I'd not heard of before. Chris Stapleton and his songs, 'Traveller' and 'Parachute' were tailor-made for such a drive. As was Israel Nash, whose pensive musings were a whimsical journey that epitomised the soul of Americana and desert road trip travelling. The song, 'Rain Plans' was particularly captivating for that part of the world.

A string of exemplary blues rock, country rock, swamp rock, and psychedelic rock tracks from lesser-known bands followed. I was struck by the gunslinging, strutting force of The Last Internationale's, 'Wanted Man', the hypnotic, otherworldly, space rock track, 'Space to Bakersfield' by Black Mountain, and the dreamy psychedelic undertones of Dope Lemon's, 'Honey Bones'. All were new artists, and each track was different, but they all heightened the experience to make the drive even more celestial and transcendent than it already was.

I asked, 'Is this the type of music you're into?'

'Yeah. Don't get me wrong, I love my roots in British music. But these days, I'm more into the dirty side of blues and rock or calming Americana, which tends to come from the States. Most of these bands have played in small venues in the UK, but out here they get huge crowds. It's what I envisage for the Cutthroats. From a business point of view, I have to lean towards indie music in Manchester, as opposed to the type of stuff I'm really into because that's where the money is. I have to separate my tastes from my business, but with the Cutthroats, I get to do both.'

'I would struggle to separate business from my own tastes. I couldn't work with something I didn't love, so it's a good job I'm loving the Cutthroats.'

Once he switched to the softer side of his playlist, I passed out as exhaustion took hold. I was so conked out that I didn't even stir when we pulled over at the rest stop. I vaguely heard Ozzie calling my name during a deep slumber, but I was well away. Life on the road with the long drives and heavy nights was starting to take its toll.

I'd been asleep for an hour. Part of me felt like I'd missed out because the region was so spectacular. I really appreciated why a road trip in the US was one of the top entries on bucket lists. Regardless of whether I was with a band or not, it exceeded my wildest dreams.

Sometimes, I found myself drifting off into some past life, conjuring up the vivid imagery of cowboys riding at full pelt on wild horses in some old western movie, complete with an Ennio Morricone film score percolating in the background.

Ozzie's eclectic playlist treated me to some previously unheard gems from past bands. It made me realise just how little I knew. The likes of Marshall Tucker Band, The Doobie Brothers, The Allman Brothers and his personal favourites, Deep Purple, were just a few older bands/artists that I'd never had a chance to fully delve into before. The road intensified the meaning behind those tracks as they etched into the memory banks forever. The landscape gave me an understanding of why Americana and soft rock was born in that part of the world. There was something spiritual and inspiring that sparked creativity. I felt the same magnetic pull as I developed a compulsion to write. I pulled out my laptop and started crafting the next blog.

An air of confidence and inspiration engulfed me as I tapped away to describe the events of the past couple of days. As Ozzie had advised, I began with the arrest and added humour to it without giving away too much. I remembered a previous conversation with Ozzie about what it took for bands to make it and the sacrifices they had to endure. I thought it'd form a thought-provoking part of the review to bring home the realities to any aspiring artists. I asked him to elaborate so I could transcribe in the car.

'It's a massive commitment to try and make it as a full-time musician. The pressures can be overwhelming, so I understand why many end up giving up and getting secure jobs. I'm sure it's always been difficult, but the competition seems greater than ever for everyone in the industry. It can often feel like you're swimming against the tide just to be noticed or heard. This is by far the toughest period I've experienced.'

'Do you think there are too many bands out there?'

'For sure, but what can you do? You can't stop people from starting up a band. What I will say is there are a lot of shite bands out there that are taking up too much air space.'

I agreed, 'I've often thought that, but I've tried to be objective by saying to myself, OK, well, I don't like this particular band, but someone else will, even if it's not my bag. I understand that people are trying to be different.'

'I think that's part of the problem and the solution. Sometimes artists try to be so different that it becomes weird, or they create sub, sub, sub-genres of a particular brand of music and further divide fans.'

'I never saw it like that before. I suppose that's why everyone *is* so divided and why there's not one colossal movement that everyone unites for.'

'Precisely,' he agreed.

'I guess it worked so well in the past because accessibility was limited, rather than the multiple channels you can get music from nowadays.'

'Definitely. Anyone can make music too. One of the problems in the twenty-first century is that you've got people who work in fuckin' tech stores passing themselves off as musicians.'

I smirked before he carried on. 'You're right about the millions of avenues you can access music. When it was only a couple of radio shows it was much easier. Plus, you had people willing to go out to find the music, and there were only a few places to go. There are too many home comforts these days, and you can find music via loads of channels if you can be arsed, but a band's bread and butter are the gigs. To earn a decent living today, that's a lot of gigs, especially as people aren't buying records like they used to. Technology, in general, has had an impact. Game consoles, thousands of TV channels and streaming sites all affect people's ability to search for new music, but we have had to use and embrace that to our benefit.'

I frantically scribed away as 'Turn to Stone' by Joe Walsh maintained the great music lurking in the background of our informative chat.

'It seems hard to succeed in the music biz as a full-time profession. I guess as a part-time writer I don't see a lot of the hard graft behind the scenes.'

'Well, as much moaning as there is, and fuck me, there's a lot, if it were all bad, we wouldn't be here. For the love, never the money, and never be greedy. But you must also understand that we *have* to make a living out of it.

'And what about the blogs? What approach fits into your philosophy? Tell the truth, lie, or omit the juicy bits?'

'That's your call. You do what feels right and what you think people want to read.'

'Well, that puts me between a rock and a hard place, doesn't it?'

'Welcome to the world of music.'

The discussion waged on as we hit heavy traffic a couple of hours outside Phoenix, which prompted Quince to call Ozzie from the car in front. They were pulling off at the next stop to get some food until the traffic died down.

Once stationary, I messaged Eva about the previous night, telling her that I'd been getting an absolute ripping from the band. A series of laughing emojis was her reply, suggesting she was unabashed, but then again, she wasn't the one in the firing line.

On my way to the toilet, Will shouted out, with no filter whatsoever and in front of a few people, 'Hey Ricky. Don't be having phone sex in there like last night.'

My face turned bright purple as two women turned and looked disgusted by me. I scarpered into the toilet as fast as I could while Will cackled away in the background.

After a quick bite at a McDonald's, Ozzie pointed out that the clock had jumped back an hour due to crossing another time zone. I couldn't keep track of all this time-hopping. I felt like I should've been driving a DeLorean.

I took up the reins for the final slog into Phoenix. Ozzie insisted that the three lads ride with me to get to know them better. I welcomed his suggestion, despite knowing the piss-taking would be unbearable.

As predicted, the ribbing was relentless as they poked and prodded. 'So how often do you have phone sex?'

'Can I join in next time?'

'Was it really a girl you knew or just some sex line?'

Those were just a few of the jibes I had to take. They held a ceasefire as soon as we navigated our way to Interstate 10, which was much of the run to Phoenix.

Kyle sat in the front passenger seat, picked up my iPod, and said, 'What the fuck is this?'

'An iPod.'

'Do people still use these? I thought they went out of fashion with flares.'

'It ain't about how you listen to your music, it's what you listen to. And I know what's on there is better than anything you lot listen to.'

'I've not seen one of these in years.'

'Years! It cost about £300 only six years ago! Times can't have changed that much.'

'They're changing too fast for you, I think.'

Quince and Will joined in with the iPod-bashing as Kyle scrolled through and played 'Opportunity Free' by the Charlatans.

'I fuckin' love this tune. Not heard it in time.'

He turned to Quince. 'You got a spliff rolled up back there? Need to take the edge off after last night.'

'Are you nuts? You can't smoke that in here. If we get pulled over, I'm fucked,' I shrieked.

'Relax, paranoid android. You're on tour with a band. Go with the flow.'

'Just make sure you roll down the windows, so I don't get baked. I'm already pushing the limit after last night's sesh without adding drugs into the cocktail.'

The smell of weed was pungent, but it did at least add a chilled vibe and suited the tunes being played.

'I've been recording conversations with Ozzie, which I'm using for the reviews. Do you mind if I leave this on while we talk and potentially use anything you say?' I asked.

They all agreed, providing anything controversial would be omitted.

'Also, I might need individual interviews with you at some point, if that's OK?'

'Yeah, Ozzie said we'd have to sit down with you. Fine by us. Not sure you'll get Dee to agree, though.'

'I'll worry about that one later. I'll try and get you guys boxed off first. Anyway, let's begin. Tell me about your thoughts on the tour so far?'

'It's going well and been a top laugh. I have you to thank after that episode last night,' Kyle taunted.

'Glad to be of service. That's not going in the blogs, though.'

Weirdly, being caught in the middle of a sordid phone sex rampage served as my baptism of fire and helped break down the barriers between us.

I asked, 'Any good leads from labels after we left? There must've been some whisperings?'

'Just the usual shit. We let Ozzie look after all that. Lynwood is the one showing the most interest. Their rep said he enjoyed the show but said fuck all after that.'

'Do you think the deal will happen?'

Kyle answered, 'I don't know. I'm enjoying this life too much to go back and get a proper job, though.'

Quince butted in, 'We better fuckin' get signed or else someone's gonna get a pasting.'

'Surely a deal will happen?'

Quince shrugged. 'Who knows? The music business is full of pricks. They come in all shapes and sizes. You get some that are genuine, but most are slippery little fuckers. This business will chew you up and spit you out and leave you on the doorstep of the Job Centre before you've even had a chance to get a decent tour going.'

'L.A. is the key gig, man,' Kyle said.

'I can't wait for that. That's gonna be the pinnacle of this trip. It's gonna be mint playing the Whisky a Go Go,' Will added.

'Fuck, I forgot about that!' I exclaimed.

'We've got a long way to go till then. Phoenix, Flagstaff and Palm Springs first,' Quince reminded us.

Kyle carried on explaining the band's situation. 'We've put everything we have into this. If we don't see any proper return, we're all fucked. Not a pot to piss in. If nothing else, I'm gonna make sure I have memories to take back with me. If I'm heading to financial ruin, I'm goin' there in style.'

'Fuck yeah,' Quince concurred as they high-fived.

I understood the need to give it their all from a music and excessive partying standpoint. Even though we were all on a budget, it felt wrong to skimp out on enjoying ourselves. The trip needed to be milked for all its life-changing worth, whether the band were successful or not.

I said, 'I still don't know how you got the band together. You guys are obviously from Manchester, but how did you manage to snag a Bermudian lead singer?'

Kyle answered, 'Us three all know each other from Trafford College. Me and Will are from Sale, although I grew up in Salford. Quince is from Stretford.'

'That's St Retford to you,' Quince joked.

Kyle smirked and continued, 'Me and Quince had been in bands separately, but we weren't happy because it was boring as shit. It was the same music as most other fuckin' bands in Manchester. When we got chatting, we realised we shared the same vision. Will was on my course in college, and we'd stayed good mates afterwards. He'd been in a band himself. When me and Quince realised we were on the same page, I invited Will to jam. Musically, something just clicked, and we came up with some top melodies. Initially, I was on vocals, but I knew they weren't strong enough to carry forward if we were gonna create something special.'

'How long were you together before Dee came in?'

'A few months. We had a lot of music written and the basis of some sort of lyrics, but they weren't good enough. We had auditions with a few singers, but none had that magic we felt the tunes deserved. We were quite happy to be patient and bide our time because we knew the tunes and the chemistry were bang on. But, as is always the case, things happen by chance, and that's exactly how we met Dee.'

'What happened?'

'We'd been watching this blues rock band we know called Gold Jacks at Night & Day in Manchester. After the show, we hung out with them at the bar. Then this loudmouth American-sounding girl came over and started telling the band they were good, but they could be better. She was proper cocky and started giving them a few pointers, especially the vocalist. We all thought, who the fuck is this cheeky bitch? He took it with a pinch of salt because I think he fancied her, but she wouldn't ease up, so much so that I began to like her and suspected she was a singer herself. She certainly had the look and the attitude. I asked her whether she sang, and she was like, "Who wants to know?" I told her we were in a band looking for a lead singer if she fancied auditioning. Her response, in typical Dee style, was, "Yeah OK, but make no mistake about it, you're auditioning to be in *my* band." I never envisaged our tunes with a female vocalist, but it didn't half work. The rest is history. A few days later, she came to rehearsal and blew our minds with that fuckin' vocal. She had loads of lyrics, so it didn't take long to fit them into the songs we were working on. They were far better than the ones I'd written. We had a decent live set to play within a month.'

'When was all this?'

'About eighteen months ago now.'

'You've come a long way in a relatively short space of time then?'

'Big time.'

'Personal question, I know, but you three seem like men of the world, and Dee is obviously an attractive woman. Did any of you try it on with her?'

'Haha, tell him, Kyle,' Quince goaded.

'I'm not ashamed. Why wouldn't I have tried it on with her? She's a fox.'

'What happened?' I asked.

'She shot me down. Proper crash and burn. But you know what, I'm glad. I wouldn't have this band any other way, considering how good we are. It would've only complicated matters, and I don't want to get into a fuckin' Fleetwood Mac dynamic. I know her too well now to get involved. She'd drive me insane.'

I nodded my head in agreement.

He continued, 'We're all good mates, and that's all it will ever be with Dee. Us three all live with each other in a right little shithole.'

'I didn't know you all lived together.'

'It's only temporary to save money. As soon as this tour was sorted, I fucked off my flat and moved in with Quince and Will. I sleep on their couch cos it's only two bedrooms, but we figured it saves money. Don't tell the landlord though, not that the miserable old fart would read a music fanzine anyway. It's worth the sacrifice if you want to achieve something. Anything we can save on needless shit and living costs that can go towards the band is worthwhile for me.'

'Does it get tough with you spending all that time together?'

'It can, but we probably don't argue any more than the average married couple.'

'All the time then?' I quipped. 'And what about Dee?'

'She lives nearby in a rented one bed studio above a salon, but she's always at ours, bossing us about one way or another and raiding our booze and fridge.'

'Ozzie said you all quit your jobs too?'

Kyle again answered, 'Yeah, but none of us gave up any glamorous careers. Ozzie said it was the only way this was gonna work. All or nothing. We saved up enough to make America happen, and we're pulling in a bit from our music. Living together certainly helps. But like I said earlier, I'm not ready for this to end, and I don't want to get a normal job. Fuck that.'

I knew the feeling all too well after my Vegas endeavour the previous year, but the guys and Dee were a little ahead of me in terms of knowing where they wanted to be in life.

'Brass in Pocket' by The Pretenders came on, and Will interrupted, 'I love Chrissie Hynde, but I didn't like her in that band...what were they called? The Arithmetics?'

I nearly emergency braked right there and then on the freeway as the car erupted with howling laughter.

'What?' Will yelled, confused as to why we were in such hysterics.

Kyle responded, 'The Arithmetics! The fuckin' Arithmetics! I'm gonna burst. I'm actually gonna die.'

He couldn't contain his gut-splitting laughter.

Quince and I were gone too. I nearly swerved into the other lane my eyes were filled with that many tears.

'You're a fuckin' beaut, you Will,' Kyle said.

'What have I said now?'

'Wrong on two counts. Do you mean, "The Eurythmics"?'

'Oh.'

'And it's not Chrissie Hynde who was in that band. It was Annie Lennox, you pleb.'

'You know what I meant.'

Kyle continued, 'The Fuckin' Arithmetics! I've gone. That's worse than when you said your favourite Bob Marley song was "Red Red Wine".'

'WHAT?' I shouted, exploding into another giggling fit. 'How the fuck are you a musician with such limited knowledge?' I asked.

Will shot back, 'I don't profess to be some fuckin' music guru, you know. I play my bass and look the part. That's all I need to do.'

He sat sulking with his arms folded as the punishing tsunami of piss-taking attacked him from all angles. His face was a picture when I said, 'I'm so happy all this has been caught on the dictaphone.'

'Please do *not* use that,' he implored.

Kyle begged, 'Oh, please do. Sound bite that bit and post it on social media.'

I didn't have the heart to stitch him up despite the temptation, but it was a recording that would keep me entertained for years to come.

Eventually, we composed ourselves, and I asked them what music they liked. Quince was straight in with a choice that surprised me. 'I love my rap, hip hop and R&B, and a bit of heavy metal.'

'Really? That's quite a contrast in styles,' I said.

'Don't get me wrong, I love my rock from a musician's point of view, but I love my old school rap. Snoop Dogg, Dr Dre and that when I'm chilling out.'

'How about you, Will? The Arithmetics?' I teased.

'Fuck you. Rock, of course, but I love my older Manchester music.'

'Kyle?' I asked.

'I'm into my rock, as you can tell. AC/DC, Led Zep, Stones, Hendrix etc. It's probably why Dee and I work so well because we like the same stuff. It's why I wanted to steer away from typical British indie music.'

I seemed to have inadvertently started a discussion and debate amongst the band about musical taste. I left them to it as I reflected on Kyle's words about the band giving up everything to be out on tour.

I'd always thought that to start up a band or become a musician, the motive couldn't be to become rich and famous. You had to do it for the sheer love and remain realistic and grounded. But passion must never be lost. That was fundamental. The band obviously shared the same ethos considering their risky actions.

It brought up my own predicament, which I didn't realise was a dilemma until I heard Kyle's fear of having to go back to the reality of a mundane job. Although I'd made the bold decision to quit my job and tour the States, there was a nagging, subconscious worry about what was next. Eventually, money *would* run out and writing for a music magazine for pocket money wouldn't be a long-term solution. I'd been thinking so short-term that I neglected to think beyond that. I had enough money to keep me going on the tour and for a short time afterwards to travel, explore and seek out experiences in America, but after that, what was next? I didn't have a clue. But I knew I had to focus on my mission and help the band achieve their goal.

CHAPTER 10

We arrived in Phoenix and pulled into the car park of a huge apartment complex. Hundreds of parked cars filled the multiple spaces, with each flat having its own designated spot.

Gaining access through a lockbox, we entered the ground floor apartment. We were pleasantly surprised to be greeted by a cream-coloured, contemporary space with plush furniture and elegant décor, a far cry from the squalor we half anticipated on the band's budget. It was deceptively spacious, boasting four bedrooms adjoined to each other. The layout was like a rabbit warren with two entrances to each room. Being on the ground floor meant we also had a patio at the back with a small fenced off garden.

'How much did this cost?' I asked Ozzie.

'You'd be staggered at how cheap it was. I didn't think it'd be this nice, though. I didn't really scan the pics. Saw the price, saw how many beds, and wasn't fussed about the rest. Airbnb is the way to go, I'm telling you.'

'Me and Kyle have already bagsied the big room,' Quince chipped in.

Will said, 'You're in with me, writer. We're gonna play tummy sticks tonight. Your arse is gonna be mine. I want you to talk dirty to me like you did with your little friend last night, whoever she was.'

'Normally, I'd oblige, but you're riddled, so I think I'll pass,' I quipped. 'But I may reconsider if you play The Arithmetics.'

Quince and Kyle laughed as they told Ozzie and Dee what Will had said in the car. Even Dee let out a minor chuckle.

'You've not had a proper night with us yet. You need to get laid with all this bishop bashing you're doing,' Will taunted me.

'I don't need you to get laid. That I promise,' I threw back.

'Check out the balls on the writer here. Anyway, I wanna know more about this girl you were talking to on the phone. She sounds hot if she's up for phone sex.'

'All you need to know is she's way out of your league.'

'That is until she finds out I'm in the best band this century. She'll be all over me like a cheap coat.'

'I bet she's not even real,' Dee butted in.

'You believe what you want to believe,' I retorted with a smile.

'Like I give a shit,' she mumbled.

'You would if you saw her. You'd be wishing she'd pin *you* up against the dumpster.'

The lads whooped, but Dee wasn't amused. She shot me a look that made me shut the fuck up.

Quince broke the frostiness, 'Check this out. Fridge has got two six-packs of beers.'

Quick as a flash, Will demanded, 'Throw one of those over here.'

'Shit load of food here too,' Quince added as he took out a cheese cracker pot.

Will shared the beers to serve as an early livener. They barely touched the sides. The ice-cold liquid was a welcomed stimulant after a long drive.

We had a bit of time to kill, so I took the opportunity to ask the band if they wanted to carry on with the interview. Dee outright refused, and she ignored Ozzie's comment that she needed to do it at some point. The lads agreed. We took up seats in the garden where the sun's scorching rays rained down.

The interview lasted half an hour and topped up what had already been said in the car, but I asked individual questions to build up more of a personal profile for each band member.

I remained outside to transcribe it and sharpen up what I'd already written about the past couple of days. I sent it to Jamie, wincing as I pressed 'send'. I was nervous that the band would be pissed off that I had revealed they were arrested, which I put down to being 'drunk and disorderly', as opposed to Dee's gob. At least I had some time before it went live and would be noticed.

Ozzie drove us over to the Yucca Tap Room, the venue for that night's gig and five minutes away. We arrived as the low, murky orange sun glossed the dusty landscape. The venue was tucked away in a shabby spot opposite a strip mall, sandwiched between a Smoke Shop and a Rocket A Go Go, whatever that was.

Despite a glowing reputation, the Yucca Tap Room didn't look much. It was a low-rise single-storey shack on the side of the road that could've been mistaken for a small storage unit, mirroring the exterior of the shops on either side of it. But if I'd learnt anything about gig venues, it was the places you didn't expect to be decent that were usually the best, and the grimier, the better.

The Yucca Tap Room was known nationally and had been around since the early seventies. It had played host to many famous bands before they hit the big time, and it still housed acts that were seeking stardom and had burgeoning reputations.

We walked in to see Elvis Presley's 1970 live Vegas performance of 'Polk Salad Annie' blasting from the plasma TV mounted on the wall. I found myself swaggering to the iconic tune as I entered, practically shaking my hips to emulate the King himself.

The bar was relatively busy and had the stereotypical grungy, laidback feeling of an American dive bar: dimmed lighting, flashing Budweiser signs, chestnut-coloured oak furniture, and an odour of booze and grease stirring the air.

We met the venue manager, an old biker dude named Rex. His voice was deep and gruff when he introduced himself. He had long, straggly hair with a beard and a thick, droopy moustache to match. His face was weathered, with deep lines entrenched into his forehead and around the eyes, formed from the many years of smoking, alcohol abuse and the litany of tales that would give the average bloke nightmares.

He showed us around the joint, starting with a separate tap and cocktail room that showed sports on the projector and multiple TV screens. It also boasted an impressive twenty-nine different beers. He ordered the barman to pull us a pint of one of the local brews, which had a sweet kick to it.

We moved onto the ample-sized venue at the back. Rex told us that the promoter had assured him that the word was out around Arizona State University, so a decent-sized crowd was expected. The young and vibrant generation were the sort you wanted in attendance. They were locked into social media and of an age that moved in large friendship groups that could spread the word about emerging bands, which was paramount for artists to succeed.

Rex then led us backstage, where two crates of beer, a bottle of Jack Daniels and Wild Turkey, and soft drinks were waiting for us.

Once Rex left, Ozzie gave instructions to the band. 'Ok guys. Get sound checked, and then you have an interview with two girls from the university for their campus magazine, so look alive and drop a charm bomb or two. Get into those beers later. There's no gig tomorrow, so tonight, do what you want after the show, within reason.'

'Two girls from the university, eh? Sounds promising,' Quince mused.

'Just keep it in your trousers, Quince,' Ozzie warned.

'I think you should be more concerned about Kyle on that front.'

Kyle raised an eyebrow.

I went outside to take the opportunity to call Eva while the band went to soundcheck.

She answered, 'I hope you're not in an empty room expecting some dirty talk.'

'Fat chance of that. I'm at the gig.'

'Good. Never again will I attempt that,' she giggled.

'Yeah, probably not the best idea considering where I was. What you up to anyway?'

'Lay on my bed meditating and listening to music.'

'What are you listening to?'

'A mixture. That Oasis track came on earlier. The one you played for me in Vegas the night we met. You know, "Talk Tonight".'

The memory of that night wrenched at my heart. Those pertinent lyrics resonated again as they did then.

'Ah yes, how could I forget? Good choice.'

'I had Genesis on just before you called.'

'It still astounds me how a Puerto Rican girl is obsessed with Genesis and their early years.'

'Hey. My Papi has great taste. He forced them on me.'

'You should listen to Cutthroat Shambles. I think you'll love them.'

'I will do. I've been reading your blogs. Your second one has just been posted. Your writing is getting better.'

My stomach sank. 'I didn't think it'd go on so soon. I'll check shortly. Do you really think it's getting better?'

'For sure. I see you wrote about them getting arrested. Will they be OK with that?'

'Ozzie said he'd have my back if there was any fallout. At least I left out why.'

'Why was it again?'

'Underage drinking at a party they were at, and then Dee was mouthing off to the copper.'

'She sounds fun.'

'That's one word for her. Sassy is another.'

'How are things with her? Any better?'

'Still not speaking to me, and she constantly makes snide remarks. She's just looking for any excuse to bollock me. Mentioning the arrest will probably be the catalyst.'

'Bollock? What does that mean?'

'In the context that I've just used it, it's English for "telling me off".'

'Ah. It's a funny word...bollock.'

'We say it for a lot of stuff in loads of situations. Getting drunk, you can say I was bollocksed. If someone's full of shit, we may say they're talking bollocks. But really, it just means your testicles. We call them bollocks sometimes.'

'I like it.'

I never noticed how funny a word it could be to those unfamiliar with our culture.

'What do the band and the manager think of the blogs?' she asked.

'The manager's cool. He gave me the green light to put the arrest in. I don't think the band pay that much attention, but the lads have said the first one was good. They won't know about the latest review for a while yet. It probably reads shit anyway.'

'Well, I'm going to give you a bollock now.'

She sounded so cute. I didn't correct her.

'For what?' I asked.

'Stop being so hard on yourself about your writing. You're doing a good job, and you're talented. Start to believe that.'

'I think I would if I had the support of Dee. Jamie at Sonic Bandwagon edits my reviews too, which deflates me a bit.'

'That's his job as an editor. Don't take that personally.'

'Maybe, I don't know. My head's all over the show. A lot's going on out here, and I feel that my hands are tied in what I can and cannot report on.'

'Have you been told not to mention certain things?'

'Not really, but I can't reveal everything the band do with the sex and the drugs, but that's what Jamie wants to read. It feels like a betrayal because I'm with them all the time. If Dee didn't like one snippet I wrote, she'd go crazy. Is it worth the hassle? It's probably best to play it safe.'

'I think you need to be true to yourself. Don't lie.'

'I don't lie. I just don't tell the truth. There's a difference.'

'Your confidence will double when you stop asking, will people like this? And start asking, is this something I love?'

Writing can be a lonely act at times, and self-doubt is a writer's pessimistic right and trait. However, Eva's faith and encouragement inspired belief and spurred me on.

'You always have a way of making me feel better when I'm conflicted,' I said.

'It's what I do.'

'It's why I miss you.'

'I miss you too.'

'I best get back in anyway and see what's going on.'

'You take care, cariño. Don't let them muchachos drag you down to their level with sex and drugs.'

'Ha. As if. I'm the sane one.'

'Call me in a couple of days if you can. Try and enjoy. I'm here if you need me.'

After I hung up, the frequent, somewhat empty feeling hit me again. I was on tour with a band, the crowning glory of my life, and Eva was a constant swirl in my head.

A text from Jamie had come through during my phone conversation. It simply said: *'Good job on the 2nd review. I like how you started it with the arrest. The Bobby and Tien aspect was interesting, but I've cut it shorter and edited a bit more. I want more backstage details tonight. I still feel there's more to be told on that front. We need interviews with the band and quotes from them.'*

It was encouraging that he approved and that I'd already anticipated the need for interviews. I responded: *'Thanks. I'll keep an eye out tonight. Interviews with the lads were done earlier. I can use bits on the next blog, but I have enough for a full interview piece.'*

I stayed outside, re-reading my review to see where Jamie had edited it. In truth, he *had* polished it, but had removed a good three or four paragraphs worth of Bobby and Tien, which pissed me off. They deserved more.

The pressure mounted to report what the band were getting up to, and I was unsure how to approach it. Maybe the only solution was to drink with them later that night, write about my observations and submit the piece under the influence of alcohol before sobering up. Hmm - perhaps *not* the best idea. Write drunk, for sure. But always edit sober.

I went back inside to see what everyone was up to. Ozzie had set up the merch stand and had stayed to man it. Soundcheck had taken place, and I was introduced to the interviewers from the university. Both were in their early twenties and were quite punk oriented. Polly was the main interviewer. She was cool looking with dark hair tied back into a short ponytail. She had nose, lip, and tongue piercings. Her loose cut black top exposed tattoos on her shoulders and on the top of her back. She was supported by her photographer friend, Ashley, whose blonde hair was highlighted by flows of neon pink and sky-blue waves.

The interview was full of flirtatious anecdotes and double entendres, which both girls giggled at. Will was the main culprit. He asked Polly, 'Does that tongue piercing help with fellatio?'

Unmoved, she responded, 'Wouldn't you like to know.'

'Oh, I think I would actually,' he replied with a wink.

I couldn't bear the obviousness of it all, so I swiped a bottle of beer from the table and ventured out to the front to soak in the atmosphere. Only two acts were playing that night, but the Cutthroats were first up and billed as the headline.

I trawled through the feedback from the latest blog post via my phone, where the likes rocketed as the minutes passed. Most people commented on the arrest and wanted to know more. At least I'd added an element of intrigue and mystery to the post. Only a few people mentioned how interesting Bobby and Tien sounded. Plenty more asked when the band were appearing in their hometown. Others stated how much they were looking forward to an upcoming gig, and some commented on how much they enjoyed the show in El Paso. The attention was building pace and felt on the cusp of exploding.

The crowd multiplied in its scores and was mainly college kids. Many were without an alcoholic drink due to the legal drinking age being twenty-one, so it was an unusual sight for us Brits. I couldn't imagine my time at university or gigs without alcohol, but I guess it was something they had to adapt to in American culture. That's not to say they probably didn't have a stash in their dorms or even have fake IDs, but to go to bars and gigs without a beer felt odd somehow.

I stood with Ozzie as Black Rebel Motorcycle Club, 'Beat the Devil's Tattoo' played to help mould the mood before the show started. The lights dimmed, and the Cutthroats arrived onstage. As usual, they opened with the energetic 'Rock N Roll Heaven' to set the tone. The repertoire of high-octane songs served to elevate the youthful crowd's intensity. The poignant ballads, 'Million Lights', 'Ready to Love', and 'Curious Morality' had me emotionally stirred as Dee transformed her image from rock goddess to ballad princess. Again, I couldn't believe how she could switch effortlessly between melodies and write such profound lyrics straight from the heart. The fact she could be so difficult made it hard to believe how gentle and soulful she could be.

She took the time to address the fans, thanked the venue, and explained that they were on a US tour, encouraging the young students to spread the word throughout the campus.

Quince and Will momentarily left the stage as Kyle took up an acoustic guitar and perched on a stool next to Dee, who had also taken up a stool next to the mic. The lights dimmed, and the blue spotlights shone on both.

Kyle began noodling into a melody, and it quickly became apparent the notes were the opening to 'Hotel California', but delivered in a slower, more mysterious way than the original. Wow! It sounded dangerous and haunting. When Dee let the vocals howl, the audience was stunned into silence. The hidden dark undertone of the song's meaning shot to the forefront of the song's essence.

After it finished, the crowd frantically clapped and cheered. Dee acknowledged their adulation by placing her hand across her heart. They played another two tracks and left the stage before being dragged back on by the glut of wails calling for an encore. They returned with two more numbers, including 'Lifetime Sunshine,' the fan favourite that explained Dee's move to Manchester from Bermuda.

As the final chorus rang out, a few college kids broke through the barrier at the front and climbed onto the stage to be with their new-found idols. Dee signalled it was OK to the security guards as seven kids danced around her and the band. Four girls and three lads shuffled ineptly, bouncing up and down with little coordination or rhythm. They were only onstage a few seconds before all of them pulled out their phones and started taking selfies with the band. I found it a bit embarrassing. What had happened to rock 'n' roll? To take up a foothold onstage with a band performing live should epitomise the notion of 'living in the moment'. Unfortunately, there had to be a showing off, look at me aspect with pointless selfies and videos to score false social media points. They missed out on the whole experience.

Dee carried on the best she could without flipping her lid, but I could see her unease. It boiled over when some idiot took out a selfie stick. That was the last straw as Dee aggressively snatched it and launched it back into the audience. Many cheered and laughed, but Dee was seething, and the selfie stick-less fool looked dumbfounded.

When the vocals finished, she abruptly thanked the crowd and stormed off, leaving the musicians to finish off the instrumentals. Security got involved and ushered the young selfie rebels offstage on the other side. The band finished, but Dee returned to take a final parting shot during the applause.

She screamed, 'What kind of fuckin' space invader brings a fuckin' selfie stick to a gig?'

It may not have adhered to the wishes of a typical PR way of thinking, but it had the desired effect as many people hailed her cutting words. I thought the way she left in a pissed off huff was brilliant, but I wasn't sure the suits and decision-makers would've seen it the same way if any were around.

I could hear Dee before I saw her backstage. She yelled, 'A selfie stick on my stage! A fuckin' selfie stick on my fuckin' stage! Is that our fuckin' fan base? If so, you can have them back. Fuck 'em. Bet they're the sort of wet wipes who wear t-shirts of bands without a clue who they are.'

Will tried to calm her. 'Chill out, Dee. We rocked it tonight.'

'That was pretty fuckin' awesome if you ask me. They loved us out there,' Kyle agreed.

Ozzie stepped in. 'Dee, forget it. Focus on the positives. You were incredible. Lots of people were telling me how good you were.'

He high-fived the band, although Dee was a little less enthusiastic.

'What did you think, Hot Shot Writer?'

'Me?' I was surprised to be asked.

'No, that prick by the side´of you. Of course, you,' she snarled.

'Honestly?'

'No, be dishonest, you dick. Of course, honestly.'

'Brilliant. I thought you were better than Tucson. You were dynamite up there, Dee.'

'Get your nose outta my arse will you.'

'Fuck me! You asked, and I told. I'll lie next time, shall I?'

'You're getting a bit too cocky, you know. Maybe you should have a wank on the phone again,' she retorted.

I couldn't help but laugh, as did the lads.

'What did *you* think?' Ozzie asked Dee.

'Good. It was better than Tucson, but I want perfection. Those selfie dickheads ruined it at the end. I don't want to end up on a fuckin' TikTok or gif post made by some fuckin' spotty virgin. Next time, no fuckin' crowd invasions with day trippers. Where are we next anyway?'

Ozzie replied, 'We go to Flagstaff tomorrow, but the gig is the day after, so it's a little break for you all. There are some people I'd like you to meet. One's a photographer, Ricky, who said you can use his shots for the gig review.'

I nodded.

Dee was still livid. 'Give us ten minutes, then bring them in. Grab me one of those beers too.'

'I'll get out of your hair. I'll be out front if you need me,' I said.

'Don't worry, we won't,' Dee jibed.

I nursed another bottle of beer while I waited for the next act to begin. Mid drink, I realised that I'd ripped the labels off the bottle, a blatant sign of sexual frustration, according to some people. There was little wonder for that agitation. I missed Eva, and I was cooped up with five other people with no privacy whatsoever.

The final act began and served to take my mind off my simmering libido. The performer was in his late thirties and sported a Mohican haircut and long biker beard. He plugged in his acoustic guitar and manoeuvred the chair to be at the perfect height next to the mic. His look made me think there was a bluesy element to him. Many of the students had dispersed, but enough remained to make it worth the artiste's while.

A man reached over to the stage and plonked a glass of Jack Daniels on the floor next to him, confirming the bluesy tag I'd given him. When the lights dimmed, the House Announcer introduced him as Matt Fryers. A small mob down at the front chanted his name and hollered as he plucked the strings of his worn, vintage guitar. The followers quietened on his request and settled into attentiveness, a stark contrast from the racket they'd made earlier for the Cutthroats.

He began his first song, and his voice was exceptional, full of emotion and pain with a rasping blues tone. He held his audience and me in the palm of his hand as we came down from the energy of the Cutthroats' performance.

He announced he was going to play a few songs from the show 'Sons of Anarchy', including the theme song, 'This Life', and 'John the Revelator.' His growly rendition of them both were terrific.

A succession of original whisky-soaked, emotive ballads followed, such as 'Last Words' and 'Searching For Answers', songs that connected with me and caressed my soul. It was an inspiring and calming performance that had me rooted to the spot for a good thirty minutes. I didn't even move to grab another beer. It was only when I saw Kyle appear from backstage that the reverie was broken.

He swaggered over and shook hands with a few people along the way whilst posing for photos with a number of young ladies that recognised him. I rolled my eyes. When he stood next to me, I said, 'You know, I'd love to be you for just one day.'

'I can set you up if you want. Tell them you're our official tour blogger. It'd work like a charm.'

'I'd feel like a fraud. I'm not riding your coattails and having your cast-offs.'

He changed the subject. 'This dude playing sounds pretty tight.'

'He's great. I'm gonna buy his CD. Everything OK back there?'

'Yeah, man. Just finishing up. Those girls who interviewed us have asked us if we want to go to a party.'

'Where? At their college?'

'No. Some dude's house. It's only a few minutes away but sounds like one of those parties you see in films. It'll be bat shit crazy, man. Bet there are loads of girls. You should come.'

'What's Dee said?'

'Don't worry about Dee. She'll be cool with you coming...but you know the rule. What happens doesn't make the blog, yeah?'

'Gotcha. But you don't want people to think you're teetotal, do you?'

'I'll leave it to your discretion what you deem as appropriate. It won't leave you with much to go on.'

'Well, don't do anything stupid, and we won't have a problem, will we?'

'Where's the fun in that?' he retorted. 'This party's an eighties theme by the way. It's gonna be cheesy as shit. We're well up for it, apart from Ozzie. What about you?'

'Eighties party? Oh, I'm there.'

My mind wandered as a frisson of excitement struck me. I had grown up watching American high school/college films and TV shows that depicted the unique culture of that particular era and time. I was envious of how they portrayed school life on screen in the eighties. It always looked like the best time. It had been a period I yearned to experience for myself, which was obviously impossible. But for one night only, I could live inside the movie of my choice. I could be the college kid thrust into a time warp in America. I could hardly contain my delight at the thought, and when Matt Fryers finished his set, I was the one dragging Kyle backstage to get the show on the road.

CHAPTER 11

In the taxi, Kyle asked Polly, 'So what's this party all about tonight?'

'One of the guys on our course has his parents' house for the week so he's organised an eighties themed party. He's a bit of a nerd like that.'

Nerd? I thought. The man was a legend in my book.

'So, it's not part of a sorority house then?' Will questioned.

'No, but we are part of a sorority.'

'What's it called?'

'Delta Beta Omega. It's a chapter of Alpha Kappa Alpha,' Polly answered.

'Old Kappa Slapper?' Will joked.

Quince and I sniggered as the joke whooshed over the girls' heads.

Dee intervened, 'Guys, grow up, yeah?'

'Don't you have sororities and frats in the UK?' Ashley asked.

'Nope. It's more sports clubs at uni, and they're very cliquey. It's for sad twats up each other's arses trying to show off and outdo each other,' Will said.

'Here here,' Quince agreed.

I chuckled to myself thinking about the sports clubs when I was at uni.

'What's it like being in a sorority?' Kyle asked.

Ashley replied, 'Oh, it's amazing. It's so much fun, and it helps with friendship and career opportunities. We started out six girls living together in our freshman year.'

'House of six women? Sounds like hell,' Quince reacted.

'I don't know. That sounds like a challenge to me,' Kyle offered with a wink.

'Oh my God. You're terrible,' Ashley responded before slapping Kyle flirtatiously on the arm.

'Were you in a sorority back in Bermuda, Dee?' Will asked.

Dee turned to him, stony-faced, 'Do I look like the sort of chick who was in a sorority?'

Will goaded, 'Good point. You were probably in a pagan cult.'

She flicked him the middle finger.

Polly interjected, 'Just around this corner, and we're there.'

The neighbourhood we meandered through was typical of middle/upper-class America. The houses were enormous with neatly trimmed hedges, fully bloomed deep green oak trees and pristinely mown sprawling lawns. Pretty flowerbeds dissected the flagged walkways that led up to each modish, cream-coloured building roofed with terracotta-coloured Spanish tiles.

We stepped out of the taxi and stood in front of a colossal house. Faint sounds of laughter, commotion and music could be heard, and the curiosity as to what lay beyond the closed door was an enticing proposition.

We followed the girls up the curved path to the gleaming white front door. Polly courtesy knocked and entered without waiting to be let in. The muffled music from outside suddenly burst into life as we filed in one by one. Upon hearing the unforgettable opening wail to 'Relax' by Frankie Goes to Hollywood, I strutted in with intent, lips puckered just as the booming synthesizer that gave the song its dynamic came into effect.

The foyer was awash with people having a wail of a time. Most had embraced the eighties theme and were dressed accordingly. Many girls wore loud and bright coloured clothing with big, hairspray-induced hair. I then realised why Polly and Ashley were dressed slightly trashy. Some took it a step further in over-the-top American style and transformed into characters from the films and TV of the era. Making up the nostalgic Comic Con-style cast was Superman, Prince Akeem from 'Coming to America', Freddy Krueger, Sloth from 'The Goonies', Cobra Kai students from 'The Karate Kid', 'Beetlejuice', and 'Teen Wolf'. There was also a group of people dressed in flight suits, donning aviators trying their best to replicate the coolness of the 'Top Gun' cast. More awesomely, a set of guys dressed in carnivorous, gothic attire emulating the vampires from 'The Lost Boys'. One had nailed the Kiefer Sutherland peroxide blonde mullet. I made a mental note to chat to them later and maybe start an impromptu chant of 'Michael, Michael, Michael.'

A projector beamed 'Big Trouble in Little China' onto an entire wall in the main living area. It really was like I'd stepped back in time. The party was vivacious, and instantly lived up to expectations.

We ended up in the kitchen, where various bottled spirits were lined up on a central tabletop with a mountain of plastic cups. The kitchen was mainly filled with girls. A few were dressed like Cyndi Lauper and Madonna. Polly and Ashley knew them well, judging by the screams when their arrival was noticed. Unsurprisingly, they were all good-looking American sweetheart types that could've been extracted from the extras section of a coming-of-age drama. Polly got their attention after the onslaught of hugs and kisses had finished.

'Everyone! I'd like to introduce you to the awesome band we interviewed tonight. This is Cutthroat Shambles from England, and they fuckin' rock!'

The girls gave another excitable cheer. Their body language changed as soon as they spotted the guys, which didn't go down well with a few lads hovering nearby. It was like instant animal attraction, especially to Kyle. I felt myself blush as several sets of eyes burnt through us. I snaked myself out of the way to let the band take centre stage and picked up a beer from the silver ice bucket by the sink.

Polly took out a pristine golden cigarette tin packed with green buds and rizlas. Within minutes she had rolled a joint, sparked it up and was smoking away at the table. It wasn't long before she passed it along, and everyone took a hit. I was not in the mood to mix alcohol and marijuana and end up panned out in a sea of paranoia, so I declined the offer.

One of the lads in the kitchen, a well-built pretty boy with silken hair, took out a small plastic bag filled with white powder, quietly showing it off to a few girls, including Dee. It seemed he wanted to demonstrate his value and switch the attention back onto himself.

I took myself out of the equation, not even wanting to witness the snortskies about to take place. I refused to put up with the attitudes of coke-fuelled arrogance. I loved the band's music, but I was disappointed that they did cocaine. I couldn't help but feel like they were acting like some sort of rock 'n' roll cliché. There was an element of hypocrisy in my own viewpoint, having done what I did in Vegas with peyote, but my argument was that a hallucinogenic to help find yourself was far more practical than a fifteen-minute arrogance booster where the effects were ultimately detrimental.

I left the room unnoticed and stashed an extra bottle of beer in my back pocket, so I didn't have to return for a while. It wasn't the best place to stick it as the ice that shrouded the bottle dampened my arse.

I headed back to the main living area and smirked at the various costumes and efforts people had gone to for one night. The music seamlessly slipped into 'Everybody Wants to Rule the World' by Tears for Fears. The whole room belted the lyrics out at full volume. Whoever oversaw the playlist had done a sterling job despite the awkward dancing it invoked. Hips moved with zero fluency, and the funky overbite was in full effect. Not that my own dancing was Swayze-esque, but I knew my limits and was more than happy to lean against the wall out of sight and absorb the experience.

I'd been stood in the same spot for a few minutes and had just plucked up the courage to introduce myself to a group of costumed strangers when my plan was thwarted. A familiar voice spoke at the side of me, making me freeze.

'Well, this is a surprise!'

The voice oozed enthusiasm. I turned to see a girl dressed in a grey, baggy 'Flashdance' jumper and pink headband, and couldn't believe who it was. Lucy, the girl I'd met in the MGM Grand nine months earlier on our third night in Vegas, stood before me. It had completely escaped my memory that she lived in Phoenix and had told me she was at Arizona State University. Even if I had remembered, the idea of running into her would've been a long shot.

'Wow! Now, this is something I didn't expect,' I stuttered.

'You're telling me. What the hell are you doing in Phoenix?'

'I'm with the band, Cutthroat Shambles. Two girls, Polly and Ashley, interviewed them for the college magazine at the gig and invited us back here afterwards, so here I am.'

'Polly and Ashley were my sorority sisters. We lived together.'

'No shit. What are the chances?'

'I know, right? Crazy. How come you're with the band?'

'I've gone into music journalism. I'm writing about them on their US tour.'

'Oh my God! That's amazing. Polly said they were an awesome band. So, they're here with you? Can you introduce me?'

'Of course, I can. They're in the kitchen.'

I led the way back into Pablo Escobar's bunker. Lucy had matured since I last saw her and had lost a degree of the innocence she carried back in Vegas, but her razor-sharp eyes were still full of fire. She was a little slimmer than I remembered, which gave her an added air of confidence. Her hair was different too. It was longer and lighter coloured, coated with a chestnut brown as opposed to the coal-black that I remembered. She'd not lost that sweet smile though. When she flashed it, the familiar dimples in her cheeks formed, and it brought me back to the night we met when she smiled at me from the bar.

Kyle clocked me walk in with her, excused himself from the girl he was chatting to and made his way over to us. Judging by his heightened, energetic mood, and the fact his jaw was swinging more than Tarzan, I sensed the powder had been dished out in my absence. I looked around to see Dee hunched over in the corner taking a vigorous snort. Will and Quince looked just as wired as they chatted to Polly and Ashley.

'Ricky, man. Who's this?' Kyle smiled childlike amid a hint of gurning, teeth grinding and sniffles.

'This is an old friend of mine, believe it or not, Lucy. She knows Polly and Ashley. In fact, they used to be sorority sisters. She wanted to meet the band... so, Lucy, this is Kyle, the average guitarist of Cutthroat Shambles.'

'Prick,' Kyle uttered before turning on the charm with a melting smile. 'It's cool to meet you, Lucy.'

She blushed as he leaned in to peck her on the cheek.

'How do you two know each other?' he quizzed.

Lucy and I smirked at each other.

'Shall I tell him or you?' she asked.

'Neither of us,' I answered.

'Wait a minute, you two haven't... bumped uglies, have you? Ewww. That's disgusting,' Kyle joked.

Lucy was coy. 'Ha. He should be so lucky. A missed opportunity I think.'

'Oh, this I have to hear,' Kyle said with intrigue.

Lucy began telling the story of our night in the MGM Grand and New York New York. When she approached the gritty part, she took pity on me. She left out the bit about us kissing before my mini breakdown that resulted in me leaving when she wanted me to spend the night with her.

After she told the story, she excused herself to go and talk to a friend who called her over, but not without winking at me first, which sent an unexpected shiver down my spine.

Kyle noticed it and leaned into my ear. 'You're on tonight bro. About time you got yourself laid on this tour. She's a darlin' too.'

'You think *she's* a darlin'? You want to see the other one.'

'What other one?'

'Eva. The girl I was on the phone to. I met her on the same trip.'

'You're a dark horse, aren't you? Eva ain't here, though. If you don't get with Lucy, then I will.'

'Oi! Hands off. You can have your pick of any in here. She's off-limits.'

I don't know why I reacted so quickly. It wasn't like I was planning to make a move... or was I, subconsciously?

'You know that only makes it hornier for me, don't you? Forbidden fruit and all that. Don't worry, I'll adhere to the guy code, but you better go for it.'

I brushed off his request with a grunt as Lucy returned with two drinks.

'Jack Daniels and Coke, if I remember correctly?'

'Where's my drink? Kyle asked.

'I believe Danni has a drink for you over there.'

We looked over, and the blonde bombshell Kyle was talking to earlier glared at him.

'Oh shit. I almost forgot about her.'

'How can you forget about her? She's a knockout. Like I said at the gig, I'd love to be you for just one night.'

'You couldn't handle being me,' he joked, adding, 'Well, do excuse me, ladies. Duty calls. I guess your request is safe, Ricky.'

'What request?' Lucy asked.

'Nothing. Ignore him. Good memory on the drink, by the way. I'm surprised you remembered anything after that night. My memory is still a little hazy. I was so drunk.'

'Oh, I remember more than you know.'

'Oh yeah?'

'It didn't sit well with me how we left things.'

'I'm sorry about that. My head was in a different place back then. I wasn't in the best shape.'

'And now?'

'It's been quite the transformation these last nine months.'

'Maybe you can tell me about it later. For now, drink.'

We clinked plastic cups, and I threw down the JD and Coke. It was strong as fuck and made me wince. My throat burned as the bourbon made its way into my system.

'Whoa. Are you trying to get me drunk?' I asked.

'Maybe.'

Her grin sparkled, and I smiled back at her. To stop myself from being hypnotised by the prolonged stare into her mysterious eyes, I broke the spell, and said, 'I still can't believe you're here. It's so good to see you again. How've *you* been, anyway?'

'I've been great. School's been going well. Not been back to Vegas since. Have you?'

'I was there a few days ago actually, but just for one night.'

I told her how that happened, then summarised the personal awakening I'd gone through in the last nine months and how the issues that plagued my soul when we met had vanished.

We were getting on great. It was like the follow-on night we never had back in Vegas. We pulled up stools at the central table in the kitchen and hogged the JD like it was our own twisted love child. She continued to pour strong concoctions whenever the cup emptied, with a very high JD to Coke ratio. Inevitably, I began to feel lightheaded as the drink flowed.

The party became rowdier, and the music volume was cranked up as 'Don't You Forget About Me', by Simple Minds played. Given its status amongst eighties high school film folklore, I fist punched the air as the 'Hey, Hey, Hey, Heyyyyy!' began. A few other guys did the same to salute John Bender.

I was in my element, blissfully locked into the nostalgic vibe. Lucy and I must've done half the large bottle of JD in by that point, and to say I was feeling it was an understatement. Coincidentally, I felt like I was on my way to being the drunkest since the night I met Lucy in Vegas.

Kyle and Dee were on the other side of the kitchen and held the interest of several partygoers. Will and Quince had gone outside as the merriments spilt out to the back garden.

'The Lost Boys' came in. I excused myself from Lucy and made a beeline for them, expressed my love for the film and praised how great they looked. They were appreciative of the comments, so I got chatting with them. They tried to guess my accent. I had to correct them when they said Australian.

Not long after, in typical American fashion, some bright spark suggested playing drinking games, and that's when things turned. Somehow, I found myself thrust into being the sixth member of 'The Lost Boys' team in a game of 'flip cup' against a team of typical jocks, who all wore yellow and blue bomber jackets (the meaning of which escaped me, it could've been from anything).

I'd seen the game played before but had never attempted it. With the way my coordination felt under the influence of Mr Daniels, I didn't think I'd be any good. All that was required was to down the beer, place the empty cup upright on the table hanging slightly over the edge, and flip it in one swift motion to land face down. Once that player completed the task, it moved on to the second player, and so on. The winner was the first team to drink and flip all their cups. It was a simple drinking game where the forfeit for the losing team was to down a shot each.

For some inexplicable reason, and despite me saying it was my first time playing, 'The Lost Boys' placed great confidence in me and stuck me last to storm us home to glory.

The game started at a frantic pace. Every player nailed the flipping of the cup within three attempts. By the time it was my turn, it was neck and neck. Everyone cheered and clapped as the hysteria grew, adding further pressure onto my shoulders. I managed to down the drink in one gulp, but the cup flipping became the real sticking point given my drunken stupor. I failed miserably with several woeful attempts as my corresponding player landed it on the second go. The opposition berated us, and I felt deflated for letting down my vampire friends.

I downed the shot of tequila with ease but was nominated for a further forfeit by 'The Lost Boys' as they blamed me for their defeat. They thought it would be funny if I chugged from a hosepipe attached to a keg of beer for thirty seconds whilst being held upside down. Then, when I was tipped back onto my feet, I had to take a hit from a bong. I was hesitant, but I couldn't look a fool in front of the band, Lucy, and everyone else. I had to fly the flag and keep the reputation of Mancunia intact.

The jocks tipped me upside down and held my ankles to balance me. I instantly felt the sea of booze splash inside my stomach. Someone placed a pipe next to my mouth. I bit it and guzzled away. Chants of 'Chug! Chug! Chug!' rang out from the spectators who wanted my blood. Thirty seconds felt like minutes as beer spilt over my face and into my hair. Eventually, I was flipped back to my feet, and an almighty rush swarmed me. My head spiralled into another realm, but I wasn't done yet. The bong was thrust into my face. I placed my mouth over the top and inhaled deeply. The back of my throat stung, but I managed not to cough up a lung during the five-second inhale. I exhaled as my hazy eyes dissolved into the back of my head. The hit was that strong I lost my footing, so much so that the jocks had to stop me from swooning backwards and crashing onto the tiled floor. Cheers blistered around as I just about managed to keep it together and stumble off away from the congregation.

It was a necessity to take a second to compose myself, so I sat down on a stool as Lucy put her arms around me to steady my rocking body. There was no way I'd see out the night after such an extreme act. I knew that I'd pay a hefty price later.

After several minutes of getting to grips with myself and riding out the storm, I saw that the party was in overdrive, with 'Ferris Bueller's Day Off' now showing on the big screen.

When 'Beat It' by Michael Jackson came on, my eyes lit up and a second wind consumed me. I stood up and headed into the main living area, uncontrollably walking in like Jackson in the song's music video with a spring in my step and my wrist shaking by my side. I did not pull it off well. Thankfully, I didn't attempt the moonwalk. Lucy watched on from afar and laughed hysterically at my foolishness. All inhibitions had been lost and I didn't care how much of a tit I looked. I think at one point I danced like David Brent to 'Smalltown Boy' by Bronski Beat, which brought strange looks from the many who weren't familiar with the original version of 'The Office'.

When 'Danger Zone' by Kenny Loggins played, all hell broke loose, and the wildness escalated. A couple of the jocks I played flip cup with had joined me, along with the 'Top Gun' guys. We jumped around in a rowdy circle with arms clutched tightly around each other, struggling to maintain our collective balance. Quotes from the film were fired off by each one of us as we transformed into the various characters. I slammed another shot down that was shoved into my hand. God knows what it was, but it was a cheeky little nip that made my face recoil as it gushed down my throat.

The scene had become one of carnage, and as more and more people arrived, it resembled something like the last days of school where anything went.

A bizarre, boozy conversation with Will transpired when REO Speedwagon's 'Keep on Loving You' came on. For some reason, I tried to convince him that being able to 'woo and seduce a girl to this song back in the eighties would be the height of coolness.'

Apart from a look of puzzlement and laughing at my inebriated state, his response was, 'Did you really just say woo?' before shooting down the theory.

The night moved at a reckless pace as drinking, dancing and observations of an American party flashed by too quick. I'd completely let myself go and freed myself from the shackles of sobriety. I was absolutely steaming and lost all sense of coolness, roaming aimlessly around the house talking shit to anyone, telling them that, 'I'm with the band' or 'I can write about you.' I sensed I was being a pest and a menace, but I didn't care. I was starring in my own eighties college film, and I was the dick who couldn't handle his beer.

Lucy sensed my downward spiral, and I was thankful she came to my rescue. I enveloped her in my arms when she neared. She steadied me and moved to save me from myself, leading me to the back of the kitchen and sitting me down on a chair away from everyone else.

'Hey, Tiger. Are you OK?' she said with concern.

My speech was a bit slurred. 'Yeah, babe. I'm fine. Thank you for looking after me.'

'Ok. You're hammered. The fact you called me babe in a creepy way shows that.'

I noticed Dee crack a smile at my dishevelled state. I unwisely started on her. 'And what are you smiling at, Dee? Miss Rock Star Superstar Wannabe.'

'You better shut up before you say something you regret. You're drinking with the big boys now,' she responded.

'It won't make a difference, will it? You already hate me, don't you? Why do you hate me, Dee?'

'You're going up a notch in my book seeing you in this state.'

'I can drink you under the table anytime,' I challenged.

'Oh, is that a fact?'

'Yep. When I'm sober in three days, I'll challenge you to a drink off.'

She laughed off my claim.

I added, 'And I'm gonna write whatever I want about you. I bet you don't even know that I wrote about you getting arrested on the latest blog. Can't take it back now. It's live. It's out there. Everyone knows.'

Her face turned. 'You what! You wrote about our arrest?'

'I didn't say *why* you got arrested.'

She stomped over, and in one quick motion, she slapped my face, which prompted startled gasps from those who witnessed the assault. Kyle caught me as I tumbled off the chair like a felled tree.

'What the fuck, Dee?' Kyle barked.

'If he's fucked us, that's the least he'll be getting,' she retorted.

'Ozzie said it was fine,' I pleaded.

'Oh, did he now? He had no fuckin' right. I told you I'd fuck you up if you fucked us over. You better run if this goes bad.'

She stormed out of the kitchen, and Kyle asked, 'Are you OK, mate?'

'Yeah, fine... I think.'

'Did you really write about the arrest?'

'Yeah, but I didn't go into any details. Ozzie told me to be vague.'

'I'm not gonna read it now but will do tomorrow. You must have a death wish confronting her like that.'

'Ah, fuck her. I'm pissed, and I don't give a shit.'

I carried on my slur, 'You know what, mate? I absolutely love you, and Will, and Quince...even Dee too. When she calms down, she'll forgive me, won't she?'

'I wouldn't count on it.'

I sat quietly to compose myself. The dry slap from Dee left my cheek throbbing and red.

The flip cup games still persevered, and Quince and Will had been dragged into one. With their team winning, the same forfeit that had befallen me landed on a guy from another team dressed as John McClane from 'Die Hard' - dirty vest, blood smeared on his face and no shoes. His friend was dressed as the blonde henchman from the same film. Once he completed his forfeit, the hit battered him hard. He stumbled back with such force he knocked over a large pan of cold chilli from the cooker and slumped to the floor. The pot planted onto his head, and the chilli slid down his vest. The kitchen erupted with jackknife laughter.

I was still in a daze but was just managing to remain compos mentis. Lucy had been dancing with friends but returned to see how I was.

She asked me, 'How hammered are you?'

'Pretty hammered but feeling a bit better. The room isn't spinning anymore, and I'm not seeing three of you like I was earlier...just two of you...and a fine two they are.'

'Ok, you're wasted, but are you too wasted to dance?'

'Nope. Might do me good to move about a bit. Lead the way, Tonto.'

Tonto? I thought.

'Fade to Grey' by Visage was playing as she turned her back to grind on me slowly, just like she did in Vegas. At one point, I attempted to text the friends back home with whom I'd been in Vegas. I wanted to let them know that 'Grindfest' was up and running again. I gave up when I couldn't see the screen through my blurred vision.

I put my phone away and leaned into Lucy's ear. 'Hey. I'm sorry about what happened in Vegas.'

'Ricky, you don't have to...'

'No, no, no. I do. Any other time I'd have gone into your room that night, but I couldn't. Something stopped me.'

And without even thinking about Eva, I said words I immediately regretted. 'But I'm not being held back now.'

She turned around to face me as 'Cry Little Sister', the theme tune from 'The Lost Boys', started up. She moved closer to me, inches from my mouth, and gazed deeply into the well of my eyes. The dark overtones of the track created powerful chemistry between us, and before I knew it, I leaned in to kiss her, softly brushing her parted lips. I pulled away almost immediately as if I'd committed a sin, but with eyes still fixated on each other, I moved in again to kiss her. This time I didn't pull back, and our passions soared. It was then, lost within Lucy's ravishing lips, that the night slipped into a blur.

CHAPTER 12

I awoke supine on a strange bed, as rough as a bear's arse. My eyes locked onto a crack in the ceiling that I couldn't deviate from. My head pounded like a power drill was penetrating my skull, my body ached, and my mouth was as dry as the bottom of a birdbox.

Without moving, my sticky eyes scoured the unfamiliar bedroom. I jolted when movement from the other side of the bed rustled the duvet, which completely covered whoever was lying there. Snippets from the previous night flooded back. I cautiously shifted my tender head to the left and peeled back the covers to confirm my suspicions. Lucy innocently lay asleep, wearing a black bra that cupped her mountainous breasts. I didn't pull the covers back any further than her torso, but I did note how beautiful and trim her body was.

I desperately tried to piece the night together. Remembering the game of flip cup and subsequent beer chug and bong hit made me gip a little in my mouth. I recalled talking bollocks to several people... and then... I remembered the kiss...oh God, the kiss with Lucy. I presumed things went a lot further, considering I was in my boxers and she was in her bra, but I couldn't remember a damn thing after the kiss.

I put my hand over my forehead, and a wave of guilt overcame me, brought on by the thought of Eva. But why? I tried to justify it to myself, surmising that Eva and I weren't even a proper couple, and I was on tour with a rock band, with her blessing, so what did she expect? *That's some cold shit, Ricky*, I thought. My inner voice reminded me of what that girl meant to me, making me feel worse. I wanted to take the coward's way out, creep out without waking Lucy and make a sharp exit. But again, the sane inner voice spoke. *That's some cold shit, Ricky.*

I turned over to look for my phone. My jeans were folded neatly on the floor next to the bed, with my plain black t-shirt pristinely placed on top. My socks and trainers were carefully placed at the base of them. How did I have the faculties to do that in the state I was in?

I found my phone in my jeans pocket and saw a message from Ozzie asking where we were. I responded, assuring him we were all fine and I'd get the band together as soon as possible and head back. The tapping of my phone disturbed Lucy.

She purred, 'Morning, Drunky.'

I slowly turned to her. 'Good morning.'

'How are you feeling?' she asked.

'Shocking.'

'I'm not surprised. You were wasted last night.'

'Oh God. What did I do? Nothing embarrassing, I hope, apart from talking shit to people. That much I do remember.'

'Nothing so bad where we had to kick yo ass outta here. Although, you did get slapped off Dee.'

The memory flooded back, and I cupped my head in my hands. 'Oh fuck!' I cried.

'Relax, Kyle said it'd be OK.'

'I'll probably get kicked off the tour now. I'll have to lay low with you for a while,' I said.

'Yeah right,' she was being sarcastic.

Gesturing to how we were both lying in bed, I tentatively asked, 'Erm, how did this happen? And did we...I take it we...you know?'

'Ha. You should be so lucky, Ricky Lever. Not with Eva on your mind.'

That threw me. 'How do you know about Eva?'

'How much do you actually remember about last night?' she quizzed.

'Not a lot. The last thing I remember was kissing you, and after that...nothing.'

'Oh, I could have some fun with this,' she teased.

'Please don't. My head hurts enough as it is.'

'You asked me for a threesome.'

'Oh no.'

'With one of The Lost Boys.'

'Oh God.'

'He was up for it, and when you both got naked, you couldn't get it up and passed out.'

'Oh, please, no.' I was mortified.

'Relax...I'm just fucking with you. You're too easy.'

'For fuck's sake, Lucy. That was Oscarworthy.'

'Well, I did think about studying drama.'

'Please tell me what happened?'

'Well, just like Vegas, you broke my little heart again.' She gave a sarcastic sob.

'I think I prefer the threesome story. Did I?'

'No. Not really,' she chuckled before revealing, 'You wanted to take me upstairs, so I brought you up here, and we carried on kissing, but you started talking about your "beautiful girlfriend, but not your girlfriend, Eva". So, I took pity on you and told you nothing more was going to happen. I stayed with you and made sure you were OK and didn't choke on your own vomit in your sleep.'

'That sounds pathetic on my part... but thank you for looking out for me.'

'Aw, you were so cute.'

'I'm sorry I broke your heart.'

'Oh, please. Don't flatter yourself. I was bullshitting you. You're easy to play with, ain't ya? I'm at college having the best time of my life. I'm not pinning all my enjoyment in life on a one-night stand with *you*, even if you are kinda cute. It would've been nice, I reckon.'

'Nice? It would've been incredible,' I responded.

She shot me a sassy look at my sudden surge of confidence.

I added, 'I've never been so happy to be rejected.'

'It was very interesting to learn that you met Eva two days before me in Vegas.'

'Hey. I was in Vegas doing what you're probably doing at college. Don't hold that against me.'

'Just teasing you again, sweetie.'

'I think you should've studied drama.'

'I'll consider it. Anyway, in another life, I'd have rocked your world. But I'm afraid you're going to have to use that creative mind of yours to imagine what it would've been like.'

'As soon as that post-night-out-morning-after-horn kicks in, I will. As it happens, I can't feel anything below my waist I'm that hungover,' I said.

'Don't be calling me for phone sex either.' She winked.

'Don't tell me those dicks told you about that?'

'They certainly did. I'm guessing Eva was the one you were talking to?'

'Right, conversation over. I'm not talking about this with you. Those fuckers.'

She giggled.

'Where are they anyway? Do you know?' I asked.

'I think they'll be around somewhere.'

'I guess not being at uni or in Vegas on a lads holiday means I'm out of practice for drunken nights like this. Then again, I've never drunk from a keg upside down and then had a hit from a bong immediately afterwards. That annihilated me. No wonder I was so fucked. I'm amazed we managed to get a bed considering how many people were here last night.'

'We *were* lucky. I had to lock the door, so no one else barged in. You passing out had its advantages.'

'I'm sorry if I ruined your night.'

'It's fine. I was done, and someone had to look after you.'

Conscious of getting back for Ozzie and the pending drive, I hauled myself out of bed and nearly collapsed back onto it.

Pointing to my perfectly laid out clothes, I asked Lucy, 'I take it this is your doing?'

'Of course. The way you left them was a disgrace. It's one of my pet peeves leaving clothes thrown about like that. You'd be lucky to have me, Ricky Lever. I'm more than just a pretty face. I'm a pretty maid too.'

I stumbled around as I got dressed and exited the room. The scene was a picture of despair. I'd seen some wild parties in my time, particularly in the university years, but this was a ridiculous level of carnage. Bodies lay everywhere like an assassin had slain everyone. The landing was cluttered with those unfortunate not to get a bed for the night. Given the theme of the night, it resembled a murderous nightmare of iconic eighties characters.

I carried on walking down the corridor and slowly opened every door I came to. Some had numerous people in and around the bed. One bed had a couple spread-eagled, buck naked, and the bottom two legs of the bed had buckled, so they were lying slanted. He must've been like a jackhammer.

The place was a lot bigger than I anticipated, so it took me a while to navigate my way around. Five rooms in, I finally saw the familiar sight of Kyle in bed with Danni, who he'd been talking to all night. Will and Quince were on the floor with three other dudes and five semi-naked girls, including the interviewers, Polly and Ashley. I didn't want to know what debauchery had occurred.

I prudently tiptoed to Will and gave him a slight kick on his shoulder. He didn't stir, so I kicked him harder. His eyes slit open, and he moaned, 'Owww! Fuck me, what the fuck's that?'

Upon seeing me, he reacted, 'Ricky, what the fuck, man?'

'We need to go.'

'What time is it?'

'Nine o'clock.'

'Ah, fuck that, I'm staying here. Fuck the band. This is my life now.'

'C'mon. Ozzie will be pissed.'

'Trust me, he won't. He expects this of us.'

'We need to go. We can't stay here all day. We've got to get to Flagstaff.'

'Chill, man. Gigs not till tomorrow. Plenty of time. For now, rest, sleep, chill.'

'You're fuckin' useless.'

I left the room and realised that I was still monumentally pissed and in no fit state to drive anywhere. Perhaps Will was right, so I went back into the room I slept in. Lucy was still in bed, so I hopped back in. I instantly fell back to sleep for a much-needed siesta to get rid of the bastard behind my eyes.

The vibration of my phone woke me as saliva drooled on the pillow into which my head was buried.

It was another message from Ozzie: *'Where are you guys? You OK?'*

It was 11.15. I forced myself up, feeling much more human than before, albeit not 100%.

I replied: *'Sorry. Fell back to sleep. We're fine. I'll rally the troops and get them back.'*

I headed into the room where I'd seen the guys and there were fewer people spread around than earlier. I wouldn't take no for an answer when I tried to rouse them, clapping rapidly to kick-start them into gear. They slowly obliged, but Kyle still protested. I asked where Dee was, and they had no clue. I felt panicked that I had to tell her what to do, which was going to go down about as well as a fart in an elevator.

Behind the second door I approached, Dee stood in a t-shirt and knickers with two other girls, who looked a bit worse for wear. Trying not to stare, I apologised and talked to her from behind the pulled door, using the text from Ozzie as bait to convince her to get ready.

She was moody. 'I've already had a text from him. I've told him I'm getting ready and on my way.'

As I closed the door, I heard her say to the girls, 'I'm sure he's trying to catch me in the act. Pervert. He got caught having phone sex a couple of days ago too...'

I thought about marching back in and laying out my defence but decided against it. I was in no mood for an argument with the headache I had. I'd only dig myself further into the mire.

I tiptoed through the living room to where there were still enough bodies to fill a morgue. I then entered the kitchen to find Lucy sitting with Polly and Ashley. The place was a state with chilli all over the sink, spilt alcohol everywhere, and what I presumed was a small pool of vomit in the corner, which I couldn't look directly at. A couple of guys wandered around, one of whom was the host and seemed untroubled by the state of the house he had to clean up. I don't think he'd seen the collapsed bed.

After a welcomed, strong cup of coffee, the whole gang staggered downstairs. We hovered by the front door as people assembled to see us off. One of the girls gave Dee an impassioned kiss, and Kyle snogged Danni, far too enthusiastically for that time in the morning, to the point where I could've added to the vomit in the kitchen.

Lucy gave me a prolonged hug, and the lads lacked subtlety as they stared on.

'I'm sorry again for what happened,' I whispered.

'There's no need to apologise. Nothing happened. I've got your details now, so I'll friend request you on Facebook and keep track of the tour.'

I gave her another hug and pecked her cheek before opening the door to leave. An extraordinary amount of paper cups, bottles, and general garbage littered the vicinity on our short walk to the parked taxi. As we got into the minibus, everyone wished the band luck and cheered as we departed.

Shortly into the journey, Kyle pointed out the guy from the party, who was dressed as Superman, doing the walk of shame down the busy road in full costume. It was such an obscure and hilarious sight.

Kyle wound down the window and screamed, 'Game over, man! Game over!' The guy was startled, but he responded by adopting a Superman pose and simulated flying down the street.

I was so tired, but there was no chance of sleeping as the lads were on top note, reminiscing about the night's escapades and how crazy it was. I bore the brunt, being labelled a lightweight, an unfair criticism given what I'd had to endure.

Will was rambling on about dancing with 'the fit blonde, who was definitely into him,' and added, 'I can't believe she passed out before I had the chance to pull her. I worked most of the night on her too.'

Kyle put him straight about the reality. 'Will, she was as thin as a smackhead's ankle. And you were dancing like a middle-aged Tory who does ecstasy twice a year and finds his best rhythm to fuckin' ABBA.'

The recollection moved on to the impromptu game of strip poker. That explained why so many people were semi-naked and piled next to each other in the room they were all in. Apparently, that was the last act before most people crashed out where they sat. Kyle boasted of his conquest. I was amazed he had the energy and the audacity to have sex with Danni despite the many people in close proximity.

The continued recollecting eventually led to one of the night's major incidents.

Kyle turned to me and asked, 'How's your face?'

Dee looked up and gave a smarmy grin.

'Can't feel a thing. You'll have to hit me harder next time,' I goaded.

'I'm sure that'll happen before this tour is out,' she snarled before burying her head back into her phone.

'So, you still want me to carry on then?'

'Not up to me, is it? Tried to get you thrown off before you even arrived. I'll be having it out with Ozzie, though. Don't worry about that.'

Trying not to show how pissed off I was, I replied, 'Good. I don't give a shit anyway. I can't be arsed with you anymore.'

I don't think she expected such a blunt comeback, but I was getting sick of her attitude. The tension between us was palpable, and the rest of the journey played out in silence.

Back at the flat, Ozzie stood at the front door like a nosy neighbour. He started to grill us as soon as we were within earshot, but Dee interrupted, 'Did you tell Hot Shot Writer that he could mention us getting thrown in jail?'

As quick as a flash, he responded, 'Yeah, I fuckin' did. And you should be glad of it because I've just got off the phone with Jamie at Sonic Bandwagon, and Emma, who does my social media. They said the article Ricky wrote is trending in a few areas and is being shared to fuck all over the show. So as far as I'm concerned, good job everyone. You clowns for getting arrested, for a shitty little misdemeanour, and for Ricky writing about it. And I'm gonna put my cock up my own arse for allowing it to go public.'

The lads welcomed the decision, but Dee couldn't allow herself to be happy and remained cold-faced, simply asserting, 'Well, next time, I want you to consult me first before any controversial shit like that goes to print.'

It was me who then developed the smarmy grin.

We found ourselves back on the road. Fortunately, Flagstaff was only a couple of hours north of Phoenix, a straight run up the I-17. The accommodation for the next three nights was provided courtesy of Lynwood. They'd referred Ozzie to a band they knew native to Flagstaff and organised for us to stay with them to help save on the costs. The band were called 'Dirt Ball Express', and they were billed as one of the bright sparks of the Arizona music scene. I was a little wary of spending three days with another band. At best, the nights would be chilled, sitting by a campfire supping a couple of beers, talking music, and getting a sufficient night's rest. At worst, and most likely, Dirt Ball Express would be just as crazy as the Cutthroats, and we'd have to endure three intoxicated nights where anything could, and probably would, happen.

I checked out the band on YouTube to get an idea which way the nights would sway. They were a rough-looking, three-piece swamp blues band, so I was more than apprehensive about spending three days with them. I was in no mood, or fit state, for excessive drinking. If the Cutthroats obliged later that night, I'd be seriously worried about their health and be astounded by their ability to hit the booze hard pretty much every night. I was learning that rock 'n' roll was still alive, but I struggled to keep pace with it.

Ozzie and Dee took the Dodge, and I assumed she would spend the next two hours complaining about me and the decision around the jail story. I had somehow been roped into driving the Chevy with the lads, which was risky because I was certainly over the limit. I needed something easy to listen to, so I found Richard Ashcroft's, 'They Don't Own Me'.

The inevitable third-degree came from the lads.

'What the fuck happened to you last night anyway?' Kyle asked.

'Don't ask. I was wrecked.'

'You surprised us. Was starting to think you were a boring old fart with no vinegar. You showed some balls doing that forfeit.'

'Couldn't let the Mancunian side down now, could I?'

'Too right. What happened with that girl anyway? You nail her or what?'

'Not exactly. Don't think I was in any fit state even if I wanted to. I'm glad I didn't, though.'

'What? Aaargh! You've gone down in my estimation now. She was fit.'

'Yeah, she was.'

'Then what was your problem.'

'It's complicated.'

'Fuck that. Is it the girl who was on the end of the phone?'

'Yeah. I feel guilty, and all we did was kiss.'

'Oooh, steamy,' he mocked.

I paused before asking, 'I know I might sound a fool asking this, but why do you go chasing it every night?'

'Do you ever see me chase it?' Kyle smirked.

'That's a good point.'

'It just comes to us. Come on, you've seen how it is. I'm not being an arrogant twat, but we're in a band. This shit just follows us.'

Will interrupted, 'Plus, at school, Kyle was a right ugly bastard, so he's making up for lost time and ridding himself of his demons.'

'Fuck off, Will.'

He reached around to give him a playful slap.

'Is that true?' I asked.

'True that I wasn't a looker. My face hadn't caught up to my chin. False about the reason why I go from girl to girl.'

'Classic psychological reasoning if you ask me,' Will said.

'Fuck off, Freud.'

I changed the subject, 'What about girlfriends? Have you ever had any?'

'Tell him, Quince,' Kyle insisted.

Quince spoke from behind me, 'I was engaged a couple of years ago, and it was a disaster.'

'We won't make Quince's mistake,' Kyle endorsed.

'You were engaged? What happened?' I asked.

'Turned out she was a bitch, so I got rid.'

'How long were you with her?'

'Five months,' Quince answered.

'So, you've all never had a serious relationship before, solely based on Quince being with a bitch for five months?'

I couldn't help but laugh, then asked Kyle, 'What's the longest you've been seeing someone then?'

'Since getting into a band, I've never seen the same girl for longer than three weeks. Nothing's gonna come between me and the music, and I want as many girls as I can get before I get old and boring like you.'

'Cheeky fucker. I'm not *that* much older than you.'

'You act like you're Ozzie's age, and at least he lived a bit.'

'I'm not that bad. I have lived a bit, you know. I've just calmed down more recently.'

'Tell me about the filthiest experience you've had then, Ricky?' Kyle quizzed.

'It probably doesn't compare to any of your experiences, considering you're in a band. I've already encountered two of you in compromising situations in just a few days.'

'And we've encountered you in a solo situation in just a few days too,' he fired back.

I laughed before asking, 'You tell me your dirtiest experience first?'

'I'll tell you one just from this tour. In Tucson, that girl stuck her tongue up my arse and gave my grundle a good licking.'

'That's disgusting. But what the fuck is a grundle?' I quizzed.

'You know, your notcha,' Kyle answered mid-laughter.

'Notcha?' I was bemused.

'Notcha arse and notcha balls. That bit in between. What do you call it?'

We all creased over.

'You mean a guiche?' Quince corrected.

Again, we howled.

'A fuckin' guiche? What's a guiche?' I questioned again, even more confused.

'I believe that's the technical term for it,' Quince answered.

'I think the technical term is the perineum,' I corrected.

'Oooh, get you with your fancy names,' Quince mocked.

'I've got a few names for it, but I've never heard it called a grundle or a guiche,' Will piped up.

'Like what?' I asked.

'Gooch. Biffins Bridge. Chin Rest. Bung Knuckle.'

The car filled with lung-busting laughter. It sparked a sequence of lad conversations, resulting in the band revealing stories from their combined sexual conquests.

The salacious stories of threesomes, multiple partners in one night in different venues, and invites to swinging parties were eye-opening, to say the least.

Then they showed me various pictures they'd been sent from the abundance of women they'd met in their band years. It didn't matter that I was still driving as they thrust the images in my face, making it difficult to focus on the road. It was mind-boggling to see so many women pose in such a way for them, with all sorts of filthy texts to accompany it.

As they scrolled through the pictures, they commented on them from their collective memory banks. On and on it went, and it astounded me. In my naivety, I thought this amount of band sexual exploits had been lost since the turn of the millennium. I assumed times had changed, and people were far more reserved than in past eras, especially with the ease with which social media could ruin reputations with one click. Turns out I was wrong. They were very much still in existence... and perhaps even worse than ever.

CHAPTER 13

By late afternoon we hit Flagstaff, and it was pointed out that we'd been travelling on the historic Route 66 - only for about fifteen minutes, but it was still another point ticked off on the bucket list. The temperature gauge in the car gradually dropped as we climbed to about 8,500ft above sea level. I couldn't believe the swing in temperature and landscape in such a short space of time, and we hadn't even crossed State lines. Flagstaff was far greener than the orange fortress we'd been used to for the past few days. Towering mountains were cloaked in snow on the distant horizon, a contrasting image to the sun thrashing down and glossing the arid surroundings in Phoenix.

We blindly followed the vague arrangements put forward by Lynwood, having not been given much information about where we were staying. Following the zip code for guidance, we drove through a leafy suburb tucked away in a ruralised setting that led to a single lane road. I followed Ozzie as we hit a bumpy trail off the beaten track. I feared it would lead to something more ominous and sinister in the arse end of nowhere, as the trail of doom submerged us deeper into the wilderness. I imagined entering a murky province, like a scene from 'Deliverance', and I'd be squealing like a pig before sundown.

'The Killing Moon' by Echo & The Bunnymen started, and my anxiety connected to the song's creepy intro. We came to a clearing with a huge, somewhat neglected, wooden farmhouse at the end of the overgrown path. A couple of beat-up transit vans were parked outside, and junk was piled up around the woodland perimeter.

We crawled up the path with caution and stopped a good way from the front of the house. I exited the car, stretched my legs, and took a deep breath. The air was polluted by smoke coming from a fire that blazed at the rear of the house.

The ramshackle door flung open. A wiry, shirtless man with long greasy hair and an uneven goatee appeared. A doobie poked out of the corner of his mouth, and the abrupt waft of cannabis beat the distant fire smoke into submission as he neared us.

'How y'all doin? You Cutthroat Shambles?' His drawled accent was strong.

'Certainly are. Are you from Dirt Ball Express?' Ozzie asked.

'Sure as shit am. I'm Gunther, the lead singer. Pleasure to meets you.'

They shook hands. I sensed from Ozzie's reaction that Gunther's hand was clammy as he grimaced once he retracted. We introduced ourselves just as a scruffy Jack Russell ran out barking like mad. It terrorised us as it constantly weaved in and out of our legs. The excitable little shit then decided to cock its leg up on the wheel of the Chevy and take a gushing piss. I shouted and chased it away, which only encouraged it to run amok and create havoc.

'Gollum! Git yo ass up in here,' Gunther yelled.

'Gollum? You called your dog, Gollum?' Will asked.

'Sure diiid.'

Dee spoke up, 'You can't call a dog Gollum. The poor fucker probably has an inferiority complex.'

Kyle whispered, 'I don't think that matters living amongst these zombies.'

Gollum obeyed his master and scarpered inside.

Gunther said, 'We got's a room set up for y'all, but I don't know how much sleep y'all gonna git wit the show tonight.'

We looked at each other puzzled.

Ozzie asked, 'Show? What show?'

'The house concert.'

'What the fuck is a house concert?' Quince piped up.

'Y'all about to find out.'

'Let me get this straight. This is where we'll be staying *and* where you'll be playing too?' Ozzie confirmed.

'Hell yeah. You folks from En-ger-land don't do this shiiit?'

Ozzie countered, 'Not to this extreme. House concerts are usually artsy folk singers who come to your house and play. I need to make a call.'

He walked away back towards the Dodge and took his phone out. I presumed the recipient was a rep from Lynwood.

Gunther continued, 'Quite's a common thing rounds here. We have shows in barns and yards. There's a stage inside. Plenty of folk rounds here loves to have themselves a barn dance. It's gonna be off the hook when all the peeps arrive.'

We followed Gunther into the house and were greeted by a festering, putrid stench that stung the nostrils. The house looked like it'd been lifted from a horror film set, being as abhorrent as any of our collective nightmares.

Piles of rubbish were bagged up and left to rot in the hallways, and dead bugs were scattered on the floor. The mixed smell of dog shit and dog piss smacked us in the face as we passed another room, making Kyle gag a little. I thought my hangover had subsided, but the squalid hellhole triggered a second wave.

We then went upstairs and were shown to our room. It was one room between six of us in a dusty, shambolic cesspit with one rusty bed. A cockroach ran across the floor, prompting Will to sing and do a little jig, 'La Cucaracha. La Cucaracha.'

Astonishingly, there was a pile of fifteen guns stacked on top of each other in the corner, a mixture of hunting rifles and pistols. Quince probed Gunther about them, and his response was blasé. 'Oh, don't you's worry about those. That's for hunting and protection. You guys don't have guns back in the UK?'

Will was blunt, 'Do we fuck. Guns aren't legal.'

'Guns aren't legal? How in the hell do you's defend yourselves if an intruder came in taking yo shit?'

'I'd give him a Mancunian love bite,' Quince quipped.

What the fuck was this place? It was crazy on a whole new level that stunned me.

Ozzie returned with a horrified look after enduring the walkthrough.

Gunther said, 'Well, I'll lets you settle in and see you's later.'

After he left, I asked Ozzie, 'What did Lynwood say?'

'They know nothing about the gig or the state of the house. They just assumed they were doing us a favour knowing these guys were staying in a large house. I don't think they expected it to be as shit as this.'

Kyle said, 'If we stay here, we're gonna need a tetanus shot.'

Ozzie countered, 'Given Lynwood sorted this for us, it'd look really bad if we bailed.'

'Fuck that. It's a shithole. Tell them to get their arses out here and stay the night. See how they respond to that,' Dee cried.

'Look, how about Dee bunks in the van, and we try and work something out in the house?' Ozzie suggested.

'Fuck that, Ozzie. How about we all bunk in the van? How the fuck are we meant to sleep here? Rats will be nibbling at my balls before the sun comes up,' Kyle burst out.

'It's not a bad shout to sleep in the van and car,' I agreed.

'It'll be freezing come midnight,' Will offered his opinion.

'That's a chance I'll take,' Kyle asserted.

The band had very few boundaries but staying in *that* house was beyond reckoning. It was a violation of the Human Rights Act. We agreed to treat the grounds like a campsite and sleep in the two vehicles.

We unenthusiastically checked out the rest of the house, eventually coming to a vast open room at the back that had been knocked through to make space for a gig. It looked like it was initially three rooms but had been shoddily renovated to just one. It could easily fit about one hundred plus people inside. It was a great idea if the place wasn't such a shithole.

The three members of Dirt Ball Express sound checked as Gollum ran riot across the stage, barking his head off. There was a sound engineer and another two grim-looking stoner dudes lurking about. They all looked like parodies of themselves - long hair, beards, sweaty, dirty, and all possessing a drawl associated with moonshine and drugs.

Kyle mused, 'It's like Antwerp Mansion[1] on steds in here. It's a glorified crack den. That's how you should open the blog about this night, Ricky: "I was standing in what could only be described as a mutha' fuckin' crack den when I was gang-raped by a gaggle of half-witted rednecks."'

I was standing next to Dee when Ozzie asked her, 'If you want to bail and go to a motel, just say so.'

'Fuck that. If nothing else, it'll be a story to tell. It'll give Hot Shot Writer something interesting to write about. Who knows? Maybe we'll be arrested again.'

'What? And risk another slap off you?' I joked.

'What's that?' Ozzie asked.

'Nothing,' I said.

'You slapped him, Dee?' He was obviously unaware of the incident.

'I barely touched him.'

'What did you slap him for?'

'Talking about the arrest in his review.'

He snapped, 'For fuck's sake, Dee. What the fuck is wrong with you?'

I jumped in, 'Don't worry about it, Ozzie. I've told her it didn't hurt and to do it harder next time.'

She walked towards me with purpose, but thankfully, Ozzie blocked her path, so instead, she flicked a finger up at me and walked off.

'Why didn't anyone tell me she slapped you? I'm only the fuckin' manager. I should know what the hell is goin' on,' he ranted.

'It's fine. I pushed her a bit because I was wrecked. It was when she found out I put the jail story in the review.'

'It's bang out of order. I'll have it out with her later. She can be a proper slapped arse at times,' Ozzie raged.

---

1   Semi-derelict Victorian mansion in Manchester that was used as a music venue.

Still taken aback by the situation, we opted to hang outside for safety reasons. We didn't want to catch a disease or get accidentally shot in the face by the moonshine-supping, gun-wielding hillbillies.

Gunther came out. 'Would any of you's like some food? We have a barbeque going back here. Got some pig's feet and chitterlings cooking.'

I nearly vomited as Ozzie answered, 'We've eaten, thanks.'

'You sure? Would you like me to skin an animal for you boys?' he drawled with a sinister laugh.

I stood motionless, petrified, my mouth agape. I genuinely thought that the animal they spoke of could be human and this was their way of disposing of the body.

'Definitely not. It's fine. Thanks all the same,' Ozzie responded.

'Give me a holler if y'all change yo mind.'

With nothing but time on our hands, Ozzie and I took the opportunity to do some work on our laptops. I finished writing the lads' interview and began writing the next blogs. I wanted to keep busy and productive to take my mind off the disaster zone we were stuck in. With no Wi-Fi, I was unable to send them to Jamie, so they sat pending in my drafts.

In the throes of writing the blog, a text came through from Eva that merely said: *'Hey. I hope you're OK and the gig went OK last night.'*

Guilt corroded me. We'd not spoken since before the Phoenix gig. She had no idea what had happened afterwards. Given that I woke up in bed with another woman, despite practically doing nothing, I felt shameful. I could only muster the reply: *'Yeah I'm OK thanks. It was good. Will speak later. I'm just writing.'*

The band had a pre-arranged radio interview with a station closer to home. Rebel Rach was a renowned music journo in Manchester and had her own radio show. She was a big fan of the band and had asked for a catch up while they were on tour. The interview was to be pre-recorded because of the time difference, but it was due to go live later that night in the UK.

The band congregated around Dee's iPhone, all with beers in hand after opening a crate from the back of the Dodge. They spoke candidly about the tour and what was coming up in the days ahead, referencing some of the more risqué moments without going into explicit details.

As time spiralled on, scores of people ambled up the path for the show, with only a few choosing to drive into the compound. They were an interesting set. It was clear that meth was a drug of choice as sunken eyes and a lack of teeth evidenced severe substance abuse.

The band attempted to make light of the situation by pointing out some of the oddballs who strode past them. They were so far removed from our own world it was frightening. A man with a weird hairline that started from the tip of his crown was described by Quince as 'having to backcomb his arse hair to give himself a fringe.'

An overweight, grotesque man in his sixties with a bushy, grey beard waddled up the trail. He nibbled on something which looked like roadkill that he'd just picked up from the side of the path. He accidentally dropped it to the ground. Wounded by the mishap, he drawled, 'Shiiiiit. I dropped ma God damn beef jerky, maaaan! He bent over to reach for it and struggled to pick it back up. As he continued to strain, his shorts fell to reveal the dirty, hairy crack of his arse, making us recoil and gag.

Quince was the first to brave the toilet for a number two. Up until that point, the bushes had sufficed for a quick piss. When he returned, his expression was one of dismay.

'I'm mentally scarred. You don't want to go in there. It's a disgrace. I can't even describe the smell. It's worse than sharing a room with Will after a curry.'

Kyle flinched.

Quince continued, 'I can't have a shit in there. I'm gonna have to venture into the wild.'

Off he went into the cluster of trees and bushes on the perimeter of the grounds. Although we laughed when he disappeared into the thicket, deep down, I was conscious that I may have had to follow suit at some point. I just hoped it wouldn't come to that as I wasn't sure my bowels would allow me to perform the act in nature.

When Quince returned, he pulled up the legs of his jeans to reveal no socks and simply remarked, 'No bog roll. Had to use my socks and bury them too.'

We pissed ourselves with laughter, but it made me even more determined to hold in any turtle's head that threatened to make an appearance.

By the time Dirt Ball Express were due on, the sun had disappeared over the trees, and the temperature dropped again. The wind was a little more savage and howled a tune as it swept through the trees.

We went inside to watch the show and get a bit warmer, strategically waiting till the last possible moment so we could stand at a safe distance at the back.

If we thought the place was catastrophic beforehand, it was nothing compared to what awaited us a couple of hours later. It was like The Wild West - boisterous with copious amounts of drinking and an intimidating tension, suggesting that it could go off at any point.

A layer of fog snaked through the corridors carrying an odour that was a mixture of cigarettes and cannabis. There was also a weird, faint, nail polish remover-type smell that I wasn't familiar with. At first, I thought it was a natural smell from the shit tip, but Kyle pointed out that it was meth. How he knew, I didn't want to know.

Perhaps the sound and venue had something to do with it, but Dirt Ball Express' brand of swamp rock was bland. It wasn't the best put together gig to showcase talent, probably billed more as a piss-up amongst friends. If they were on Lynwood's radar, there was no reason why the Cutthroats couldn't be signed. Most of the electric sockets were overloaded and hung from the rafters, looking like they needed someone to physically hold them together throughout the show. The behaviour of the locals was likely drug-induced, as they heavily stomped and rocked their heads like mental patients to a beat that wasn't in tune with the band's rhythm.

After the second song, I needed to use the toilet. Rather than go back outside to the bushes, I stupidly braved the nearby facility. I was anxious that whatever twisted image awaited me in there would sear itself onto my memory forever. God knows what state it was in after everyone inside had been let loose to do number ones, twos and whatever threes and fours constituted in that part of the world.

I shimmied my way through a few people and tried not to rub shoulders with them. I reached the toilet and tentatively kicked the door open with my toe. The smell attacked me instantly like a blast from a hairdryer. I winced as it felt like the niff wrapped itself around me with a python's stranglehold. I took a few steps forward, and my foot splashed into the puddled floor. The walls were black and grey, definitely not its original colour. The bath may as well have been chucked out for all its use as the rim was stained golden brown.

I mustered one more step inside but couldn't go any further. I bottled it and fled outside to find a patch of bush in the dark and hoped that a grass snake wasn't out hunting for worms.

As I completed my final jiggle, the sound of bottles smashing caught my attention. The noise became more profound as the music cut short, replaced by a string of commotion. I buttoned up and ran back into the house to see groups of people scuffling near the front of the stage. It resembled something out of the film 'Road House'. With no security to tame the crazies, an explosive situation potentially brewed. Kyle, Quince and Will looked on, seeming to enjoy the disorder.

Dee's reaction was different. She fumed, 'Fuck this shit, Ozzie. I'm outta here, I'm done.'

'She's right. This is ridiculous. We need to leave here before those guns get used,' I concurred.

'I'm way ahead of you. Ricky, please tell me you've not had much to drink,' Ozzie asked.

'Fuck all after last night. I'm still suffering.'

'Pussy,' Dee interjected.

'Now's not the time to take the piss, is it?' I responded.

'It's always a good time.'

Ozzie snapped, 'Pack it in, you two. Let's bail and get a motel somewhere. I don't care if it eats into our budget. There's no way I'm staying around here for three nights.'

The fighting continued as we left, and my last image was a member of Dirt Ball Express swinging a guitar from the stage down onto some poor fucker's cranium.

On our way out, I asked how the ruckus started. Will answered, 'Someone probably wasn't happy that their sister was sleeping with their brother and had left them out of it, and then the cousins got involved.'

As we exited the shack, the unmistakable red and blue flashing lights of a patrol car pulled up in front of us. The refulgent headlights blinded us as two cops stepped out. 'Hold it right there!' one of them barked.

'Arrrgghhh! For fuck's sake! What now?' Dee screamed.

'Looks like I'm gonna write about us getting arrested after all,' I joked.

Dee wasn't impressed.

Another man, dressed in civvies, appeared. 'Officers, those aren't the renters of the property.'

Ozzie responded, 'If you want the people renting this place, you'll find them inside. Nothing to do with us, officer.'

Kyle mocked Ozzie's conforming tone. 'Fuck me, Ozzie, you may fold under questioning.'

Will and Quince laughed at the Goodfellas reference.

The man who greeted the cops pulled out a document and stated with authority, 'We got an eviction notice here. We're here to remove these people from the premises. Six months they haven't paid the rent, despite multiple warnings.'

'So, no one called you about the disturbance?' Ozzie asked.

'What disturbance?'

Dee interrupted, 'What disturbance? Can you not hear what's going on in there, Deputy Dog?'

'You better watch your mouth,' the cop directed.

Ozzie shot, 'Dee, are you nuts? You've already been arrested for that gob of yours. Keep it shut.'

I shouted, 'You need to get inside...quick. I think you've got bigger problems than an eviction notice.'

'You just wait here,' he commanded.

Both cops entered, guns drawn. I envisaged some sort of Wild West trigger-happy shootout was about to play out.

Within minutes, two other cop cars arrived.

Shortly after, a few culprits were ejected, thankfully with no shots fired. The police had a few locals cuffed and lined up on the grass.

The bailiff eventually entered the house, and we could hear his outrage from outside. Every sentence started with, 'God Damn...', and was usually followed by expletives about the state of the place.'

Gollum barked incessantly from inside the house. I couldn't help but laugh when I heard the bailiff constantly yelling, 'Someone shut this damn dog up!'

Gunther and his fellow band members were escorted off the premises and were ordered to remove their crap. They also had to answer some difficult questions about the pile of guns the officers had found. We never got to hear the explanation.

The situation calmed down, and order was restored. The officers briefly questioned us, but once they were satisfied we were innocent bystanders and clearly not from around those parts, they let us go sometime around midnight.

We trudged back to the vehicles in silence, trying to comprehend what we'd just experienced. Ozzie joked, 'So, shall we still stay here then? Might be a few beds free now.'

Ozzie searched his phone and found a motel called The Canyon Inn about twenty minutes away. It was cheap, and more importantly, available. It also turned out to be closer to the gig venue the band were due to play the following night.

The Canyon Inn was located towards the centre of Flagstaff, taking us back to a certain degree of normality after our engagement with the cast of 'The Evil

Dead'. The area was surrounded by numerous independent fast-food outlets, but not the globally known conglomerates that dominated the industry. They still served pretty much the same shit – burgers, fried chicken, fries, and doughnuts. It hit home just how reliant on fast food America really was and why there were such obesity problems.

The Inn was a decent spot to stay and thankfully wasn't in the middle of nowhere like Bates Motel. The single-storey block layout with front doors that opened directly onto the car park was the quintessential image of an American motel. I'd always wanted to stay in a remote motel after seeing them so many times on TV. Knowing my luck, The Canyon Inn probably doubled up as a drug den/whorehouse, though.

Ozzie said the cost hadn't eaten too much into the budget, but he had pulled a fast one. He should've booked three rooms, but to save money, he'd booked two. I gladly volunteered to sleep on the floor, given the earlier alternative.

The rooms were basic, boasting two imposing canvas pictures of Route 66 on the wall above the beds. It was kind of a cool sight to remind us of where we were.

On our way to the two adjacent rooms, Ozzie spoke, 'Ok, everyone. Listen up. I was gonna wait till tomorrow to confirm but fuck it. I figure we could do with some good news after what's happened tonight. I had a phone call this morning from a mate of mine who runs a management agency based in the UK. They have a band currently touring the US, but they're going to have to cut the tour short. Because he knew we were here, he asked whether we'd like to fill in for their final two tour dates, and I agreed.'

'Cool. The longer we're out here, the better for me. Where and when?' Kyle asked.

'You sure you want to know?' he teased.

Together the band egged him on to spill the beans.

'The first is...drum roll, please... Las Vegas!'

The band gasped in excitement.

'Fuckin' nice one. That's mint. When's that?' Quince asked.

'The day after the L.A. gig.'

'Aww man, we can't get fucked up in L.A. then?'

'You wouldn't be getting fucked up anyway on such an important night. You'll have plenty of time to get fucked up in L.A. before the Whisky show.'

'Where's the gig?' I asked.

'Count's Vamp'd Rock Bar & Grill.'

I replied, 'I've never heard of that. Can't be on the Strip, surely?'

'No, it's a little out of the way but has a great reputation. It's a proper rock venue by all accounts. It's only a support slot for another band, but the pay is decent, and it gives us more exposure.'

Kyle agreed, 'Good work, Ozzie. Vegas. I've never been. I can't wait.'

Will and Quince echoed Kyle's sentiments.

'Ricky, you'll have to show us around, considering you fancy yourself as Lord Mayor of Vegas,' Quince joked.

'Gladly. You won't be able to keep up with me in Vegas. That's my home turf.'

'You don't want to challenge us to a drink off.'

'Where are we staying?' Dee butted in.

Ozzie answered, 'Looks like we can get a few cheap rooms in New York New York.'

Butterflies fluttered in my stomach. New York New York was where so much of my trip nine months earlier happened. It was where Eva had returned to surprise me for our final Vegas tryst. I then remembered that I blew her off somewhat with my earlier reply. I took out my phone and sent her a message: *'Sorry. It's been a crazy night. I'll explain tomorrow. Miss you.'*

'And where's the second gig?' Dee asked.

In my flustered state, I'd forgotten about the second announcement.

'Well…who wants to see where Dee comes from?' Ozzie teased again.

'What do you mean?' asked Will.

'Have you heard of the Bermuda Festival?'

'Erm no,' Will answered.

'You're shittin' me! You've got us a slot there?' Dee said.

'Not just any slot. Only the same stage as the Red Hot fuckin' Chili Peppers. And because I'm *that* fuckin' good, I've managed to keep a decent slot and not be thrown way down to the bottom of the undercard.'

'That's mint! When do we go onstage?' Kyle asked.

'Fourth from the end.'

'That's fuckin' mega!' Kyle screamed.

'It's going to be the biggest audience you've played to guys,' Ozzie added.

While the band revelled in the excitement, I quietly asked Ozzie, 'Do you want me to come with you for this? Both Vegas and Bermuda?'

'Yeah, man. Why? Do you not want to?'

'Of course, I do. I need to check the flight cost. I'm not sure Jamie will front them after you told me he's a bit tight.'

'A *bit* tight? If you stuck a lump of coal up his arse, in two weeks you'd have a diamond. Don't worry about it yet. We'll sort something out.'

I didn't bring up how this would affect the Eva situation. Flying beyond the East Coast to Bermuda could possibly mean I wouldn't fly back again. I had to think it through before committing. But it was another great opportunity and part of the unpredictable travel plan I had my heart set on. To see Bermuda would be astounding and somewhere I'd never considered visiting beforehand. I guess that's what travel entails sometimes. You just have to go with the flow and end up wherever the current takes you.

Quince pulled out a bottle of Brandy and said, 'Wasn't a total loss going to that shithole. Look what I nabbed.'

We applauded his efforts as he offered it around.

'I think we all deserve a cheeky shot of this,' he said.

No one complained. With no shot glasses, we used the glasses and coffee cups provided in the room. Quince swigged directly from the bottle.

The tipples continued, and the brandy was polished off in no time. On the final round, Will stood up. Through garbled speech, he said, 'Ok. For the final shot, I'd like to make a toast and drink to something in honour of this fucked up night and that shithole we've just been to.'

We all stood with him and held out the glasses.

'To guns 'n' roaches and eviction notices!'

We applauded his wit and downed the shots in one.

CHAPTER 14

As usual on this trip, I must've only got a couple of hours of sleep. It wasn't jet lag this time. It was the discomfort of sleeping on the hard floor under a desk, coupled with Quince and Ozzie's collective snoring that sounded like a ferry docking.

Ozzie had left the room at some point in the middle of my slumber, but Quince was still away with the fairies. He continued to snore loudly with a full bed at his disposal to stretch out his hefty frame.

I felt exhausted and likened the feeling to my six-day binge in Vegas. My body was being put through its paces again with the excesses of life on the road. Although I barely drank the previous night, I was suffering from the travelling, sleep deprivation, and dealing with the general shit the tour continued to throw up.

The sun beamed down from up high, but the air remained cool, forcing me to put my zip-up top on for the first time during the day on the trip.

I headed over to the hotel reception, where the free breakfast was located. Breakfast was basic, consisting of coffee, juice, bread, and a selection of Danishes and jams, but it was all that was required. Ozzie was working at a table with a coffee and a plate full of crumbs in front of him. He'd just finished a phone call as I arrived.

'Hey. How'd you sleep?' He sounded upbeat.

'Absolutely shite. Surely you couldn't have slept well?'

'I got what I needed. Just a couple of hours is enough.'

'Fuck that. I'm a wreck if I don't get at least seven hours, and I'm five short. I'm feeling the pace. This rock 'n' roll world is tough to keep up with.'

'Ah, you get used to it. This is only the beginning for you.'

'At this rate, it'll be the end of me.'

'Haha. You've got to toughen up if you want to succeed on the road. At least you're getting on well with the lads. I still can't believe Dee slapped you. I've not had a chance to give her a proper bollocking about that, but I will.'

'I doubt she's going to change her opinion of me now. What's done is done. But yeah, I think I've made inroads with the boys, and we're well past the awkward stage now. I suppose being caught in the act helped, as well as the party in Phoenix.'

'I've heard about Phoenix, you dog.' He grinned at me.

'What have you heard?'

'Just that you ended up in bed with some girl.'

'Well, not quite like that.'

'Oh?'

Whereas I didn't reveal much of the truth to the lads about what happened between Lucy and me in Vegas, I felt compelled to tell Ozzie the full story. When I said I didn't sleep with her at the party, he gave me a look to suggest I was lying and holding out on him.

I put him straight, 'Honestly. I was completely off my tree and probably passed out before I had a chance, but if I was even ten per cent less drunk, I reckon I could've... I might've...I probably would've.'

'Don't be too hard on yourself. You're not in a relationship with this... Eva, is it? How many people in your position would've gone off with the first girl who showed them a bit of attention because they're with the band?'

'I guess you're right. All this just happened so fast. I can't believe I ran into a girl I nearly slept with in Vegas. Of all the girls to run into, it had to be her.'

'But nothing even happened, and you said you were a mess. Being held upside down drinking kegs and smoking bongs, I hear. No wonder you're still struggling.'

'You really did get the gory details, didn't you?'

I changed the subject. 'Have you spoken to Lynwood yet about last night's fiasco?'

'I didn't have to say much. They called me when they heard the band had been evicted and apologised to me. They even said they'd cover some of the costs for the hotel, which is good of them.'

'Do you know what happened to Dirt Ball Express?'

'Not too sure. They got evicted, I know that.'

'They'd probably be living in better conditions in jail.'

'Haha. I couldn't care less. I have enough on my plate with this tour and sorting out some of the acts back home who are mithering me.'

'Any news on a potential deal for Cutthroats? Surely the Phoenix gig has scored brownie points, and getting the Vegas and Bermuda gigs can only mean good things?'

'They're keeping their cards close to their chest on this one. Just got to keep the momentum going and see what happens. Looks like they'll wait till we hit Los Angeles.'

'Speaking of Vegas and Bermuda. I've got a phone call to make,' I said.

'To your lovely lady friend?'

'Yup.'

I ventured outside to call Eva. On top of breaking the news to her that our potential meet could be further postponed, I still felt guilty about spending the night with Lucy. I hoped her intuition wouldn't tell her something was bothering me.

Eva was enthusiastic when she answered. 'Hey you. How are you?'

'I think my body might be broken, but I'm getting through it. How are you? Work OK?'

'I'm OK. Work is good. How's the tour?'

'Interesting night, but aside from that, I've got something to tell you.'

'Oh?'

'The tour is being extended. There's an extra gig in Vegas, believe it or not, and there's also a trip to Bermuda afterwards. I've been invited to carry on covering the band.' I cringed after revealing the plan.

'Wow! That sounds amazing.'

'You're not pissed off?'

'Hell no. That's an incredible opportunity for you. You must go. You'd be loco not to.'

'But we had plans to meet.'

'We've waited nine months. I'm sure we can wait a little longer.'

'I guess. It's not ideal, is it? I'm desperate to see you.'

'If we don't get to meet this time, I'm sure we will, one day.'

'It won't come to that. I'll make sure we meet,' I promised.

'Whatever will be, will be, cariño,' she theorised.

'It's a fantastic opportunity, I know, but a part of me doesn't want to go. I've had my heart set on seeing you after all this is done. To have that taken away has made me a little sad. If I fly to Bermuda, I'll be closer to Manchester than San Diego. I don't know how much flights are, so it might not be *that* easy to come back. It just feels like I'm drifting further and further away from you, and if that's the case, I don't want to hold you back.'

'Hold me back from what?'

'Moving on and getting on with life. Being with someone who at least lives nearer to you... I don't know... I'm being battered from pillar to post out here, physically, mentally, and emotionally and I don't know what I'm thinking anymore.'

'I'm in no rush to move on with another man if that's what you're thinking. I don't want anyone else. Hell, I wasn't even looking for a man when I came to Vegas, but there you were, ruining my plans,' she teased.

'Ha. I wasn't looking for a girl too, but things... sort of happened.'

'They did. Look, I'm happy where I am in life and I love you being part of it, but if you want to call it quits, I'd understand. But just so you know, I don't want to call it quits with you.'

'I don't want that either. Just ignore me. I'm exhausted, and I don't know what I'm saying.'

'You need to rest, or you're going to make yourself ill.'

'I hear you. It's hard, though. It's so intense out here. I never realised what a tour entails away from the glamour. Let's get the tour out of the way, and we'll discuss *us* afterwards. Deal?'

'Deal. Let's not mention it again until the trip is done.'

We carried on talking. I told her what happened at the house in Flagstaff. She laughed, the kind of frenetic laugh that stopped time. She understood why I was so drained and not thinking straight, given what I'd had to endure in the past twenty-four hours. She had to go to work (Eva worked with war veterans), and we agreed to speak soon, without setting a specific time.

Her parting words were, 'You don't choose a life. You live one. Do not hesitate to go to Bermuda and live life. Chances like this only come around once in a lifetime, cariño.'

Her wise words stuck with me as I went back into reception and slumped on the chair opposite Ozzie, who was still on the phone himself organising some of his acts from back home.

After he hung up, he asked, 'Everything OK?'

'Yeah. I'm great.'

Sensing I wasn't exuberant, he asked, 'How's your girl?'

'She's good.'

'Did you tell her about Bermuda?'

'I did.'

'And?'

I paused, then said, 'The other day when we talked outside the house in El Paso.'

'Yeah?'

'You said, don't be like you. If the girl's special, don't do what you did. What did you do? If you don't mind me asking.'

He shut his laptop. 'I don't mind you asking. It was a long time ago. In a nutshell, I stayed in the music game, and Mia got out, not that she was ever in it for a career.'

'She was in the music scene too?'

'Yeah. We're going back to the nineties here when we met. She was still at uni in Manchester, but she was from Bournemouth. I met her at a gig at Dry Bar. I even remember who played that night. It was a band called The Cornelius Crane. They were class, you'd have loved them, proper Americana tunes...I digress, sorry. Anyway, she was doing some voluntary promo work for a small label, gaining work experience. We hit it off instantly and started seeing each other regularly until we were official.'

'What happened then?'

'She finished uni and stayed in Didsbury. She got a job working in marketing for some company. She still did a bit in music, but she did less and less as her career soared. Music had become sort of a full-time job by then for me despite struggling to make ends meet, so I was working the odd bar shift in my local when I could. But our social life was top.'

'I can imagine.'

'Anyway, we'd been seeing each other for a while. We started talking about the future, moving in together, marriage, kids, and all that bollocks. After a year or so she got offered an opportunity down in London that I guess she couldn't turn down. She asked me to move down with her, saying that the music thing was never gonna get me anywhere, that I should chalk it down to a great experience and get a "proper job darn sarth". I guess I couldn't believe she wanted me to jack in my passion to become something I'm not. Call it pride, stubbornness or whatever, but it made me more determined to stay up north and prove her wrong. We argued a lot after that. Petty shit really, and most of it was my fault cos I was a pig-headed bastard back then.'

'At least you proved her wrong.'

'The sad thing is, she was probably right. Was all this worth it? Maybe it was, but I wonder from time to time what my life would've been like if I'd upped sticks and moved down south. I was too scared to move out of Manchester back then, probably still am. London never has, nor ever will, appeal to me, even if I might've done alright in music down there.'

'Surely you don't regret not going?'

'I said the other day that you can't have regrets in life, and it's not like life has been downhill since she left, but I do wonder, what if, when sat alone in my gaff late at night reflecting on life's ups and downs from time to time.'

'Has there been anyone since Mia?'

'Nah. Not the way I felt about her. Couple of short-term girlfriends, but there isn't a love like a first love, is there? I never really moved on from her, and to put work and music before another woman helped justify that in some way.'

'I can understand that.'

'Why do you ask all this anyway? Has Eva given you an ultimatum? Her or the tour?'

'Quite the opposite. She's encouraging me to go to Bermuda, but if I go, the chances of seeing her anytime soon diminish.'

'Only you can make that call. I'm more than happy to have you in Bermuda with us. If you want to come and can afford it, then do it.'

'Well, that's another thing. The cost.'

'Financial or emotional?' he asked.

I contemplated both and could only muster an indecisive shrug at the question.

There was plenty of time before we were due at the gig later that evening. The switch in accommodation left us only a couple of minutes drive away from the venue. Everyone else had remained asleep, and Ozzie advised me to leave them to it so they could recharge the batteries. He had a lot of work to do around organising the logistics of Vegas and Bermuda. He was also dealing with the never-ending phone calls from people demanding his attention back home.

I polished the reviews from the Phoenix gig to the eighties party (where I left out my own drunken downfall and Dee's slap) to expand on the hellhole we'd been subjected to. With Wi-Fi restored, I submitted the blogs in three blocks, including the lads' interview, so they could be staggered over the coming days. It gave me a bit of breathing space before the next lot were due.

I should've really caught up on some sleep and rest as per Eva's recommendation, but with having the day to myself, I intended to be alone away from the band and reconnect with myself.

I sifted through the abundance of leaflets that inundated the reception counter for anything of interest. Grand Canyon was the obvious advertisement plug, but having been there nine months earlier, I wanted something a little different. It didn't take long to find the perfect tonic for the madness of the tour, and it was something that would help bring an element of peace to my overworked mind. It was an excursion to a Navajo Indian reservation. America wasn't exactly rich in the sort of history England and Europe were accustomed to, but the Native Americans provided an offering to appease my cultural and spiritual curiosities.

I asked the receptionist about the tour, and she said she could check the availability for that day. She confirmed my booking and informed me that I was being picked up half an hour later at the motel.

A twenty-seater executive minibus pulled up in the lot. A burly man, who resembled Grizzly Adams, disembarked to greet me in a husky, smoker's voice, 'Hello, friend. JR's the name.'

'I'm Ricky. Nice to meet you.'

'You sure got lucky booking this at short notice. I got another pickup at a motel down the road, so I could fit you in.'

'I really appreciate it.'

I climbed onto the bus. A few people sat quietly, none below the age of fifty, all dressed like teachers on a school trip. Perfect. I'd had enough of the rowdiness of youth for the time being.

JR got on the mic that echoed around the bus. He told us that before we visited the Navajos, we were going to some lava fields in a patch of land left decimated by a volcanic eruption at Sunset Crater. Afterwards, we were going to visit the Wupatki Indian Reservation before making our way to a Navajo site. I didn't read the print properly on the flyer. I assumed it was just a visit to the Navajo Reservation, but I was getting my money's worth.

JR was knowledgeable. He educated us about various points of interest on our travels, including the history and reasons for the geological formations on the nearby mountain ranges, such as The San Francisco Peaks.

He preferred to take the back roads to the lava fields, which were made more captivating by the majestic brush with nature. Bristlecone pine forests blanketed the back roads, and in the distance, the mountain tops were lathered with snow. It looked more like Canada than Arizona. That part of the world was simply a treasure trove of natural beauty and colourful topographic nuggets.

Just as I was chomping on some Danishes I'd taken for the road, we stopped at the lava fields and were free to roam through the pathways. JR warned us not to fall because it *will* hurt, and we *would* bleed. Touching some of the formations as I moved through, I could see why. The black, razor-sharp rock that had been present for hundreds of years was a Health & Safety Officer's wet dream.

We continued the picturesque journey and seemed to be the only vehicle travelling that road. JR explained that other sightseeing tours ignored the route because the area was so close to the Grand Canyon, and they preferred to take the direct road via the interstate.

JR revealed more about himself. He was married to a Native American, which explained his in-depth knowledge of their culture and history. His former profession was a film location scout. He revealed that he'd worked with Mel Gibson on 'Maverick' and 'Braveheart'. On the subject of films, he told us that the route we took was used for many of the scenes in 'Easy Rider' and several Westerns. It was evident why a film director would use such surroundings to help capture a film's essence.

We arrived at the Wupatki Indian Reservation, a beautifully preserved archaeological and heritage site. The old ruins and historical arenas invoked a feeling that I was insignificant in this world. The formation of the sandstone buildings, dwellings and structures was breathtaking. It gave me an appreciation for the ingenuity of the natives and how they were able to construct such buildings in those times. I could barely assemble a flat pack, so it was mind-blowing how these people managed to build these back then.

We trekked through the beaten footpaths and found our way to the bottom of the site. The Native Americans believed that a spirit lived below ground, called 'kachina'. The myths stated that it could tell what the weather would be like in the coming days. The kachina was said to lurk beneath a blowhole that ran for miles upon miles through a network of underground caves. If a scarf was placed over the top of the hole and got sucked in, the pressure was high, so the weather would be good. If the scarf blew out, then the pressure was low, meaning the weather would be bad. The blowhole was still active, and when one of our party put her scarf over the top, it was being sucked in, hence the good weather. Science tells us why the phenomenon happens, but hundreds of years ago, the Indians believed this to be the work of the demonic spirit and its mood. I chuckled to myself when I likened Dee to a kachina.

Whilst we stood marvelling at the sea of sand that bathed the lands, JR alleged that the Mormons attempted to settle in the same parts as the Native Americans, but the indigenous folk were against that. They tricked them into taking a special cacti drug and sent them wandering through the plains, battling through a trance till they hit Utah. The story may have been tongue-in-cheek Wupatki humour, but I hoped there was an element of truth to it.

The next stop was the Cameron Trading Post for a late lunch on a Navajo Ranch. I ordered a traditional Navajo Indian stew. It was delicious and was sure to set me up all night, given how filling it was. The portion size was ridiculous, made all the larger by the piece of bread that complemented it. It wasn't just any kind of bread, like a Warbies toasty. Instead, it was the biggest slab of customary Indian fried bread imaginable. It looked like a frisbee, was greasy as hell, but tasted sensational.

There was a shop on site filled to the brim with authentic Indian crafts and holistic nuggets. Knowing Eva's affiliation to spirituality, I bought her an authentic Indian bracelet and some chakra stones. Who knew when I would get round to giving them to her? But I promised myself that I would give them to her in person one day.

The informative and much-needed tour concluded, and we headed back to Flagstaff. I was dropped off at Canyon Inn. Ozzie was in the same place I'd left him, laptop still open, and his phone was pressed against his ear. An empty cup of coffee rested on the side, and I wondered how many he'd gone through. He broke from his call as I headed over.

'Ah, so how are the Native Americans?'

'That was well worth the trip. I needed that. You should've joined me.'

'Wish I could, but duty called.'

'Where are the others?

'The lads went up the road looking for a place to get some food a couple of hours ago. They said to bring the stuff to the gig, and they'd meet us there as they'll be right by it. I think Dee is still sleeping.'

'I thought she'd be back drinking.'

'Nah, she needs to rest that voice of hers. She can be sensible when necessary. Can't say the same for the lads.'

He closed his laptop, stretched out and proclaimed, 'I need a break. Do you fancy a walk up to Walgreens to stock up on a few things?'

'Sure. Scope the area out a bit.'

CHAPTER 15

After a three-minute drive, we arrived at the gig venue, the Green Room. Dee was enraged when she heard that the band had been out most of the afternoon, and she spent the journey making her feelings known.

'Those dicks better not be pissed. They know the fuckin' rules - they can't get hammered before a show.'

'They'll be alright, I'm sure,' Ozzie tried to allay her fears.

'I've a bad feeling. Been a while since we've had an incident. We're due one, and it usually happens when I'm not around beforehand,' Dee said.

A stressed-out man puffed heavily on a cigarette by the doors as we pulled up in the car park at the rear. He made a beeline for us when he saw us take equipment out of the van.

'Are you Ozzie?' He looked flustered.

Ozzie replied, 'Yeah. Frankie, I presume?'

Without replying to Ozzie, he snapped, 'So, you're in charge of those animals in there?'

Dee butted in, 'What the fuck have they done?'

'Done? They're a disgrace.'

Dee pushed passed Frankie and stomped through the door.

Ozzie continued unloading the Dodge and said, 'Just give me a sec and we'll sort out any issues.'

Moments later, Dee reappeared, her face florid with fury. 'I don't fuckin' believe it.'

'What is it?' Ozzie asked.

'They're fuckin' wasted. All three of them. Why did you let them go off on their own, Ozzie? You know what they're like.'

'I'm not their babysitter, Dee. They only went for food somewhere. How bad?'

'Far worse than that gig in Stoke. Will is jabbering like fuckin' Chewbacca on speed.'

'For fuck's sake! I don't need this shit.' Ozzie rubbed his temple with his fingers.

I wondered what the hell happened in Stoke that didn't involve making pots.

'Are they going to be in a fit state to play tonight? You can kiss the fee goodbye if they can't even stand up on stage,' Frankie raged.

Ozzie sighed. 'Let's not be hasty, Frankie. I'll go and see what the deal is and have a chat with them.'

Dee got back in the Dodge and slammed the door shut. I followed Ozzie into the venue, quietly relieved that Dee's anger was not directed at me for a change.

Upon entering backstage, the scene was decadent and chaotic. The room was poorly lit and felt cold, and a musty, damp smell tainted the air. The carpet was old and worn, and you could feel the hard concrete beneath the surface. The walls were stained from old cigarette smoke, and a mustard-coloured gloss ridged its way across all four corners.

Will was topless and sat on an armchair, snorting coke off the perky breasts of a pretty flame-haired temptress who straddled him. His pupils dilated as he came around to make eye contact with Ozzie and me. More than one empty vial rolled around the remnants of white powder on the table in front of him.

Kyle and Quince sat at a table on the other side of the room and looked plastered. The empty bottle of Johnnie Walker next to them suggested why. Two other guys dressed like glam rock throwbacks, with silver and blue sequins, sat opposite them. Three more girls stood nearby and looked stoned as fuck with narrowed, reddened eyes, swaying to 'Funnel of Love' by Wanda Jackson that shot out from the speakers.

I continued to scan around and nearly jumped out of my skin when a guy riding a unicycle darted past me from my blind side. It got weirder when I saw a woman dressed as a rainbow-coloured unicorn floating about, completely off her tree on some intoxicating drug. The oddness continued on the far side of the room, where a few artsy-looking dudes were dressed freakishly – like they were part of some new age cult born out of the fires of the Manson Family. It was like an Andy Warhol party, full of the weirdest of the weird, and I couldn't get my head around how the band had come to be in such peculiar company.

'Who the fuck are these people?' Ozzie asked a wired Will.

'They're the band on after us, believe it or not. Two of them are yoga masters. Look.'

He pointed over to two hippy dudes sitting in the corner on yoga mats meditating and stretching away, displaying a level of flexibility that made my groin ache.

Ozzie wasn't impressed. 'Oh, that's great, so not only are they in some weird fuckin' band, but they can suck themselves off whilst clipping their own toenails.'

I couldn't contain my laughter, despite not being the appropriate time.

'I bet their set is gonna be proper freaky, man. Like Jethro Tull on crack,' Will replied.

I looked at the poster of the stage times on the door to see that the kooky band were called Cats of the Moon. What the fuck kind of band name was that?

Dee stormed back in and went ballistic like a jilted bride. 'You fuckin' set of pricks. You know you're not meant to get pissed or do drugs before a show. You don't fuckin' listen! If you fuck up tonight, I'm fuckin' done. Get your shit together and get these fuckin' morons out of here!'

'Ah, chill out, Dee,' a bleary-eyed Kyle responded. 'This is the band playing after us. They're our new friends. They might be a bit strange, but fuck it, it's a laugh, innit?'

Dee was exasperated by Kyle's casualness and stormed toward him. Ozzie moved fast to thwart her path, keeping her at bay and putting himself between her and her prey. She gave up the ghost after hurling a few expletives and left the room in a huff.

Ozzie echoed Dee's words, making his disappointment known. 'You've got an interview with a local rag soon. How the fuck are you gonna be in any fit state to do that?'

Kyle pulled his face in defiance. Ozzie took exception and got angrier. 'Don't give me that cocky arse face you always get when you've had too much booze, Kyle. You've already jeopardised the gig tonight. The least you can do is give a semi-professional interview to the people who can help make you. Sort yourselves out, get ready for soundcheck and try to remember what fuckin' notes to hit.'

Ozzie left, and I followed to help bring the gear in. He remained silent, so I didn't engage with him. Dee sat seething with her arms folded in the back of the car.

When soundcheck arrived, it was painful. It took forever as the guys were sluggish. I wouldn't say they were completely wasted and falling over, but they looked and sounded drunk enough to be nowhere near their best. Kyle had a slight wobble about him while adjusting his guitar strings. Dee's agitation was boiling throughout, but she refrained from making a scene when the journalist and photographer were pointed out to her.

The sound engineer and staff had an inkling something wasn't quite right as the band laboured through. With Frankie looking on anxiously, Ozzie tried his best to deflect attention to more business-like matters - ticket money and setting up a merch stand.

Once soundcheck was finally completed, the guys went backstage, and Dee headed towards the bar to find a corner table on her own with a bottle of water. Ozzie decided to let her fly solo on the interview to avoid any confrontation with the others. He also didn't trust what the boys might have said to a young, good-looking female photographer while inebriated.

I went backstage to keep tabs on them for what it was worth. They remained obstreperous as pills were dished out by the cult leader of Cats of the Moon, which escalated matters. I eyed Kyle with a few in his hand, and he slurred his excuse, 'These are uppers. They'll wake me up ready for the show.'

Quince looked to have already taken his share of drugs as he bombed about the room, chatting at 100mph, His eyes bulged, and white residue stuck to the side of his nostril.

On his return, Ozzie was gobsmacked when he saw what was happening.

'Fuck this! I'm not being around them when they're like this. They won't listen to reason in this state,' he growled before storming out, leaving me alone in the freak show.

Will bounced over to me, full of unnatural energy. 'Tricky Ricky. Do you think we're out of order getting blitzed? Do you?'

'I'm not saying anything, Will. Just try and put on a good show, yeah?'

He exuded a condescending drunken attitude I despised in individuals and wouldn't leave me be.

'Are you gonna put this in one of your blogs? About how we're just a set of pissheads.'

'You know I wouldn't do that. How did you get so wasted in such a short space of time?'

'Been on the whisky since two o'clock.'

'That explains it then.'

'Makes me chaff in this heat.'

'Too much information.'

'You told everyone about us being arrested, so what's to stop you from writing about this?'

'Yeah, but the arrest story worked out for the best. This episode wouldn't be in your best interests, would it?' I was getting annoyed.

'You're boring. You're no fun. Here you are with a rock 'n' roll band, and you won't even have a bump or get pissed with us. You're the enemy, aren't you? A fuckin' narcotics agent. Grassing us up to the world about our drug and alcohol abuse. You couldn't even bring yourself to fuck that girl in Phoenix.'

That hit a nerve, and I snapped, 'Fuck off, Will. Sort yourself out, you're a mess! And you two as well!' I directed at Quince and Kyle.

They both responded with a sarcastic, 'Ooooohh-hhhh!'

I continued to rant, 'People have put a lot on the line to get you here, and you're gonna fuck it up. Look at you all, coke and pills before a gig with your jaws going ten to the dozen. So fuckin' cliché. I've got news for you. It's been done to death in rock's heyday, no one thinks it's cool anymore, and most of those that did, ended up in rehab. Why do you do it? Ego not big enough? You're on the cusp of something special. Do your job, and if you want to get fucked up afterwards, so be it. It's pathetic.'

I had to endure another bout of verbal diarrhoea as I stomped out of the door. You can't reason with people when they're already in the grip of a drug binge. I felt empathy for the people tasked to deal with the drugged up, boozed up rock egos of the past. Beyond the stage and larger-than-life persona, it was a nightmare, like babysitting grown men. I had an uneasy feeling that reminded me that rock 'n' roll doesn't always go so swimmingly, and it wasn't meant to. The gigs had been going too perfectly, and there was no way that could be sustained.

Whilst at the merch stand, Jamie messaged me. He complimented me on the three recent submissions, saying that the writing had improved. He was happy with what I'd described offstage with Dirt Ball Express, although I didn't name the band directly for fear of a legal backlash. He was also happy with the interview with the lads, but he emphasised the need to lock Dee down into an in-depth one-on-one. Easier said than done. He wasn't aware of the tension between us. He said he'd post the interview the next day, but the gig review and travel blog had already gone live. After having a quick scan, I could see he'd sharpened it up, but bits didn't feel like my work. He was the boss though, and there was no way I could complain. I was buoyed by the content of the early comments, which expressed laughter and shock at what had happened at the Dirt Ball Express house concert.

The unknown question of the band's playing ability lingered in my mind as the support band came onstage. They were a rockin' blues rock band called Gorilla Riot, and they gave an exceptional account of themselves. They benefitted from arriving a little late and not having to tolerate the craziness backstage for too long before they went on. I knew that an on-form Cutthroats were better. But given their current condition, I was worried that most people would go home talking about Gorilla Riot rather than the Cutthroats, and deservedly so. Not only that, how would I spin it in the blogs if the performance was a proper fuck up? I was caught between professionalism and band loyalty yet again.

Dee decided to get ready in the van, preferring to stay away from the lads after her interview. She was nearly ready when I went to get a few more CDs from the Dodge. Her token burgundy cowboy hat that had become the trademark of the tour rested next to her. She looked striking, dressed in black with make-up expertly applied.

She caught me staring and taunted, 'Take a picture, it'll last longer.'

I gulped and apologised, 'Sorry. Just that…you look good.'

She flashed a hint of a smile as she messed with her hair in the mirror.

I panicked and had to get out of there, saying, 'I'll leave you to it. Have a good one.'

'Fat chance of that,' she murmured.

I hoped her quality and staggering looks would divert focus from the band's potentially substandard performance.

Shortly after, I gave her a quick heads up that they were due on in five minutes. She followed a few steps behind me and ran into the guys en route to the stage.

She refused to acknowledge them. It was painfully obvious they hadn't sobered up.

Kyle joked, 'What? No huddle or rendition of "With a Little Help from My Friends"?'

Face looking dead ahead, eyes narrowing, she answered, 'Go fuck yourself, Kyle.'

'Wow! First time with no rendition beforehand. Don't know why you insist on doing it before every gig anyway.'

Dee shot him a hurt look that implied a nerve had well and truly been struck. I noticed her fists clenched tightly, and I readied myself to intervene, but she refrained from acting on any impulse.

Her jaw tightened, and she said, 'If we weren't about to go onstage, I'd knock you the fuck out.'

Her face was so serious that Kyle backed off, and he kept his mouth shut. I'd never seen a glare like it. Dee gave him one last warning just before they entered the public domain. 'Do not fuck this up!'

I doubled back and took up a place by Ozzie at the merch stand.

The 450-capacity theatre was about three-quarters full, but it exploded when the guys started their piercing instrumentals. Quince began the rumbling drumbeat, and Will and Kyle followed. Instantly, I could tell something was off. The guitar from Kyle was lackadaisical, and the usual harmony between Will and Quince was non-existent. Dee burst from the side of the stage and greeted the audience with a sparkling smile and wave. A torrent of clapping and cheers manifested. I hoped her pipes would bring it together and mask the subpar instrumentals.

'How y'all doing out there?' she roused, transformed from the bloodthirsty femme fatale she had portrayed moments earlier.

The fans popped as 'On Your Knees' was in full flow. Dee belted out the lyrics with authority, but she tailed off towards the end due to the ragged rhythm that wasn't keeping time with the song's pace. They were too slow for what Dee demanded and it threw her off tempo. Her agitation was palpable, especially when she had to quietly remind Kyle what the next song was. It was palmed off as a comedic incident, so the fans didn't notice, but Ozzie and I saw the truth. They salvaged a smattering of pride by nailing a cover of 'Zombie' by The Cranberries, but it was short-lived as the mediocrity manifested again. Kyle was the main culprit for the sloppiness. He missed notes and mis-hit strums. His eyes glazed over, and his teeth were grinding from the drugs that gripped him. He couldn't even bring himself to play up to the females at the front, one of his more alluring characteristics that connected the band to their audience. Instead, his head remained bowed and disengaged. Dee shot him dirty looks from time to time, but she couldn't make her feelings known publicly.

The set whimpered out, but they were still brought back out for an encore. Disappointingly, this ended with an average rendition of their final, romping hit, 'Lifetime Sunshine'. The crowd applauded, but it was subdued compared to the usual adoration of previous gigs. They knew they'd witnessed something that didn't live up to the hype.

Backstage was toxic, and the band were divisive during the inquisition. I arrived while it was in full swing.

'For fuck's sake!' screamed Dee. 'That was fuckin' atrocious! You lot should be fuckin' ashamed of yourselves!'

'Ah fuck off, Dee. So, we had a few drinks, a few lines and pills. What's the big deal?' Kyle responded.

Dee immediately went for Kyle, but Ozzie was quick to get between them. I jumped in to stop it from going further as profanities continued to be hurled from one side to the other. Will and Quince were quiet, sat in shame, accepting the error of their ways.

Ozzie snapped, 'You were awful. You better sort yourselves out. Do you want this or not? This isn't some fuckin' pub gig in the arse end of nowhere. This isn't a game! This shit is real! You can't go and get hammered before a show and expect people will pass it off as "rock 'n' roll". Fuckin' grow up! I don't even know who was out there watching tonight. If Lynwood had anyone out there, we're fucked.'

Dee refused to let it go, 'I told you before. If you guys fuck this up, I'll knock you all the fuck out, I swear.'

'You couldn't knock a wank out, Dee,' Kyle parried back.

Big mistake! Dee saw red and launched herself at him again. Ozzie couldn't catch her in time, and a monstrous right hook cracked across Kyle's face, sending him flying off balance and crashing to the floor. Ozzie dragged her away kicking and screaming as her rage wanted a second shot.

Kyle stood upright and shrieked, 'What the fuck, Dee!' - and then went back at her. Luckily, Quince was on hand to stop him from getting anywhere near, using one meaty forearm to halt his movement. Dee wrestled herself free from Ozzie and headed for the exit. Before she left, she turned and shouted, 'You can all go and fuck yourselves. I'm fucking through with it all. We're done!'

'Drama Queen!' Kyle shouted back.

She picked up a can of baked beans sat by the cooker and hurled it in the direction of Kyle. He ducked, but Will was powerless to stop it from striking him on the top of his head. He screamed in agony as it bounced off him. Dee slammed the door shut as she left. Will held his head and groaned as speckles of blood oozed through his fingers. He yelped, 'I'm bleeding!' and nearly passed out when he saw the blood on his fingers. Ozzie had to catch him and sit him down as he swooned.

'Take it easy, soft arse,' Ozzie said as he looked and surmised, 'Ah, it's nothing. You won't need stitches.'

He ripped off handfuls of kitchen roll and handed them to Will to apply pressure.

He then addressed the boys. 'You need to have a long hard look at yourselves. I'm not putting my money and time into people who are more interested in boozing and doing drugs.'

'Leave it out, Ozzie. It's one night. It's not that big a deal,' Kyle argued.

'You're not getting it, are you? This tour is under scrutiny, and we're only here a couple of weeks. Things can change dramatically. I don't think you know how it all works. This isn't the sixties where this sort of shit is welcomed. Labels don't want a set of pissheads they can't manage anymore.'

'Shouldn't someone go after Dee?' I asked.

'Ah, fuck her. She's being a dick,' Kyle said.

'She'll be OK. Dee can take care of herself,' Quince added.

'Maybe you should go and find her?' Ozzie said to me.

'Me?' I was surprised. 'Surely, I'm the last person she wants to see?'

'I've got things to sort out here. I need to see Frankie and square things up after that shit show, and no way should any of these three go and talk to her.'

I mulled it over for a second, and although not exactly enamoured by Ozzie's suggestion, I knew someone had to watch out for her while she was so incensed.

'Fine. I'll see if I can find her and make sure she doesn't do anything stupid, but I'm not talking to her. I'll just watch her from a distance.'

'You sound like a stalker,' Kyle remarked.

'Not the time, Kyle,' I said.

As I opened the door, something dawned on me, and I had to ask, 'Who the fuck brought a can of baked beans backstage anyway?'

Quince answered, 'Think they were meant to be someone's dinner...dirty bastards.'

I headed out into the bar and looked around but couldn't see Dee. The audience had dispersed, and only a few peculiar folks remained for Cats of the Moon's set. I asked the barmaid if she'd seen Dee. She pointed to the front door, saying she saw her storm out a few minutes earlier. Minor alarm bells rang as to why she would leave the venue and where she was going.

People were smoking outside, but there was no sign of Dee. I asked two lads if they'd seen her. 'Oh yeah, dude, she went that way.' They pointed down the street that housed numerous shops and bars. Very few people could be seen, but none resembled Dee from the back. I didn't like the idea of her being alone. Rather than go back inside to tell Ozzie, I found myself in a game of cat and mouse searching for her, unaware of what reaction she would throw my way when or if I caught up with her.

I paced in the direction she was last seen. My first port of call was a bar about thirty yards down the road. The place was practically empty. I shouted to the barman, 'Didn't happen to see a girl come in here in the last ten minutes, about this high? Kind of pretty, probably looked a bit moody?'

'No, can't say so, Mister,' replied the old-timer.

I thanked him and left.

I was unsuccessful in the next two quietish bars. I hit a slightly busier one which sounded more raucous as 'War Pigs' by Black Sabbath smashed out from the door. I cautiously made my way in, conscious that I looked a little out of place wearing khaki cargo shorts and a white t-shirt.

I stepped inside and heard a commotion to the right of me. Two big guys leered over a table. I thought nothing of it until a familiar voice bellowed from behind them.

'Just fuck off right, and when you get there fuck off again, then fuck off some more and keep fuckin' off, and then fuck off again,' Dee snapped.

One of them droned, 'I like this one, Chad. She's got some fire in her belly.'

'C'mon, let us join you and buy you a drink,' Chad said.

'Fuck you!' Dee shouted.

'Ye right Doug, she full 'o' fire. I like a little fire.'

The man attempted to grab Dee by the arm, but she swiped it away and yelled, 'Don't fuckin' touch me, you smelly piece of shit!'

Without thinking, I flew over and barked, 'Get the fuck off her,' throwing a right jab at Chad. The force of the blow caused him to let go of Dee, but he only stumbled back a step or two. I was in trouble. The other man, Doug, was bigger. He came at me from the side, fists raised, foaming at the mouth. I didn't have time to get my hands up and move into a defensive position, but I didn't have to as Dee stood up and toe-bunged him right in the balls. The force with which she connected made me flinch.

I then turned back to Chad, who came at me again. He lunged and clasped both his hands around my neck making me fall back. I fought hard to remove his meaty, clammy claws off me, but I struggled. His face was inches from my own and his breath stunk of whisky and stale tobacco. I continued to grapple with him. The only option I had was to take Dee's approach and bring my knee up to his groin in an uncivilised, but survivalist move. As soon as it connected, he moaned loudly and instantly let go. He dropped to his knees and released his hands from my throat to cup himself. I swung my right hand at his cheek with all my strength. He fell backwards, but Dee wasn't content with seeing him fall. She lost it, hovered over him, and booted him relentlessly in his stomach whilst snarling and spitting at him. I intervened and pulled her away for fear that the other punters would see us as the instigators and seek revenge. Rather than hang around to find out whose side they were on, I picked Dee up in a fireman's lift and carried her out. She was ready to stay and fight everyone in there, so to drag her out was a feat.

Outside and yards away from the bar, Dee scrapped to free herself. 'Ricky, put me down for fuck's sake. Who are you? Forrest Gump?'

I set her down. 'And who are you? Rhonda Rousey? I think we need to get out of here in case Bebop and Rocksteady come after us, don't you think?'

'Fuck that. I want round two with those fucks.'

'Dee! Don't be stupid. They'd have killed us if we hadn't gone for the bollocks.'

She relented, and we moved faster down the street. I constantly checked to see if we were being followed, but no one came, so we slowed down to a steady walk.

Dee stopped right in front of me and blocked my path. 'Thanks. Seriously.'

'Don't mention it. Are you OK, anyway? How's your arm?'

'It's fine, I'm OK. How about you?'

'I'm OK… apart from the fact I can still smell that piece of shit on me.'

I nursed my neck from where his hands had been wrapped around my throat.

Dee looked at it. 'Doesn't seem to be any bruising. Looks a bit red, though. I can see his finger marks on you. You didn't have to get involved. You could've got really hurt.'

'Anyone would've done the same.'

'Yeah, but you're a writer, not a fighter,' she joked in a Michael Jackson voice that made me chuckle.

'Not just any writer…a Hot Shot Writer,' I joked. 'I'm just glad you're OK, and I turned up when I did. You shouldn't have wandered off like that.'

'You're not my Pops, you know.'

'And you're clever enough to know you shouldn't wander off into strange places on your own.'

'Ok, OK. I hear you… *Pops*.'

'Why did you go to *that* bar anyway? There were three quieter ones better suited.'

'I wasn't exactly thinking and went for the loudest one, hoping to pick up a biker chick for the night.'

'Good choice,' I said with sarcasm.

She smiled and asked, 'So, will this little incident be reported?'

'Oh, definitely. This is going in.'

She shot me a look.

I added, 'Of course, it won't. I don't think we should mention it to Ozzie either.'

'You might be right about that. He'll go sick at me.'

We continued to walk down the street back towards our motel. The few seconds of silence broke when she said, 'Thanks again, and… thanks for the awesome reviews.'

A warm fuzzy feeling engulfed me, and I felt myself blush.

'You read them?'

'Someone had to check you weren't some illiterate fucktard, didn't they?'

'I have an editor for that, trust me.'

'And I also apologise for slapping you.'

'Considering the whopper you gave Kyle, I think you held back on me. But don't worry about it. Shit happens.'

'You were actually quite funny.'

She moved towards me. 'C'mon, let's hug it out, bitch.'

We embraced, and it was a sweet moment to savour.

'What now?' I asked.

'I don't know about you, but I need a drink after that and I'm not going back to the Green Room. I'm fuckin' done. The band. This tour. I need to get away.'

Oh shit, I thought.

'C'mon, Dee. You don't mean that.'

'I do. They've massively overstepped the mark. I'm not putting up with shit like that. I don't care what they do after gigs but beforehand is unacceptable. They were a total disgrace, and Kyle's attitude is a God damn joke, especially with what he said about huddling and singing, "With a Little Help from My Friends" before the show. Fuck him.'

'Why did that offend you so much?'

'Never mind.'

'Let's talk about it. I'll shout you a drink in a quieter bar.'

'I've got a better idea. How much have you had to drink? Can you drive?'

'Not had a drop, so yes, I can drive. What are you thinking?'

'Everyone's getting on my tits. I need a break from them all. We're not far from the motel, and I don't want to be around the guys tonight or tomorrow, for that matter. Let's go back, get our stuff and go for a drive away from here.'

'Are you crazy? It's late. Where are we gonna go?'

'Sedona.'

'Sedona?' Where's that?'

'It's only an hour south of here. Where's your sense of adventure?'

'Ah, now she's in San Diego,' I said in my best Eddie Hitler voice. She looked blankly at me. I think the TV show 'Bottom' was lost on her.

'Dee, until half an hour ago you wanted to string me up by my balls, and now you want to go AWOL to the middle of nowhere with me?'

'I'm a crazy rock star, remember? My mood changes with the wind. But why not go to Sedona? Aren't unplanned trips what it's all about?'

She was right. Unplanned adventures were all part of life's mystery and excitement. We had a couple of days off before the next gig in Palm Springs, so it was an ideal opportunity, despite the circumstances.

'Fuck it, let's do it. But at least allow me to let Ozzie know you're OK,' I said.

'Not yet. Wait until we're on the road. He'll only try and talk us out of it, and seeing how soft you are, you'll agree.'

'Hey. I've just proven what kind of backbone I have by bailing you out of the shit. But if he gives me a bollocking, I'm saying you kidnapped me.'

'Kidnap implies I'd demand a ransom. And you ain't worth shit.'

'Oh, thanks.'

CHAPTER 16

It didn't take long to walk back to the motel and round up our belongings. Although the animosity seemed to have been resolved, I still felt nervous around Dee. I was wary of her artistic temperament that could rear its ugly head at any point.

She eased into the passenger side. 'Ok Hot Shot. Drive.'

'Still calling me that name then?'

'Most definitely. And put some decent tunes on.'

That won't be a problem,' my tone turned cocky.'

I was safe in the knowledge that all I had to do was press play on the iPod, knowing that something worthy of the road awaited. 'Evil Woman' by Electric Light Orchestra was the track that played. I strained to hide my amusement.

'What the fuck are you grinning at?' Dee snapped.

'Nothing. This song reminds me of someone, that's all.'

She punched me in the arm. Christ, it hurt. For someone so small, she didn't half have some power. I felt the throb in the bone.

'What was that for?' I cried.

'You know God damn well what that was for.'

'I didn't say you, did I?'

'You didn't have to.'

She grabbed my iPod and sifted through it.

'How old is this device?' she scoffed.

'The lads said the same. Don't take the piss out of my bible. It's a classic.'

'You need to update.'

'I can't believe I'm living in a world where owning an iPod is seen as prehistoric when there's a CD player in this car.'

She ignored me before saying, 'Now this is a track. Get your foot down. You're driving is about as slow as a tax rebate.'

'I Can't Wait' by Stevie Nicks started as we hit the freeway. As she requested, my foot pressed to the floor.

She reclined the seat, took her shoes off and rested her feet on the dashboard.

'Whoa! What the fuck?' I yelled.

'What?'

'Those Griffin feet. We've got a lot of driving to do, and I don't want to smell your cheesy wotsits for the rest of the drive. Look at those sweaty toes. Look at the state of them. They look like little bollocks.'

She jack-knifed with laughter, and it stunned me.

'Fuck, Dee, I didn't even know you had teeth, never mind a laugh in you.'

She turned away, battling to contain her giggles by digging her fist into her lips.

'Well, wonders never cease. The great and power-ful Dee Darrell might actually have a personality and a sense of humour that goes beyond bitchy and moody.'

Her toes curled on the dashboard.

'Wait till I write this in my review.'

She turned to me, eyes watery, 'You better fuckin' not.'

'I wouldn't dare cross the great Dee Darrell. Nope... not this Hot Shot Writer Dickhead.'

She burst into a laugh so powerful I nearly swerved off the road. Her whole body shook to amplify the sound. I couldn't believe my eyes and ears.

After a couple of seconds, she calmed and said, 'I'm sorry, again.'

'For what exactly?'

'Giving you a hard time and slapping you. I have trust issues.'

'Oh, that. Ah, no sweat. I can handle it. I'm just glad we're sweet now...aren't we?'

'Don't push it. For the moment, we are, but that can easily change, so don't piss me off.'

'I'm only here to serve your best interests, you know. There's no way I'll screw you guys over. It's not in my nature.'

'I'm starting to believe that.'

'I do understand why you didn't want an unknown coming onto the tour and that it takes a lot to trust someone. I just want you to know that I'm not like a tabloid journalist looking for gossip or setting people up. I just want to help, and I'd never betray confidences.'

'You've got to understand that there are so many dicks and sharks in this industry we have to be wary of everyone that comes into our circle.'

'I get that, but you can trust me.'

She sat quietly for a minute before asking, 'Tell me a little about yourself, Hot Shot. What's your story?'

'What do you want to know?'

'The usual shit. Where you from? Where you been? Who've you fucked? All that bullshit.'

I gave her a brief overview of my background but stopped short when I remembered the lie we'd fed to Dee and the band about how long I'd been in the industry. After telling her that she could trust me, lying to her was hypocritical, so I decided to come clean and hoped her mood wouldn't turn. At least she had nowhere to go and couldn't storm out of a moving car in the dead of night.

'Listen, Dee, I said you can trust me, and I want to be honest with you.'

'You got a confession, Hot Shot? I'm not absolving you of your sins.'

'Well, you know how I said I'd been working behind the scenes for a few years in music, and I have experience of the industry in that way?'

'Yeah.'

'Well, that's not entirely true.'

'No shit,' she oozed sarcasm.

'Why do you say that?'

'I know you've only written a few reviews and have been around for less than a year.'

'How do you know that?'

'I know all. You don't strike me as someone who's been around that long. I've already told you, when it comes to Manchester, I know anyone worth knowing, and you ain't one of them, sweetheart.'

'Oh, thanks for that. Nothing like knocking my confidence.'

'Sticking with me won't do your credentials any harm.'

'Check out the big balls on the rock star here.'

'Balls bigger than yours.'

I didn't dispute that.

'I appreciate you fessing up. I was wondering who would cave first, you or Ozzie. I'm disappointed Ozzie didn't say anything.'

'I think he's still gunning for you after slapping me, so call it even.'

'Hmm. Maybe.'

'He was just trying to protect me and the tour.'

'If you'd written a load of shit, I'd have brought it up by now, but you haven't, so there's no reason for me to kick off, is there...yet?'

'Is that a compliment?'

She smiled without answering.

'Do the lads know?'

'Do they fuck. Unless it's a big pair of tits or a cracking set of legs, they don't notice shit.'

I laughed and changed the subject, 'Tell me how you came to be in music? When did you know you wanted to become a singer?'

She clammed up, and her face dropped. 'Maybe another time.'

Something in her eyes suggested a deep discomfort. I sensed she *really* didn't want to talk about it, so I left it hanging before probing from a different angle, 'Why do you sing "With a Little Help from My Friends" before each gig?'

'Not now, Hot Shot. Just enjoy the tune.'

Still holding my iPod, she flicked to 'Thank You', by Alanis Morissette to provide a chilled antidote to Stevie Nicks' rocking mood enhancer. Dee sang the song perfectly whilst staring distantly out of the window into a tsunami of inky blackness.

Still glaring out of the window, she asked, 'You got a girl, Ricky?'

I stayed silent.

'Don't panic. I'm not asking you on a date. You're not really my type.'

'Cheeky fucker! What's wrong with me?' I argued.

She looked me up and down and pulled a face. 'You're not exactly an edgy rock 'n' roller.'

Her look of disgust hardly boosted my self-confidence.

'I'll have you know I've done plenty of edgy things.'

'Oh yeah, like what?'

'Once, I did thirty-four miles per hour in a thirty zone. What do you make of that?' I joked.

'You're practically a modern-day James Dean ain't ya? A Rebel Without a Clue.'

'I could tell you about my time in Vegas, which is edgy for normal folk, but I suppose for crazy artistes like you, it'd be child's play, so I won't bore you with the details.'

'Thanks.'

I shot her an arsey look that was met with a cheeky smile.

'Anyway, you haven't answered my question? Do you have a girl?'

'Yeah, I got someone…in a way.'

'Is this the girl you mentioned in Phoenix, who you claimed I'd want to pin me up against a dumpster? She rolled her eyes.

'Yeah, that's the one,' I snickered.

'What does she think about you being here?'

'She's incredibly supportive about it. If you want to know the full story, then I'll have to go back to the Vegas trip. Don't want to bore you, do I?' My tone turned sarcastic.

'Fine, go on then. Let's hear it.'

I revealed how Eva and I met and the circumstances around it. It felt strange talking to Dee on a deeper level after our differences. Her guard dropped when she was away from the pantomime theatrics of the band. I started to relax around her. That was until she gave her honest opinion about one of the most heartfelt moments of my life.

'Sounds like a shit rom-com.'

'I knew your pleasantness wouldn't last long,' I replied.

'I'm just playing with you. It seems like you're a bit of a pussy if I'm honest.'

'Say what you think, why don't you?'

'I call it like I see it.'

'It's not as easy as that. She lives in San Diego, and I live in Manchester, and I'm about to go to Bermuda with you guys. Long-distance relationships rarely work, do they?'

'Don't they?' she casually responded.

'We agreed not to talk about it while I'm on tour. She probably thinks I'm going to have a different girl every night.'

'As if you could.'

'You like putting me down, don't you?'

'You set them up too easy for me.'

'You want to see a picture of Eva? That'll show you what I'm capable of.'

'No.' She shot me down with ease, again.

'Well, fuck you then,' I reacted.

'Cool your jets, Hot Shot. Let the dog see the rabbit.'

I dug out my phone and found Eva's Facebook page. Her profile pic was set against the backdrop of the sandy beach in Puerto Rico from when she visited family three months earlier. She was dressed in a white floral print dress. Her hair was waving in the wind, and an angelic smile captured her essence, a smile that always melted me. I passed my phone to Dee.

'She's kind of pretty. You do surprise me.'

'See. I'm not a total gremlin after all.'

'You must've drugged her. What's wrong with her? She can't be normal.'

'She's plenty normal. But I get your point. She's way out of my league.'

'She must have a screw loose somewhere.'

'Coming from such a stable and self-confessed sex goddess like yourself,' I said.

I must've touched a nerve. 'Eva Espinoza. I'll remember that name and request her as a friend and see if I can turn her.'

'Like fuck you will.'

'I've turned the best of them. But don't worry. I'm not having your sloppy seconds.'

I grimaced at the concept before admitting, 'I am a dick, though.'

'I know that... but why specifically?'

'Because I kissed that girl, Lucy, in Phoenix, and although it didn't go any further, I feel proper shit about it.'

'So, that was her name, Lucy. Quite the minx, from what I remember. Not as foxy as the chick I ended up with. She was hot.'

'Can't say I saw her. I was too fucked up.'

'Yeah, you were,' she giggled. 'But seriously, you felt like shit just because you kissed someone?'

'Yep.'

'You wet wipe. I'd focus on the fact that you didn't go any further with her. That's probably harder to do judging from my experience with men...and women.'

'Well, being too drunk and the fact I kept talking about Eva stopped it.'

'Haha. Did you really?'

'Apparently so. Lucy told me that one of the reasons we didn't end up sleeping together was her choice because I kept going on about Eva.'

'Haha. You fuckin' loser,' she mocked.

'That's a bit harsh.'

'I can just imagine how pathetic you must've been crying over some girl you're not even properly in a relationship with and completely screwing yourself out of a screw. I bet she felt wonderful hearing you ramble on with yourself like an extract from a teenage girl's diary.'

Dee had a way of not sugar-coating things that made me see how absurd the scene must've really been. She keeled over in stitches at the concept, and I found myself chuckling along with her.

'Anyway, what about you?' I asked.

'What about me?'

'You're more complicated than me. You're bisexual, right?'

'Yeah, so what?'

'No judgement. Just that...no one's safe around you, are they?' I jibed.

'You are,' she shot back before digging me in my arm right on the bone. I gritted my teeth to show no pain, but it didn't half sting.

'So, come on then. Anyone special in your life? Male or female?' I probed.

'Just drive, Hot Shot.'

'You're the boss, rock star.'

She found 'Shine on You Crazy Diamond' by Pink Floyd. As soon as the haunting opening faded in, she said, 'I don't want to hear a word from you while this song is on. Just relax and enjoy the moment. No interruptions.'

She closed her eyes and tilted her head back. It was an epic song to have soundtrack a night-time drive in the middle of the divine desert. With hundreds of stars dotting the caliginous sky, it felt like we were dancing on the astral plane.

The driving enhanced the experience, and it had a profound effect on me, serving as a place for reflection, cleansing and philosophising. Certain things in life can't be understood until those desert roads are driven on. I'm not sure I understood myself, but the beauty is that I didn't need to know. The connection was ethereal and from beyond this world. It made me nostalgic for a life I've never lived and will never have. Whether it was the topography, the music, or touring with a band, I didn't know. Perhaps all those factors contributed to the unearthly sensations. There were no boundaries or restrictions, and it was one of the greatest senses of freedom a person could experience.

Our midnight drive to Sedona passed in the blink of an eye. Forty-five minutes was child's play compared to the daunting eight-hour marathon to Palm Springs that awaited us two days later.

Sedona was heralded as one of the most picturesque places in the world, not just in Arizona, but arriving so late meant we couldn't make out any of the scenic beauty. The moon's glow teased shadowy outlines of rock formations that dented the sky in the distance.

We hit the heart of the quiet town. With minimal lighting, I could just about make out the saloon-style theme of each precinct. Dee used her phone to book us into a cheap motel on the outskirts of the centre. She had also messaged Ozzie after several missed calls and messages from him. She allayed his fears by saying where we were, and not to expect us back that night or the night after. Alarm bells would be ringing at the prospect of Dee and me together after all the bickering and sniping.

At the motel, the manager handed us one key for the one room. I'd assumed Dee had booked separate rooms, but it was a twin. Having seen her enviable endurance levels, I fully expected her to be wanting to go and find a bar somewhere. I was pleasantly surprised to hear her say, 'I'm beat. I'm going to bed, but you better be up early tomorrow because this sobriety isn't lasting two days, and I want to see this town for all its worth.'

I was more than ready for bed after the long, pulverising day. I dived into bed while Dee brushed her teeth in the bathroom. I never even heard her come out.

CHAPTER 17

The following morning, Dee was full of energy and dragged me up at around 7:30, demanding that we explore the exuberant nugget of Sedona. In normal circumstances, I'd have pissed and whinged at the prospect of driving at stupid o'clock in the morning. Too many drab and bitter grey mornings in Manchester had influenced that torpid mentality. But, in the bucolic American West, I needed to push past the exhaustion barrier and experience a town described as 'the most beautiful place on Earth'.

We were back on the road and drove aimlessly within the aesthetic jewel as the sun blazed intensely, a stark contrast to the coolness of Flagstaff. The lazuline sky bounced off the sandstone cliffs and reddish-hued monolith ranges that littered the landscape. An iridescent kaleidoscope of colour tinted the terrain. It looked like a CGI enhanced image from another planet that had no business being on Earth.

The roads were curved, making it difficult to drink the scenery in, so I pulled off into a rest area to take a lengthier look. Dee and I stood entranced, locked into some sort of meditative spell as the geological phenomenon etched itself into the memory banks. There was little wonder why Sedona had such a magnetic pull of spirituality and a sense of well-being.

Dee broke the silence, 'Just beautiful, isn't it?'

'I'm hypnotised. This is idyllic,' I agreed.

'Kind of like how I imagine heaven to be.'

She went back to the car and rummaged in her bag to pull out a notepad and pen.

'What are you doing?' I asked.

'If you can't be inspired to write lyrics looking at this, you might as well give up.'

'I know what you mean. I feel like even I can write a song sat here.'

'You just stick to your reviews and leave the professional music to me,' she bantered.

I left her to it whilst I took numerous pictures on my phone.

Ozzie messaged me to ask if we were OK. I let him know things were fine and not to worry. I didn't bring up Dee's superficial intention to quit the band.

Back in the car, we meandered around bends, navigating through the pictorial vista. The contemplative song, 'A Horse with No Name', by America, fittingly played as we drove through the heart of the sacred lands.

Eventually, we came across the entrance to Slide Rock Park. Dee told me to pull in as she'd read about it online. Visitors could get into the river and slide downstream because the riverbed was so smooth from the algae that coated it. My initial thoughts were, *fuck that*, but Dee had a way of getting you to push your own limits.

Our walk to the river through the park was spectacular. We were surrounded by soaring cliffs, the building blocks of Sedona that seemed to shapeshift when gazed upon. It was like taking in the most natural drug to heighten the senses, a dose of nature. It was ineffable, a place that really had to be absorbed first-hand to appreciate its power and beauty.

We hopped over massive boulders towards the top of the river that marked the start of Slide Rock. People gathered to weigh up the mini gauntlet. I was hesitant at first and talked myself out of it, using the weak excuse that I didn't have a towel and a suitable change of attire.

While I mulled it over, Dee had already stripped down to her purple panties. I sharply averted my eyes until I heard a splash.

She shrieked, 'Fuck! Fuck! Fuck! That's fuckin' freezing!'

Once she adjusted to the cold, she screamed with adrenaline-fuelled elation as she glided downstream with the current. She leapt up after reaching the bottom, tits swinging about like a nudist, arms aloft in celebration.

'You're crazy!' I shouted.

'Are you getting in or what, Hot Shot?' she bellowed.

'Hang on a minute. I'm not as senseless as you... I take it it's cold?'

'Freezing, but so what. Say yes to everything and embrace all opportunities in life.'

She was right, but I dithered.

Bored with waiting, she shouted, 'Rickyyyyy!'

'What?' I snapped.

'I can see your vagina from heeerrrree! Mother Goose, you pussssyyyy!' Her 'Top Gun' reference didn't go unnoticed. Even a few bystanders giggled. I refused to be upstaged and not partake in something more daring and out of the ordinary, so I stripped down to my boxers. There was no chance I was going stark bollock naked. Luckily, my underwear was well-fitted, and there was no fly hole, so the boys couldn't sneak out of the barracks. Dee wolf-whistled and mocked me by imitating the tune to the 'The Stripper', with a series of 'Da, da, da's', complete with a jig and hand clap.

I made my way over to the starting point and slipped flat on my arse due to the wet surface. The onlookers were more than amused, and Dee's cackle echoed through the gorge. Whilst in a heap, in a bit of emotional and physical pain, I eased my way into the water like an injured seal that lacked any grace or elegance. I slithered in and began my descent through the gauntlet, sunglasses still on to salvage a bit of coolness. It was freezing, and I fought to catch my breath as I hurtled through the water that splashed into my face. But what a rush it was as I rode every bump and hump with gusto. I made it down to the bottom, where I crashed with such force that my sunglasses flew off. I was submerged beneath the surface for a few seconds, and panic set in as I scrambled to find my footing and gasped for air. Finally, I managed to stand, and I slicked my hair back whilst wiping the water from my eyes. Fortunately, my sunglasses floated next to me, and I threw them back on as if I'd been composed throughout.

'Took you long enough,' Dee said, looking unimpressed and impatient.

'That was class. I wanna go again.' I was like a giddy school kid.

'Ok, easy "Adrenaline Junkie". I'm gonna jump in from that ridge.'

I looked up to see the jumping-off point about twenty feet above the water. With my newfound sense of adventure, I didn't dawdle. We both jumped in a couple of times each. I felt liberated, regressing to my more carefree, daredevil childhood days.

After several more slides down the gauntlet and jumps from the ridge, we headed back to the car, where I noticed that my skin was as smooth as a nineties R&B song. Frolicking about in the natural water must've acted as an emollient cleanser to unclog my pores. Remarkable what nature can do to your body and mind.

With no towels, we drip-dried before getting back into the car. My underwear was soaked, so I looked forward to the inevitable chafing later. I brought it up to Dee, and she nonchalantly responded that she was going commando. She quickly whipped off her knickers by the side of the car without anyone seeing.

Back on the road, she asked, 'Have you heard from any of the others yet?'

'Just Ozzie. I've told him not to worry. How about you?'

'Ozzie has been panicking, trying to ring me. I've messaged him to tell him to leave me alone and I'm fine. Did you write about last night's gig yet?'

'When have I had a chance? I've seen a couple of reviews from local fanzines, though.'

'And?'

'It ain't pretty. Think they picked up on the lads being pissed. You came out looking OK, but the two I read weren't exactly glowing.'

'Ah well. I don't give a fuck. Don't write your review today. You're here to keep me entertained, and as you sort of work for me, you have to do what I want to do,' she ordered.

'Oh yeah? And what might that entail?'

'We should take the car back to the motel, and we'll come back into town, get something to eat, and then drink all day and get fucked up.'

'Sounds appealing, actually. Fuck it, let's do it.'

CHAPTER 18

It didn't take long for a quick turnaround at the motel. The most important part for me was changing my underwear to stop the chafing. I subtly swiped Dee's moisturiser to rub onto my groin, arse, and 'grundle' as Kyle described it.

Once I was ready, I stepped out of the bathroom to see Dee dressed coolly. She showed where her roots lay with a Led Zeppelin vest top, denim shorts, black boots, purple-tinted aviators, and her burgundy cowboy hat.

We landed at a Tex Mex Bar, taking up one of the many seats outside as the restaurant was crammed indoors. With the sun sizzling, I couldn't understand why people chose to sit inside. I was starving after capering about in the river. I licked my lips when I scanned the menu and eyed the steak section. After declaring my choice, Dee shot me a look of disdain, revealing she was a vegetarian. I contemplated changing my choice to suit her needs, but the description of the steak drenched in a peppercorn sauce with creamy scalloped potatoes, mushrooms, onion rings and sprouts with bacon on the side sounded too damn good.

Dee went straight for a beer with her meal, whereas I opted for a Diet Coke, which she turned her nose up at.

'I thought we were getting shit-faced. What's all this Diet Coke nonsense about?' she quizzed.

'It's a marathon, not a sprint. Don't worry, I'll catch you up.'

'Trust me, you won't.'

I rolled my eyes and said, 'Anyway, we need to talk about the blog. You know I have to interview you at some point for the magazine.'

'Not now, Hot Shot. We're having a break from that. Let's just enjoy being here and live in the moment.'

'Ok, but can we talk off the record then? Not in a journo to singer capacity, but as a *friend,* maybe?'

'As a *friend*?' she repeated with a raised eyebrow.

'Well, you drag me into the middle of nowhere at midnight, so I assume that's what we are now? We're certainly not enemies anymore, are we? And as you've said many times, I'm not your type in *that* way, so it must be friendship.'

'Damn right, you're not my type. But you're still in a trial period for friendship, so don't go blabbing to people that you're my *friend* just yet. I do have a reputation to uphold, you know.'

I smiled at her coolness.

'What do you want to talk about?' she asked.

'What do you want from this?'

'From what?'

'Music. And don't give me the bullshit journalistic answer of world domination and all that crap. What is it *you* want?'

She took out a cigarette.

'I didn't know you smoked?'

'Only the odd one every now and then when I'm relaxed. I swiped these off Ozzie.'

'He's gonna be pissed. No wonder he keeps calling.'

'He's got a sleeve of two hundred with him. You want one?'

I'd quit smoking months earlier as part of the plan to take back control of my life and save money to enable me to travel. The craving took hold under the circumstances, driven by the chilled, tranquil surroundings. I plucked one from the pack, and she lit it with her Zippo in one swift motion. I inhaled and dissolved as the tobacco rushed straight to my head.

Dee took a deep puff of her cig and exhaled nonchalantly. She turned to be sitting side on to me, so her elbow rested on the back of the chair, legs folded. She flicked the ash in the ashtray and answered my question. 'There's no secret formula to what I want. I want to be successful but to remain true to myself. I'll never sell out and become the pawn of some dogshit commercial label that wants to control and popify us and have us pose on the cover of fuckin' Heat magazine. That's not what I want from this.'

'I get that. Artistic integrity is important to you. I'm glad you hold those values.'

'I do this for the art, the love, and for the people to hear my words. I'm not in it for the money or the fame. That's just a by-product of it that doesn't interest me. I'm not materialistic at all. I love the simple things in life, like music, travel, nature, and books. That's what turns me on. But I *have* to be a performer. There's nothing else I want to do in life. If not, I may as well not exist. I don't have a choice but to do this.'

She spoke with such passion that I empathised with her need to succeed.

She carried on. 'You know, I was too little to remember, but my mom said I went nuts for 'Tiny Dancer', by Elton John. Apparently, I used to dance around to it all the time. She predicted back then that I'd be onstage in some capacity.'

'Why did you come to England?'

'I was attracted to the music history. I had a choice between the UK or here in the States. I was looking at Los Angeles, actually. Funny, isn't it? It took me emigrating to England to find my asshole bandmates, and here we are with a shot of making it in the States. If that's not some sort of twist of fate, what is?'

'You're talking like the band is still together,' I smiled.

'Yeah… well… we'll see.'

'Let's say you do carry on. Do you think you'll make it?'

'What does "make it" even mean anymore? Financial longevity isn't a given these days, even if we get a two or three-album deal. We're good enough to hold our own, but talent alone isn't enough these days. It's all about who you know and how lucky you get.'

'It's a shame that's how it is. But you have Ozzie working for you.'

'We do, and he's been great and has contacts, but he can't force people to make decisions.'

'What will you do if it all doesn't work out?'

'It's not an option, and I don't even think about it not working out. This *has* to work out at any level to earn a living, even if I end up on a fuckin' cruise ship singing Dusty Springfield covers. I ain't goin' back to a temp office job to be a goddamn dogsbody for the rest of my life.'

Her reluctance to settle for mundaneness reminded me so much of myself.

'I know what you mean. I've been there with the same worry and lived in that nightmare. Luckily, I got out when I could.'

'But music journalism can't pay that much?'

'True, but it's a start. This started out as a solo road trip. It was my "sticking two fingers up to the world" adventure. I guess I've not really thought beyond the tour and have been stuck in the live-in-the-moment mindset for now.'

'You should keep that approach.'

'So should you, even if you don't get signed.'

'We could both be fucked together. I can be the resident cabaret singer at some dive bar in Fucksville, and you can review me for the local six-page newspaper.'

After a brief pause, I asked, 'What's your biggest fear, Dee?'

She took the last puff of her cig and extinguished it in the ashtray, 'Failure!'

The dreaded fear of failure and having to suck it up and get a normal job was a fear I knew all too well. The enormity of the trip's importance was again driven home for all of us. Every gig, every action, the pressure to perform and impress was constant. The Cutthroats simply had no choice but to succeed. Their whole future depended on the outcome. At least I had a degree of breathing space, but to keep the train rolling, I had to write, and I had to write well enough to hold and build up a consistent audience.

Up until the day before I left Manchester for San Francisco, I was a music journalist on the side with the security of a day job. When I walked away from the day job to travel and write, that security was removed despite the financial cushion I'd built up. The money I earned from writing reviews was not enough to sustain a living. Would I try and survive in the music industry somehow? How was it even possible? It was a super competitive industry in every aspect, where full-time work was hard to come by. I could easily be thrown back into office life as soon as the red approached on the bank balance. I wasn't ready to do that. I'd come too far in my mind to retreat to what I was escaping from. I had to develop a tough mentality like Dee and refuse to let that be my path.

She returned the question, 'What's *your* biggest fear then?'

'The same as yours. Failure and ending up back where I started and being miserable.'

'Ok. Let me put it another way. What does success mean to you? Chief Editor of a music mag?'

'Fuck knows. I really don't know. I guess just to keep writing until something pops, or if any other position comes up in music that takes my interest. I have no idea what that is, though.'

'Maybe Ozzie can find you something with him.'

'I think Ozzie has his own issues and just about stays afloat.'

'There's plenty of roles in this industry.'

'True, but none have really taken my fancy. I've enjoyed the sanctuary and solace of writing. I think that's my niche.'

'We all shine the brightest in peripheral light,' she hypothesised.

The statement struck a chord.

'I like that theory. I'm not one to put myself out there and deal with lots of people face to face. I like to hide behind the screen, whereas it seems to come naturally to you.'

'Years of experience and practising in front of a mirror with a hairbrush,' she said.

I laughed and carried on, 'Regards writing, I don't really have a plan. I've been going with the flow and learning as I go along, but it did bring me on this tour, so maybe fate *is* on my side. Before I was told about this tour, my life revolved around the initial reasons for this trip. I was so focused on saving up for a travel adventure that I couldn't see beyond it long-term.'

She countered, 'Life's too short to always play it safe. You must take risks. If all this doesn't work out, then it doesn't work out, but at least you tried, and no one can take away the fact you toured the States with a band and wrote about it. Not a bad thing to have on your epitaph, is it?

'Haha. Not at all. I've got a little bit put aside, but it won't last forever. Sooner or later, something's got to give. I'm scared I'll end up back home and be in the same situation as before, albeit richer from the life experience. But I'd rather have a passport full of stamps than a house full of stuff and a partner who caresses my soul than one who manipulates my spirit.'

'That's quite profound... for you.'

'Thanks. And I've not even had a beer yet. I guess I'm desperate not to end up back at a desk job after being involved in something as great as this. But perhaps that's what all this is meant to be. To have an ultimate life experience, scratch an itch and tick off number one on the bucket list. It's more than what most get to experience, I suppose.'

'If your will is strong enough, it won't be the end. But never forget or underestimate these experiences, and never let anyone take them away from you.'

'If all else fails, I could just live off the land and travel illegally around the US for the rest of my days, like a nomad,' I joked.

'Not a bad idea. That's always been a dream of mine and my fallback plan. Have you ever seen "Into the Wild"?'

'Seen it? I *love* that film.'

Into the Wild is a book/film about the exploits of Chris McCandless, a rebellious and enlightened young man. He gave his sizeable education fund to charity so he could live as a nomad travelling around the West of America. His aim was to reach the wilderness in

Alaska and settle in an ultimate sanctuary haven. It's a fascinating, inspirational story, and Dee's allusion to it tickled the fantasy realms of the traveller within me.

She mused, 'Imagine doing what he did? Giving up all that money for a real adventure and living off the land. I'd love to live like that.'

'I'd love to do that too, although I don't think I'm built for such a harsh existence, however liberating it sounds. I'd have to do it in a camper van at the very least. I saved up for nine months, so I could have some basic home comforts whilst travelling, like a bed and a means of getting about. Camping as a way of life with rattlers and bears sneaking up on me is where I draw the line.'

'You shithouse,' she taunted.

After we ate, I switched to beer, much to Dee's delight. They were going down too well as the conversation flowed. As I guzzled my third, she pulled out a notepad and pen and scribbled away.

'More inspiration?' I asked.

'You never know when it hits you.'

'Let me see then?'

'Never!'

She slapped my hand away and ordered me to grab the attention of the hot waitress and get another round in.'

I signalled to the cute brunette with the pinned-up hair to bring us two more beers.

We continued to sit outside drinking. The more we drank, the more that laughter became a staple of our conversation, mainly brought on from the stories she shared about the band since its inception. I felt privileged to be let in on a circle of trust that barricaded them from outsiders.

'You see, they're not all bad. You've had some good times,' I stated.

'Sometimes.'

'You're not quitting the band, are you?'

'I've not decided yet.'

'You need them just as much they need you, and you have a dream to realise. This is rock 'n' roll. The road isn't meant to be smooth. It's meant to be bumpy as fuck in a rickety old wagon trying to negotiate some ridiculous twists and turns along the turbulent way. Every great band in history has had shit, so what makes you exempt?'

'That's probably the truest thing you've said.'

'See, more than just a Hot Shot Writer Dickhead, as you so eloquently put it.'

'Eloquently? Don't be using your fancy words on me just because you've had a few beers.'

The sun seemed to spiral out of control beyond the rocky ridges, plunging us into darkness in minutes. It then became apparent why no one wanted to sit outside. The temperature suddenly dropped to a level like Manchester in January.

There was live entertainment inside provided by an alternative-folk band named Houndmouth. We had struggled to really hear them through the glass doors, but after deciding to go inside and hang by the bar to get warm, we managed to catch the last song of their set. They dedicated it to the beautiful town of Sedona, saying the song was called 'Sedona'.

Dee and I stood in silent appreciation for the few minutes they played. What an incredibly beautiful song to capture the town's soul and its spiritual and calming quality. The pace and tone gave the track such depth and understanding. Based on that one song alone, I purchased their debut album from the desk by the side of the stage.

Two more rounds followed before Dee suggested moving on. I agreed, so we asked the waitress for recommendations. She suggested an Irish Bar called Mooney's. The temperature had further plummeted as we exited for the short walk around the corner.

Mooney's was relatively busy for a midweek night. An old, slick black guy wearing a trilby was perched on a stool in the corner. He strummed his beaten, oak-coloured guitar and gave a powerful, wailing rendition of Muddy Waters', 'Champagne and Reefer'. The bar encapsulated all that was great about dive joints: dark, dirty, with a certain charisma that made you want to lick the spilt whisky off the floor. This was coupled with the cajoling stench of cigars and liquor that greased the air. It was my type of establishment and one I'd craved to experience after watching how several films and shows had depicted old juke joints.

The dirtiness of the singer's voice and twang of his guitar suited the backdrop. It called for a chaser to go along with the beers we ordered, as impending drunkenness blurred our vision and clouded our minds.

I caught Dee staring at the gritty singer, lost in a chasm of her own thoughts. She spoke quietly to not interrupt him, 'Have you ever been in complete misery and despair, Ricky?'

The look on her face was one rooted in deep-lying pain.

'Haven't we all? Why do you ask?' I returned.

'No reason.'

I sensed the avoidance.

'What happened for you to feel like that?' she asked.

Memories of the pain I felt pre-Vegas nine months earlier sprung to mind.

'My ex did a number on me last year, just before I went to Vegas.'

'It hurt that much?'

'Yeah, it fuckin' hurt.'

'Break ups can be harder than death sometimes. What happened?'

Since my return from Vegas, I'd not spoken to anyone about what happened regards my ex, Mandy. Any talk of Vegas had been around the positives and Eva. I'd not felt any reason to divulge past pain from something that I was well over and had ended up meaning nothing. Given the nature of the night, the spiritual setting we were in, and Dee's need to understand, I revealed my story. I hoped it would help heal whatever anguish she was evidently feeling. I told her what transpired before Vegas to make that trip so important. I ended by saying, 'But out of pain comes something beautiful. I genuinely believe that.'

'How did it all change for you out there in Vegas?'

'I took a trip to the desert armed with a few peyote buttons. Not the wisest move, but somehow it worked. What an experience, though! I saw things that I'm not sure were real or a hallucination. Almost like these mind-expanding drugs did just that, expanded my mind to open a portal that's very real but undetectable without a helping hand.'

'Sounds fun to go shrooming in the desert. I'll have to try it someday.'

'I'd air on the side of caution. People have been known to have bad trips. I'd only advise it as a last resort to get answers to any deep questions you may have. I felt like I had no other option at that point. But you know what, it wasn't really the tripping out on peyote that changed me. I'm not denying it facilitated the change, but to see things clearer about who I am and would become, that revelation came later that night.'

Dee seemed engrossed in my story as I continued, 'I was walking out of New York New York after Eva had returned on my last night. I was on my own, and it was nearly morning. "Rocket Man" by Elton John was playing. There's a lyric in that song that stuck with me. It was the final piece of the jigsaw that liberated me.'

'What line was that?'

'I'm not the man they think I am at home.'

'Why did it strike a chord?'

'Because I'd been living a lie for so many years and everyone had me pigeon-holed, especially my ex. Even my friends and family, to some extent. I kind of retreated into myself after university. I always had dreams of living like a free spirit, but I guess I never got to fully express myself to live that way. It's very easy to get sucked into the mundane way of life after uni because of the debt it leaves you in and the pressures to earn money.'

'I can see that.'

'But now I'm living it and surprising people along the way. No one anticipated that I would write for a music mag and up sticks to travel around the States on my own, let alone write about this tour.

Dee leant in and nodded along. 'Sounds like this Vegas trip was an absolute blast. I've never been, but I can't wait to get there after Los Angeles.'

'I can't explain to you how monumental it was. We went through so many highs and lows with everything you can experience out there. Maybe it was heightened for me because I was going through some shit, unlike my three mates, who just surfed the wave constantly without any hiccups. Plus, I met Eva, which made my time a little more meaningful. It felt like my whole life was mapped out, and Vegas was this pivotal catalytic moment that connected everything to send me on the path I was meant to be on.'

'You're quite philosophical and spiritual deep down, aren't you? I had no idea.'

'Well, I am several beers deep at this point. I'm probably talking shit.'

'Ha. You're not.'

'It's always been hiding in the background, but since Vegas and Eva, I'm more aware of it. But *you* must be philosophical and spiritual too as an artist, especially with some of the lyrics you write?'

'I've always had a connection with the holistic. I believe that where you move musically is a strong indication of where you're moving spiritually and emotionally. It signifies how your personality is evolving to be who you're going to become. Music is the most profound journey.'

We carried on theorising while the blues singer yowled away in the background. He stopped half an hour later and spoke in a hoarse voice, 'Okay, it's that time of night where we open the mic for any wannabe singers out there this evening.'

I looked at Dee. 'You getting up and strutting your stuff?'

'Fuck it, why not,' she shrugged.

'I was joking.'

'I wasn't.'

She raised her hand, and the guitarist pointed to her. 'We got a young lady down here who fancies herself as a singer. She don't half looks the part too with that fine-looking cowboy hat,' he drawled. 'What's yo name, sweet thang?'

'Dee. Dee Darrell. And what's yours, fine Sir?'

'Yo can call me Whisky Charlie. Whatchoo gonna sing for us, Dee Darrell?'

'Actually, I thought I may play the guitar and sing, if that's OK with you, of course? May I borrow this fine-looking instrument you've been playing?'

'Yo most certainly can. Take good care o' her. I could use a trip to the bar, so be my guest, Ms Dee Darrell.'

She shouted, 'Barman, pour this man a whisky and put it on my tab.'

'Yo too kind, sweet thang.'

When she turned on the charm, Dee had a way with people that was effortlessly cool and magnetic. I didn't know she could play the guitar, so to see her pick up the acoustic was a shock. I was intrigued as to what she would play and whether she was any good or not. I had no doubt she would be if she had the balls to get up and play at the drop of a hat.

She hopped her short frame onto the wobbly stool, plucked a few strings to check the tuning and brought the mic closer. She cleared her throat. 'Thanks to Whisky Charlie. Let's have a quick round of applause for his set, shall we? He's been awesome.'

Claps and wolf whistles rang out, and Whisky Charlie tipped his trilby to the punters. Once the applause died down, Dee was back on the mic.

'Ok. This song is a special song for someone here tonight. Someone who's a bit of a Hot Shot back where I'm from.' She nodded over to me, and I felt a mixture of embarrassment and warmth at her declaration.

She played a few introductory strums before the serenading began. *'She packed my bags last night pre-flight... Zero hour nine AM.'*

The opening to 'Rocket Man' by Elton John began. I completely crumbled under the sentiment and nearly welled up. When she hit the chorus, goosebumps showered me, especially when her gaze fixed on mine as she belted out, *'I'm not the man they think I am at home.'*

The background chatter fell silent as the attention fixed on the little girl with the immense voice, who sang with such passion and natural flair that it was impossible to ignore her. I looked over at Whisky Charlie, and he was mesmerised. He gave an approving thumbs up to the bar staff behind him, mouthing, 'This girl's good.'

The emotion and intensity on Dee's face as she sang was extraordinary, and the onlooking, boozy punters connected with it - so much so that when the song ended, the applause was overwhelming. None was louder than my own as I stood to demonstrate my gratitude.

Dee placed a hand across her heart. 'You're all too kind. Thank you so much. I am in a band by the way, and we're currently touring America, so be sure to check out Cutthroat Shambles. We're on all the usual social media channels. You'll know about us soon enough.'

I guessed she wasn't disbanding the gang after all. I couldn't help but praise her when she sat back down.

'That was unbelievable! I never knew you played the guitar.'

'I'm not the woman you think I am, am I?' she joked.

'I can't tell you how much that meant. I'm speechless.'

'Ok, calm down, Hot Shot.'

'You know what, you have a career as a solo artist if it doesn't work out with the band.'

'Good to know.'

'Who would've thought when you delivered that slap at the eighties party that we'd be in this situation a few days later?'

'Life is full of surprises. You never know the twists it'll take, especially when you're in a band.'

'I take it by your last comment onstage that you're not quite ready to quit just yet?'

She just shied away, but I knew the truth.

Whisky Charlie was back on the mic and asked the listeners to applaud one more time for Dee Darrell – applause that was rapturously delivered.

'I need a drink after that. Same again?' I asked.

'Sure. Keep 'em coming.'

I signalled to the barmaid for another round and caught her checking Dee out in the most inappropriate way.

'I think you're in there. Barmaid, totally checking you out.'

'She's cute. But you're my date tonight. That's not an invitation by the way.'

'You're not my type anyway. You're getting too soft. I preferred you being a bitch to me,' I teased.

She nudged me in the arm.

Whisky Charlie announced he was taking a break. He flippantly remarked that he couldn't follow Dee's performance immediately after. Any potential singers in the bar must've felt the same because no one volunteered to step up to the mic.

He requested that the jukebox be fired up for half an hour to keep us entertained. In keeping with the theme, Howlin Wolf's, 'Smokestack Lightnin'' blasted through the airwaves, followed by a few more iconic numbers from Muddy Waters, Lightnin' Hopkins, and Buddy Guy.

'I still can't believe you rattled that song off and knew how to play it,' I said.

'A woman of many talents. It's how I started off back in Bermuda.'

'What's Bermuda like?'

'It's beautiful, but as you can imagine, not a lot of scope to be a rock star.'

'Who were your influences growing up?'

'Freddie Mercury was, and still is, my man.'

'I can see his influence in the way you sing and perform. Raw power and showmanship.'

'Best frontman of all time in my opinion, and my dog is called Freddie too.'

'Why am I not surprised? Who's looking after Freddie while you're here?'

'He's with my mom back in Bermuda. It pained me not to bring him with me to Manchester when I moved.'

'At least you'll get to see him again soon when you go back over.'

A few more gulps of alcohol followed. I still sensed Dee's deep-rooted ache. With more booze giving me Dutch courage, I brought the topic back up.

'Dee, you asked me earlier whether I'd ever experienced real pain and misery. Why did you ask me that?'

'I was curious.'

'Are you sure there's something you don't want to get off your chest? You know you can trust me.'

She frowned, her demeanour changed, and she fired back, 'You wanna know why I got into music? Why I'm hell-bent on success? Why I'm overprotective and defensive to strangers? Why I have demons?'

I sat in silence as she eyeballed me. 'I'll tell you why. I made a promise to someone a long time ago.'

'Who?'

'My best friend back in Bermuda.' She turned away and wiped her eye.

Sensing her emotion, I softly said, 'Look, Dee, you don't have to...'

'Fuck, I don't know why I'm telling you this. Even the band don't know.'

'Tell me what?'

'FUCK!' she cried.

'Maybe there's no safer place than being in Sedona with someone who can be considered a confidante.'

Her eyes puffed up.

'Me and Michelle were thick as thieves as kids. We did everything together. Sang together. Wrote music together. Went to university together. Came back together. Made plans for the future together.'

Feeling overwhelmed that I'd opened a huge door, I delicately said, 'Dee. It's OK. What happened?'

'We had plans to move to the UK or the US after university and go for it as singers and guitarists, individually or in a duo. We vowed to never stop chasing our dream and to support each other no matter what. We were saving up, and then one day...' Her voice trailed off, and she shot up and ran to the bathroom.

I felt shit, like I'd opened a door not ready to be opened. Sensing the intensity of the moment I ordered another whisky each and took a large swig of mine before she returned with bloodshot eyes and a sniffly nose.

'I'm sorry, Dee. I shouldn't have....'

'It's fine. I need to get it out.'

'Only if you're sure.'

'It's been long enough. We were due for rehearsal at my house, and Michelle never showed up. A few hours went by, and her phone kept going to voicemail. I just knew something was wrong because it wasn't like her. Later that night, I got a phone call from her cousin, who told me that Michelle had been killed in a car accident. A couple of young punks had stolen a car and rammed straight into her at an intersection as she crossed.'

The tears began to form again as her voice broke.

'She was my fuckin' best friend and soul mate, and she got taken from me too early. I never even got to say goodbye. You want to know why I'm here doing what I'm doing and why it's so important to me? We made a vow to give it our best shot and become professionals. Just because she isn't here anymore doesn't mean I can't honour that.'

A lump was caught in my throat. 'I'm so sorry, Dee. When was all this?'

'Three years ago. Before that incident, I was a good kid. Rarely drank, never took drugs, never got in trouble, and never hit anyone. And now? Well, it's a natural reaction that helps ease the pain I deal with every day. It's why I can be a bitch when I don't like something. I just react aggressively, and I struggle to control it.'

'It sounds like you're still suffering from the trauma, and I don't blame you. Did you ever speak to a therapist or anything afterwards?'

'They sent me somewhere, but I didn't give it a chance. I bailed after the first session.'

'Maybe you need to try again. You can't keep it all bottled up.'

'I've managed so far.'

'You've evidently struggled by your own admission. It doesn't have to be a fight all the time. Maybe that's what this tour means for you. Maybe it can be your way of saying goodbye to the ghost.'

'I'll never say goodbye. It's all I see when I'm up there onstage. I see her all the time. Call it hallucinating or whatever, but I sing to her. All I want is to make her proud and achieve what we set out to do.'

'And you're doing that. She *will* be proud, I'm sure. You've done phenomenally well to get this far, and the journey is far from over.'

'You want to know why I sing "With a Little Help from My Friends" before every show? It was her favourite song. By singing it, I feel like I'm summoning her to come and watch me from beyond the grave. Sounds ridiculous, but that's how it feels.'

'And that's why you looked like you were going to kill Kyle when he dissed the ritual.'

'He's lucky I didn't rip his fuckin' stupid head off.'

She fell silent, and I really felt for her. She truly was in a pit of emotional strangulation. The horror and pain she must've gone through and was still dealing with dwarfed anything I'd ever experienced. My shitty little break up a year earlier was nothing in comparison.

We continued to drink and talk about Michelle as Whisky Charlie took up his place again to provide a sombre, bluesy soundtrack to Dee's heart-wrenching tale.

Eventually, she punched herself out, so to speak, and she slurred, 'I think we've had enough booze for tonight. I'm emotionally exhausted.'

'Thank you for trusting me with this. I know how hard this must've been for you. I swear I will not breathe a word.'

'Perhaps you were right. Coming to Sedona was the right setting.'

'They do say it has spiritual powers.'

'I think the bar's closing soon. Let's stop at a store on our way back. I'm buying a bottle of whisky for the room. You're driving tomorrow, so I don't care.'

True to her word, we found a 7-Eleven store, and she bought a small bottle of cheap whisky. I didn't realise how smashed I was until I planted face-first into my pillow, still fully clothed.

Dee sat by the desk, whisky in tow. She tried to get my attention, but I was done and could only mumble words that made no sense. Her earlier declaration that she could drink me under the table was completely correct. She was a monster. She pulled the covers over me, and I felt her soft lips kiss my cheek as she whispered in my ear, 'Thanks, Hot Shot.' As I slowly drifted off, I could hear the liquid being tipped back and forth from her bottle.

CHAPTER 19

I awoke early to see half the whisky bottle had been annihilated. Dee was lay on her side on top of the covers, vest top still on, bottoms off, and red satin knickers that barely covered her arse on display. I once again averted my eyes.

Considering the amount of alcohol I'd supped, I felt fairly compos mentis and fully functional to drive. Rather than disturb a snoring Dee, I made a start on the review of the last couple of days. I span the atrociousness of the band's performance to a positive, focusing on Dee's illustrious singing and how she was a born star in waiting. I made light of the band's casualness and unprofessionalism, attempting to create some sort of synergy with the exploits of the past to help drum up the interest. I wrote a hell of a lot about Sedona to deflect attention. It was a naturally descriptive town which I used to my advantage. I didn't mention that it was just me and Dee who experienced the delights. Instead, I generalised the two days as if we were all present in perfect harmony. There was no way I would reveal the fallout with the band, and especially Dee's own demons.

Once finished, I sent it off and woke Dee. She looked frightening at first sight with mascara smeared eyes. Her thick, unbrushed hair resembled a bird's nest.

'Christ, you look rough,' I tittered.

She groaned as she stretched and flicked the finger at me.

'Here. Made you a brew,' I said.

'You'd make someone a great wife.'

'We need to get on the road. I've had a text from Ozzie saying they'll meet us in Palm Springs. We're about seven or eight hours away, so c'mon, let's go.'

'Alright. Give me a minute. Need to get my shit together. Was Ozzie flipping out?'

'Think he's more pissed off with the guys. He told me he's laid into them more than once since we left, but they're ready to apologise. It's just up to you to accept it.'

'We'll see what mood I'm in when I see them. They better grovel on hands and knees for what they did.'

'I'm sure they will.'

She asked, 'Have you written a review yet?'

'I sure have.'

'Have you fucked us over?'

'Dee...really?'

'I know, I know. Trust issues. Speaking of which, not a word about last night.'

'Lips are sealed. But I'm here if you want to talk, yeah?'

She nodded as she dragged herself up and limped into the shower.

We were back on the road before morning had fully bloomed. The gruelling slog into new territory, and a new State, my first real glimpse of California, awaited. Palm Springs was the destination, a place steeped in Hollywood stardom from its heyday in the fifties and sixties. It was the location where stories that involved Elvis, Marilyn Monroe and JFK manifested.

The Sat Nav had flagged up heavy traffic on the quickest route to Palm Springs, so we were forced to head north and arc around Flagstaff before dropping down into California. It wasn't like it was a hardship to drive in such aesthetic surroundings.

Dee and I had spoken about the idea of travelling the previous night, relaying the stories told by past icons who'd endured such challenging but life-affirming journeys. We'd spoken of Chris McCandless from 'Into the Wild', but the conversation turned when she pulled out the book she was reading: 'Wild' by Cheryl Strayed. It was based on a true story about a woman's solo hike on the Pacific Crest Trail to help overcome a difficulty in life. Her character reminded me of Dee in many ways - a strong woman whose struggle with grief was used to fuel something extraordinary. I'd seen the film, and to mirror it, I played a song from the soundtrack, the wonderfully crafted folk ballad, 'El Condor Pasa', by Simon & Garfunkel.

'How're you doin' after last night?' I asked.

'I'm OK. I've kept that in for far too long. It needed to come out. So, thanks.'

'Don't thank me, thank Sedona.'

'We need to come back again and explore it more.'

'You're on. But only when you're rich and famous.'

'If we come back when I'm rich and famous, it won't be the same because I'll be mobbed.'

'I hope you're right.'

A multitude of softer tracks aided our journey. Dee had found 'It's Too Late' by Carole King on my iPod, and that was the song that played as we left Sedona.

She commented, 'I love this song. A love song for grown-ups, written by a grown-up. None of this teenage bullshit singing about someone not liking a post on fuckin' Facebook.'

We passed through Kingman, a strange town that acted as a gateway for those visiting Vegas, the Grand Canyon, Sedona, Flagstaff and other nearby parks and points of interest. Once again, the scenery was seductive and ever-changing. The forestry and snowy tops of the cooler Flagstaff and North Arizona were swiftly replaced by a warmer, arid, desert-like climate as we bombed southwest towards California.

We stopped for a quick break at a service station in the middle of nowhere. I checked social media to see that my review had been posted along with the lads' interview. A few people at the Flagstaff gig accused me of being biased or blind to the truth. One said the gig was '...a shambles as the band's name suggests.' A few other posts on the Cutthroat Shambles page said the band were 'drunken bums' and 'soccer hooligans.' I don't think they understood what true hooliganism was. I opted not to let Dee know what I'd read.

Back on the road, Dee carried on the conversation from the previous night, 'Have you given any thought to what you're going to do after this tour?'

'Give me a chance. I was blootered last night and hardly had time to think.'

'I've had some thoughts.'

'Oh yeah? Was this while you were guzzling the whisky?'

'It's when inspiration is at its most potent even if the execution isn't.'

'Haha. Absolutely true.'

'You speak so passionately about your Vegas trip and the shit you were going through and how you met Eva.'

'Yeah?'

'Why don't you write a book about it?'

The suggestion threw me off guard.

'Write a book?' I sneered. 'I've never considered that.'

'Maybe that's where your future lies. Music writing may only take you so far, so you'll need something that could bring more longevity. You're gaining experience in music, and maybe that's the first phase of an overall career in writing. You said yourself about how Vegas has shaped your life. Maybe this is a continuation of that. You've just spent a day in Sedona. Surely the essence of that place has inspired you on some level as it has me. Perhaps it was destiny that brought us both there, so we could confront our demons. Aside from telling you about Michelle and feeling a release from that, I wrote enough for about four songs last night.'

'Really? I thought you were just getting pissed.'

'I was, but I was writing and thinking what you could do. I'm a woman. I can multi-task. You can't.'

'Drinking, writing songs and planning my life is impressive even for the average multi-tasker.'

'I read a load of your reviews last night on Sonic Bandwagon too. And re-read the blogs you've done for us. I like your style. You're very descriptive and can draw a reader in. I'm not blowing smoke up your arse, but I think your writing is better than Tommy's, the writer who was meant to tour with us. I think if you write the Vegas trip as a novel, you'll surprise yourself. Loads of people will love that shit. Just don't make it too rom-com.'

'You really were having an inspirational night. I'm flattered you read my old reviews, and thanks for the kind words, but don't forget I have been edited a bit by Jamie.'

'I can still hear your voice and see *you* in the words. All Jamie's doing is shortening and correcting grammar. You'll have an editor do the same thing with a novel. You should give it a go.'

'It's an interesting thought, but there's no way I'm ready for something as big as that. I write one to two-page reviews. A novel is a completely different kettle of fish.'

'Don't underestimate yourself. What did Vegas teach you? That anything's possible if you put your heart and mind to it.'

'Weirdly, back in my youth, I did have ideas of writing a script one day. A novel, though? Different, but kind of appealing now you mention it,' I mused.

'You could even write something based on this trip in the future. Collate all the blogs from Sonic Bandwagon and make it into one rock 'n' roll journey, and we'll play the launch for it. How cool would that be?'

'Whoa! You're getting a little ahead of yourself. I've not even put pen to paper on the first novel yet. And you'll be too famous for me by then. I won't be able to afford you.'

'I'd never forget those that helped us on the way up.'

'Cos you might meet them again on the way down,' I finished.

'Precisely. But don't sell yourself short. You have a lot of plastic celebs releasing books that sell millions.'

'That's just the way of the world, isn't it? Reality TV stars are the new rock stars.'

'Fuck, don't say that. Makes me shiver. I'm already pissed off with this TikTok culture and influencers being portrayed as an art form. Anyway, something to think about while you're taxiing me about.'

I couldn't deny that writing something with a little more substance and length, like a novel or a script, intrigued me. But Dee was right. Since Vegas, I felt my experiences were part of a larger plan. Maybe the definitive conclusion would be to write about all those life-changing encounters.

We cheered when we saw a sign that welcomed us to California as we crossed the mammoth border bridge over the Colorado River. Dee harmonised, 'California Dreaming,' by Mamas and Papas at a pitch-perfect tone.

As we pulled off the bridge, I felt compelled to mark the seminal moment with a song from the playlist. There was an abundance to choose from, from the heavy to the soft, from the strutting to the melancholy. Given I was a big fan of the show 'Californication', I played a reflective, slow-tempo track from the end of the sixth season, which signified a drive to L.A. through the desert. It was Beth Hart's, 'My California', and it somehow seemed the most appropriate way to glide into the Golden State. Shortly after, Dee opted to play Albert Hammond's, 'It Never Rains in California.' It sparked an inspired run of 'California' songs that we agreed to take turns in choosing.

The terrain and driving conditions changed dramatically in California. The roads collapsed into one lane. We climbed and clambered, twisted and turned, and ploughed into a harsher desert moonscape than the scene in Arizona. Intimidating, vertiginous mountain ranges with jagged edged ridges circled us, acting as a warning about the perils of the territory.

I saw a sign for 29 Palms and made the connection to the Robert Plant song. I never knew it was an actual place until Dee educated me, telling me that he wrote it on tour whilst driving through California.

We ended up on a road that was as straight as an arrow with a steady incline. It went on for that long the horizon fused with the road. Cars looked like ants at the tip in the distance. We had no idea how far away they were. It was an unbelievable stretch that seemed interminable with each passing mile. It must've been close to fifteen miles later that we hit a slight curve at the pinnacle. It was perplexing that we could see that far so clearly.

Dee feverishly scribbled on her pad as inspiration took hold once again. The desert backdrops were a natural aphrodisiac to her creativity.

'The mood took you again?' I asked.

'This place is just a beacon of inspiration.'

'Is that how it's done?'

'In this case, it is. It opens something up inside, trust me.'

'Can you read it out to me?'

'Certainly not. No one outside the band reads my words until they're on an album or sung onstage.'

'How do you write such strong lyrics anyway? Where does it come from?'

'Where do you think?'

'Michelle?'

'Correct.'

'Sorry. I shouldn't have asked that.'

'It's fine. I'm not going to hide behind it anymore. She needs crediting for most of my songs.'

A few moments passed, and I asked, 'What is it about music that you love?'

'Aside from being a stimulus to any emotion a human can feel, it's a natural facilitator to do whatever you want and disregard the rule book. It's the medicine of the mind.'

'What does it mean to you when you're singing onstage?'

'I can't describe it sometimes. When the songs I wrote from the heart are sung back to me. Wow. When you know that every little riff and key change makes the crowd erupt and to know you were part of creating that, well, that's pretty special. People don't know that you can change someone's life through song. To have the ability to do that is an unbelievable feeling.'

'I'm envious you have that power.'

'It's a rush. I can't deny that. How about you? Why do you love music?'

'I agree about how it stimulates every emotion and fits every mood. I love how music can make me tap into another world, like a portal to my past, present and future. I visualise scenes with words and melodies and relate them to moments. It's like a soundtrack. It's hard to describe. For instance, I'm driving now, and we've got "When the Levee Breaks" on by Led Zep. It's probably the most epic song to listen to on this road. My mind starts to wander and taps into all sorts of nooks and crannies, and I get locked into a vision of my own movie.'

'I can go with that. There's a song for every occasion, every moment, every mood.'

Dee continued to scribble away, so I left her to it as my thoughts ventured into how the music, coupled with the driving, was so soul-stirring. It was a part of the trip that I felt a strong kinship with. There was an overwhelming sense of transcendent liberation whilst racking up the miles.

From an early age, I'd always envisioned driving through America with nothing but the music and the scenery for company. The reality exceeded the expectation, and I wasn't prepared for just how emancipating the sensation really was.

The quietness only lasted ten minutes before a slight apprehension crept in. I calculated that we had about two hours of driving to do, and most of it would be spent in the barren desert surroundings. The fuel gauge was less than a quarter, which I believed to be plenty until we neared our destination and found a fuel station. Stupidly, I brought it up with Dee, who argued my calculations, creating an air of panic. The last thing we needed was to run out of fuel in the desert of all places.

Time slithered on, miles ticked by and the gauge slowly depleted. We appeared to be no nearer to a fuel station or to leaving conditions as remote as I'd ever experienced. There was literally nothing, just desert plains sculpted by rugged mountain ranges with no evidence of civilisation bar the road. The desert in Arizona at least had the odd trailer park located every few miles or so. There was nothing like that on the edge of California. I remained hopeful, but Dee continued to voice her concern. The biggest indication that nerves were taking over the positive vibe was when Dee turned the music off, a classic sign of anxiety. It was the first time music hadn't played through the stereo since I first drove the Chevy.

'Why didn't you fill up? We're going to be stranded, aren't we?' Dee's temper boiled.

'Stop panicking. We'll be fine,' I tried to reassure her.

'I knew you'd be the death of me. I reveal my deepest and darkest secret, and now it's out in the world, I'm going to perish with *you*, a Hot Shot Writer Dickhead.'

'There's no need for that,' I retorted.

I was quietly confident, but the long roads that had been my companion and spiritual guide now showed their hazardous side. The Sat Nav told me the freeway approached, so I was sure a fuel station would be close by. It made sense after a slog through nothingness. The problem was that the yellow light on the dashboard then alerted us to our possible doom. On hearing the first ping, Dee launched into another scathing verbal attack and highlighted my stupidity for not filling up sooner.

'I don't believe this. If we break down, it's not being stranded in the middle of nowhere you should be worried about. It'll be me pounding the shit out of you that you need to be concerned with.'

I laughed, albeit a nervous laugh.

'It's not fuckin' funny, shit for brains!'

I was still confident, but the biffle of all biffles was in the back of my mind. My mates back home would have a field day if they ever heard about it.

We reached the interstate and prayed that some sort of civilisation would magically appear. If we broke down, we'd surely be able to flag down a car to help us. Although, they may need to save *me* from the beating Dee promised. Ten minutes elapsed, and still no sign of fuel.

Nerves became a little tauter as the dashboard continued to warn us. Dee's worries started to play on my mind and corrode my own judgement. I started to question my own calculations. Fear consumed me as I asked myself, *what the hell do we do if we break down?* I began to think of every conceivable and exaggerated ill-fated scenario of being stranded. Psychotic hitchhikers, rapey vagrants, dehydration, but more believable, a brush with the terrifying wildlife that roamed the territory. The fear of being face to face with coyotes and scorpions and snakes, oh my, left me nauseous.

Snakes were the worst. There was a very justified phobia about being face to face with an angry rattler. I knew that if we broke down, the slippery fuckers would sniff out my anxiety and decide to slither out from under rocks to toy with my emotions. I had to stop thinking about such unlikely scenarios, but it proved difficult.

I eventually snapped, 'Where the fuck are these fuel stations, for fuck's sake!'

We'd driven close to a hundred miles without seeing one.

'You're an absolute dickbag.'

'Write a song about it,' I retorted.

'Yeah. I've always wanted to write a murder ballad about a schizophrenic psycho roaming the desert looking for stranded tourists. I'll make sure he slashes you first while I make a break for it.'

'It's the fuckin' snakes that worry me more.'

'Snakes I can handle. Better not be any fuckin' turtles, though.'

I turned to face her with a puzzled look. 'Turtles?'

'Don't get me started.'

'You're afraid of turtles...the slowest thing in the world... but you can handle snakes? You're an odd one.'

'They freak me out. Why are they here? Why do they have a shell and live in it?'

'I'm guessing evolution.'

'Well, evolution is flawed when it comes to turtles.'

'Just turtles? Or tortoises too?'

'Oh yeah, they can get fucked too.'

'Well, I happen to know for a fact that there are desert tortoises out here.'

'You what?'

'Honestly. Google it.'

She frantically searched on her phone, and upon realising I was right, she wailed, 'Fuck me!'

'I've never heard of this before. An irrational fear over turtles and tortoises.'

Just as I was about to continue my probe, my eyes caught a sign. It blissfully boasted, 'Services 4 Km'. I half expected it to be a mirage, and the relief was palpable.

'Hooray! We're saved! We're not gonna die! The snakes and tortoises can go fuck themselves,' I cried.

But then a kiss of death, a twist to the tale. The car began to splutter and shudder as we coasted down the freeway.

'What the fuck is that?' Dee asked.

'Uh oh.'

'WHAT?'

'Erm, we're not out of the woods just yet.'

'You and your big mouth,' she shouted.

'Me and my mouth? Coming from you? Gob bigger than the kitchen sink here.'

'If we break down, you're walking, and I'm staying in the car away from any tortoises.'

'On your own? So Mr Psycho McSlashYourNeck can have his wicked way with you?

'I'd like to see him try. I'd fuck him up.'

I rolled my eyes.

It was a nervous couple of minutes as the car coughed and spluttered down the freeway like the Trotters' Reliant Robin. I felt Dee was on the cusp of throwing a punch at any moment. If I wasn't at the wheel, she might've done. I could feel her malevolent gaze pierce through me from the corner of my eye.

The exit approached, and I burst into fits of laughter and cheers, more out of nervous relief. Dee remained unimpressed. We crept into the entrance, and I half expected to see ZZ Top appear singing 'Gimme All Your Lovin' by the pumps. The car practically conked out as we skulked to the forecourt.

Dee yelled, 'You're one lucky bastard, Hot Shot.'

'Fuck it. It was funny, wasn't it?'

'That statement is the lie you tell when you regret an act of stupidity.'

'Huh. I never looked at it like that.'

She said nothing.

'Maybe I should just fuel up. To the top, yeah?'

Inside, I grabbed a coffee, bottles of water, and a big pack of M&Ms from the kiosk as a peace offering. At the till I eyed a small tortoise soft toy. I chuckled as soon as I saw it and couldn't resist buying it to wind Dee up.

After fuelling up, I opened the car door and threw the toy on her lap. She shrieked and nearly jumped out of her skin.

'What the fuck?' she squealed.

I didn't expect the prank to go down so well and creased over laughing my head off.

'Fuckin' idiot,' she screamed as she beat me around the head with it. She repeated herself, this time with a smile, 'Fuckin' idiot. I hate you.'

I pulled my bottom lip up and offered her the chocolate and coffee, saying in a childish voice, 'Peace offering? I'm sorry.'

She took them and turned away from me, saying, 'Not forgiven.'

With a full tank, calmer nerves and just over half an hour to go, we descended into California and onto Palm Springs.

CHAPTER 20

Palm Springs was another resplendent image to behold. Gargantuan grey-brown rocky foothills surrounded the area. It looked like the city had been hollowed out to create an expansive amphitheatre in the middle of the mountains. There was so much lushness as exotic palm trees and lavish greenery flooded the famed resort.

We pulled into the aptly named Musicland Motel on the outskirts of the centre. Ozzie had already told us where to go and what rooms we were in via text message, so it was just a simple case of parking up and finding the three rooms next to each other on the ground floor.

Dee caught my arm as we neared. 'Remember, not a word to Ozzie or the boys about what happened in that bar in Flagstaff. Or about what I told you in Sedona. Or about my fear of turtles and tortoises.'

I laughed at the latter comment. 'What happens in Sedona stays in Sedona. Are you ready to see the guys?'

'It should be them who need to be ready and worried.'

I knocked on room number sixteen, and Ozzie answered.

He was ecstatic to see us. 'Here they are, the Happy Wanderer and Lord Lucan. Nice of you to finally join us. Are you OK?' he asked Dee as he hugged her.

'Yeah, I'm fine. I just needed time away.'

'I understand, kid. As long as you're sorted now.'

'I am. So where are they then?' Dee asked.

Upon hearing Dee's voice, the lads funnelled out from the room next door and moved towards her. Will was the first to approach. He gave Dee a warm embrace and then whispered, 'Sorry, Dee.'

Dee pulled down his head and saw the graze beneath his hair. She apologised for throwing the can of beans at him.

'Forget about it. Shit happens. Fuckin' good shot, though. If we were at the funfair, I'd have given you a coconut and a big fuck off teddy bear,' he responded.

'You're a fuckin' coconut,' she jibed.

Dee then took a moment to look Will up and down and said, 'What the fuck happened to you? You look like a flump.' His skin was a bright shade of pink from sunburn.

'Out in the sun all day yesterday, weren't we? Burnt to shit, and I had no sun cream.'

'You look a mess. Ozzie, do something with him later. Stick some fake tan on him or something.'

Quince pushed Will out of the way. 'Come here, you fiery bitch.'

His burly frame swallowed her up when he lifted her off the ground.

'Are we good?' he said.

'Put me down, you big galoot. We're good, we're good.'

When Quince dropped her, Kyle stood next to her, looking sheepish. They momentarily stared at each other before Kyle broke. 'I'm sorry, girl. I've been a right prick. Won't happen again, I swear. I don't know what came over me. I was wasted and well out of order.'

'Better fuckin' not do…but you're forgiven…this time.'

'Come here,' Kyle said before he enveloped her in his arms.

As they broke, Dee clocked the slight bruise on the side of his cheek from where she'd hit him.

'Seems you've got a memento from that night,' Dee observed.

'Good job that's all it is. Don't want these looks being distorted now, do I? Makes me look more badass anyway,' he responded.

The three lads offered their apologies to me too.

'Forget about it. Water under the bridge,' I stated.

Dee roused, 'Are we gonna get this tour back on track then or what?'

'Hell yeah!' Kyle answered.

It felt like we'd never been apart.

Ozzie spoke, 'I have some good news to tell you. I wanted to wait till we were face to face rather than tell you over the phone, but Lynwood wants a meeting with you at their offices in Los Angeles. Things are looking up.'

Dee showed her gratitude, 'That's great, Ozzie, truly is great. Thanks.'

'Hey. It's all your doing. You're easy to sell.'

It then dawned on Dee. 'Oh, by the way, Ozzie, you little liar. I'm disappointed you didn't tell me that Hot Shot Writer here is a rookie and has only been writing a year.'

'You told her?' he directed at me.

'Sang like a canary,' Dee said.

'I thought it was best,' I answered.

'Well, I've been wanting to have a go at you for slapping Ricky, so I guess we're even,' Ozzie shot back at her.

'What about having a go at her for punching me,' Kyle piped up.

'You deserved it. That's the difference, you clown.'

Kyle was quick as a flash to change the subject.

'Anyway, forget all that. Got a top story to tell you both.'

'You're gonna love this one,' Quince echoed.

'Is this another sexual conquest story? If it is, I don't want to hear it,' Dee said.

'Just listen to it, yeah,' Kyle demanded in excitement.

'Go on then,' Dee sighed.

'Well, last night we had a few beers and got chatting to some Norwegian girls in Flagstaff. Proper fit they were. Anyway, I brought one back to the room while Quince and Will stayed out. When she was in the bathroom, she came back out with Will's STD cream and asked what it was. I don't think Warticon translated in Scandinavian.'

'Did you tell her?' I asked.

'Did I bollocks. It's hardly a mood heightener, is it? Plus, I was too scared she'd think it was mine.'

'So, what did you say it was?'

'I lied and said it was some special toothpaste that whitens your teeth. I assumed she thought nothing of it because she put it back, and then we did the business and all that. Anyway, this morning, it was nowhere to be found after she left.'

He could hardly contain his laughter.

'She didn't!' I said.

'She fuckin' did. She only stole it and has probably cleaned her teeth with it this morning.'

We all howled in fits of uncontrollable laughter.

Will said, 'Good job that the warts have cleared up, or else I'd be well pissed off about it. I even felt confident enough to whip it out last night without fear of the inquisition about what the spots on my dick were.'

Dee and I winced.

We dropped our luggage in the rooms. Dee caught up with her bandmates and told them about Sedona. Ozzie cornered me away from the rest. Before he could quiz me, I spoke first, 'Everything OK with the band?'

'I think so. I bollocked them. They just got over-excited in the afternoon. That weird band, Cats of the Moon, didn't help matters with their drugs. Should've seen their set afterwards. Freaky shit. I thought they were trying to summon Lucifer or something.'

'Haha. I'm glad I didn't see it. They'd have probably given me nightmares.'

'That woman dressed as a unicorn floated about the stage banging a tambourine. She was their version of Bez from Happy Mondays. I might sign them for a laugh and stick them on in The Castle Hotel. Really freak people out.'

'Knowing some people's tastes, they'd probably be a hit,' I guessed.

'Haha yeah. Anyway, things got out of hand after the gig. Backstage was a mess. Kyle threw up, so we got billed for it, or should I say, *I* got billed for it. But I'll be taking it off their end, no question about that.'

'How much did that set you back?'

'I just gave them two hundred dollars for smashed glasses, a clean-up crew, the hassle caused, and covering an unacceptable performance.'

'That's a pisser. You don't need shit like that.'

'No, but it's fine. What about you and Dee? Everything OK? I take it you're both sweet with each other now?'

'Yeah, thankfully. I don't think I could've taken the tension for much longer.'

'So, what happened to change her mind? I knew she'd come around but not to the extent where she'd drag you off to Sedona. You didn't...you know...did you?'

'Fuck no! Not even close. It wasn't like that.'

'I didn't think so, but I had to ask. I'd have been surprised if she'd gone for you.'

'What does that mean?'

'No offence, but you know. She's that... and you're...'

'I'm what? Boring? Look like a bulldog chewing a biscuit?'

'You know what I mean.'

'It's a good job I do, isn't it,' I chuckled.

'What happened anyway?' he asked.

I smiled, but not my best poker face. 'I'm sworn to secrecy, but we're all good. That's all you need to know.'

'Fair enough. It's good to have you back. Has Jamie been onto you?'

'Not since he posted my review and the lads' interview. Did you see it?'

'Yeah, I did. The interview was spot on. The lads enjoyed it. I thought you span the Flagstaff gig quite well too. Pity, it was a lie. Haha. I've seen a few keyboard warriors have disagreed and voiced their opinions. Can't be helped.'

'Ah fuck 'em. I'm here to serve the band. When forced to pick between truth and legend, print the legend.'

'Tony Wilson quote. I like it. I loved that dude.'

'You met him?'

'And then some. He was a top guy and was ace to me when I was coming through the ranks.'

'Well, you'll have to tell me more about that some-time.'

I left Ozzie and the band to it while Dee showered and changed. I hadn't had a chance to speak to Eva since Flagstaff, so I took the opportunity to update her on the situation. She was pleased that Dee and I had reconciled.

I told her about Sedona, and she responded, 'I've never been there, but I've heard it's lovely and highly spiritual.'

'It is. You'd love it. I promise that one day I'm going to take you there.'

'I'm going to hold you to that Mr Englishman. I've been following the blogs. I'm enjoying them so much. I saw people contradict what you said about the gig in Flagstaff. Was it really that bad and different to the review?'

'It was worse than you can imagine. It was awful.'

'It's good that you stayed loyal to the band and didn't sell them out.'

'I couldn't back-stab them like that, even if the lads did piss me off.'

'You're sweet. I'll look forward to your next piece.'

'I'll try and get it done tomorrow. I'll catch up with you in a couple of days anyway. We'll be heading to the gig soon, and we need to be up early for Los Angeles.'

'You're going to love L.A., especially Sunset Strip.'

'Have you been?'

'I've been a few times. You probably won't get a chance to go to some of the places I've been to, but if you're on the Strip, you'll see all you need to. You'll be like a kid in a candy shop.'

'I can't wait.'

'I was in Los Angeles when I decided to come back to Vegas to see you.'

'Ah, of course. How could I forget? Well, maybe I'll have a similar revelation.'

'Don't you dare abandon this tour for me. Call me in a couple of days. Enjoy the show tonight.'

I always felt like I was glowing after speaking to Eva. She had an effect on me that enriched my mood. I strolled over to reception with a joyful smile and a spring in my step as I waited for the band.

I chatted to the owner of the motel, who stood behind reception. Incredibly, he was from Rochdale, and his sister lived in Bolton. We were both in shock to find we were from the same neck of the woods. It made me realise just how small a world we live in.

He was an Indian fella called Nilesh, and he was in his late fifties. He was of average height with a thin frame, and his hair was short but thinning on top. I asked, 'How does someone from Rochdale end up running a motel in Palm Springs?'

'I came travelling here many years ago and fell in love with the place. I stayed on to work, and here I am, twenty years later.' His accent had lost none of its Lancashire taint.

'Did you travel alone?'

'I did, but I met my wife, Advika, here. She's originally from Portland. I was only meant to be in Palm Springs for the summer, but she convinced me to stay. Best decision I ever made. I couldn't imagine living in Manchester again, not after experiencing this place.'

'Far too cold for you now, I'd have thought.'

'You're not wrong.'

I momentarily wondered whether I'd suffer a similar fate: fall in love with the American West so much that I'd stay indefinitely.

'What brings you over here anyway?' he inquired.

'I'm touring with a band and writing blogs about it. They've got a gig at the St Patrick's Day festival in town shortly.'

'It's going to be lively down there tonight. You'll have a great time.'

'I've heard that Palm Springs is a retirement community. Is it going to be full of oldies?'

'Quite the opposite. You're in for a treat. I won't get into specifics, but it's Spring Break out here now, and there's a tennis tournament going on too, so there'll be plenty of younger people about.'

'Sounds like we've come at the right time.'

Our drive to the centre took a mere five minutes, and it quickly became evident that this was a St Patrick's Day festival like I'd never seen before. The Americans went overboard with the bunting and celebrations, which added to an atmosphere already rippling with hysteria.

Well-constructed street fairs with shimmering lights created a striking impact. A plethora of bars, restaurants, and quirky gift stands were set up along the pedestrianised precinct, which served as a tourist trap. People of all ages congregated outside the many drinking stations. Market stalls dissected the streets selling all sorts. Music from many musicians and jukeboxes flared out from all the bars, street corners and outdoor stage areas. Irish flags swarmed all over the centre as green, white, and orange cloaked the buildings and streets. Nilesh was right. Coupled with Spring Break and a tennis tournament, Palm Springs was one rocking place. The myth about it being a boring retirement community was dispelled. It was far from that ideology.

I commented to the band, 'Do a U2 cover tonight, and these people will cum in their pants.'

After we'd checked into the aptly named Paddy's Pub, the venue where the band were playing, we took the opportunity to wander about and soak up the festivities.

With a strong country and western theme to the festival, every parody of the genre came to life. Big hats, big hair, handlebar moustaches, and some very suspect mullets were braved. Dress sense was typical. Double denim with bollock-busting sky blue Wranglers, and checked shirts tucked in to showcase belt buckles depicting bulls or eagles. Cowboy hats were also aplenty, making most folks resemble Marlboro Man about to mount a bucking bronco.

A colossal line dancing square was set up in the town centre, with Josh Turner's country & western ballad, 'I'm Your Man', providing the rhythm for the dancers. Kyle mocked the cheesy opening lyrics about locking the doors and turning the lights down low, stating that was his intention later.

Will joined the clan from the side and took the piss with his own ungraceful interpretation of the dance. He predatorily eyed up the radiant mature ladies with their Dolly Parton accents, dressed in quintessential country attire. The checked shirts tied at the stomach, denim shorts, and shin-high cowboy boots had pulses racing. I had to practically drag Dee away when I saw her gawking on the sly.

We found the Hair of the Dog pub recommended to me by Nilesh back at the motel. It was one of the livelier pubs on the square. We ordered a round of beers, and Quince was quick to allay Dee's fears, saying they'd agreed to have only one beer before the show.

Once pints were in tow, Will informed us of his plan, 'I'm diving headfirst into those MILFs after the show now that my problem has cleared up. What about you, Ricky?'

'What about me?'

'You fancy an older woman tonight?'

'Never been something I've thought about.'

Kyle overheard my admission and said, 'Really? You're missing out. Especially the divorcees who've been married since they were fifteen to someone twice their age. Now they're single at forty-five with a lot of pent-up sexual aggression to get rid of. That's where I come in.'

'To help them make an even bigger mistake than marrying the prick she was with,' I quipped.

'You're just jealous.'

'You're just a predator. It'll catch up with you one day. You'll be on the Warticon like Will.'

'That's a risk I'm willing to take.'

The pint went down far too quickly, but the lads remained true to their word and had only one drink. On the way back to the venue, we stopped for burgers from a van that enticed us with the smell of greasy onions. Dee just stuck with a cone of chips.

The Cutthroats weren't the main band performing at Paddy's Pub, but they had a prime-time slot, third from the end. Ozzie reminded the band how he'd pulled some strings to bump them up the pecking order after their initial mid-afternoon slot, highlighting how good a blagger he was.

Paddy's seemed to be *the* place to be. Although the outdoor stages attracted more footfall, it seemed the best indoor venue for the festival. It was an all-in-one pub/bar/venue/nightclub that was inundated with partygoers and pissheads having the wildest of times. The atmosphere was electric, made more intense as Foo Fighters', 'Best of You' belted out. Most of the punters sang and headbanged along. Given the soaring night temperature and relentless energy the festival harnessed, the venue turned into a sweatbox. A glut of

'Real (Desperate) Housewives of Palm Springs' types had filtered in after the line dancing had finished. Kyle gave me a nudge and had the most excitable grin plastered across his face. He reiterated his desire to 'snag a cougar tonight.'

As the Foo Fighters song finished, the next band appeared. They were called Bite The Dust, and their style of raucous and gritty blues rock appealed to those driven by whisky and hard booze. Their sound invoked a compulsion to reach for the hard stuff and kept the ferocity of the crowd bubbling.

There was a reinvigorated buzz about the band when we went backstage to get ready. With differences settled and little alcohol consumed beforehand, I sensed a special performance was forthcoming. It needed to be, given it was the final warm-up gig before the big one at the Whisky a Go Go. Perhaps the argument in Flagstaff was needed to revitalise the dynamic and clear the cobwebs.

Ozzie and I went back out front, where he had managed to set up a merch stand amidst the bedlam.

A little later, the lights dimmed, and the band were announced. A deafening roar rang out, and they flew out of the blocks with 'Rock 'N' Roll Heaven', delivered to their customary high standard. Business as usual. Dee was on form, desperate to erase the ghost of Flagstaff, strutting with ardour in front of the mesmerised audience. She was vocally on point, devilish in appearance, and oozed sex appeal.

Kyle, fuelled by the prospect of playing to a bunch of cougars and having a point to prove after his abysmal showing in Flagstaff, was the best I'd seen him all tour. He was in his element and played up to the bystanders with a combination of smug stage antics and murderous riffs that hypnotised the females at the front.

Will and Quince more than played their part. Their thunderous bass lines were so reverberating and forceful, that you could probably feel the vibrations in Jamaica.

The entertaining forty-five-minute set ended as quick as a flash. A cover of Bon Jovi's 'Blaze Of Glory' captured the imaginations of the rowdy crowd to round off a phenomenal performance that assailed the senses. Even though I'd seen the same routine several times, I enjoyed it just as much as the fans, who screamed and applauded the band as they departed the stage.

I manned the merch stand while Ozzie went backstage. I turned into a right Del Boy wheeling and dealing, selling loads of stuff. It was about half an hour later when Ozzie returned. I handed him the cash, and he grinned, 'This should put a dent into that bill from Flagstaff.'

He went on to say that it was pandemonium backstage, and he'd been accosted by several people who all wanted a piece of the band. Some were from the business side, some were fellow creatives, and others were general fans who hung around outside trying to get a look in.

The band appeared in the distance and negotiated their way through the gauntlet of picture requests and handshakes. Beers were dished out, and the three lads gulped them down quickly with the shackles of the pre-gig rules loosened. True to his word, Kyle dove into a sea of older women who had swooned over him throughout the show.

The final act took to the stage, a well-known local covers band called 'The Wildkats'. They were the perfect catalyst to create crazed hedonism across the venue's dancefloor. The likes of the Eagles, Tom Petty, and Lynyrd Skynyrd formed the core of their offering.

It was refreshing to see everyone dancing and singing in unity, especially the younger generations, who gave their heart and soul to the cause by belting out each song. Back home, it was a rarity for that generation to sing the lyrics of some of the lesser-known classics of rock. The likelihood was that most wouldn't even know who these bands were, let alone the lyrics to their songs.

I smirked to myself when the band played 'Don't Stop Believin'', by Journey. As it was the adopted theme song for America, the place erupted and went insane. I questioned what our equivalent was, probably 'God Save the Queen'...by The Sex Pistols - of course.

It had been an incredible night, but the mammoth eight-hour drive had left me knackered, so I decided to turn in early. Ozzie said he'd come with me after enduring a similar drive. To my surprise, Dee followed. There was no way the lads were leaving due to the attention they attracted (I heard the phrase: 'Oh my God, I love your accent,' on more than one occasion).

Back at the hotel, an hour or so into sleep, the sound of forceful pounding woke me from my deep, much-needed slumber. I was disorientated for a few seconds until I came around to reality. I looked around the room and realised it was coming from Kyle and Quince's room next door through the wafer-thin wall that my head lay against. Whoever it was, was having a whale of a time. It became apparent it was Kyle, as I could hear his excitable voice shouting all sorts of horrifically graphic and cringe-worthy sex-fuelled remarks. I assumed or hoped that Quince wasn't in there with him. Ozzie lay in bed on the other side of the room and didn't flinch.

The constant jack-knife, coke-fuelled (I assumed) slaughtering from next door didn't slacken. After fifteen minutes, I'd had enough of the bed being slammed and having to listen to low-budget porn dialogue. I jumped up without a clue what I was going to do. I had to get out of the room, especially when the 'yee-haw' and 'ride me cowboy', percolated through the walls like I was in a proper wild western whorehouse surrounded by wenches and gunslingers.

I exited the room and saw a glimmer of light through the curtain of Dee's room next door. I gently rapped on the window.

'Who's that?' she shouted.

'It's Ricky. Let me in.'

She answered, dressed in a Ramones vest top and knickers.

'What the fuck do you want? You better not be after a booty call or anything.'

'Don't be silly. Can you not hear Kyle in his room?'

'He's two doors away.'

'Believe me, I wouldn't be surprised if you could. Some poor woman, well, lucky actually, is taking a right drilling from him.'

'He's insatiable, that boy. So, what do you want? Just because we shared a room in Sedona, it doesn't mean we're making this a regular thing.'

'I know that, but c'mon, Dee. Given the circumstances and after the day I've had, I need sleep.'

'Go on then, come in. Will hasn't come back, so just get in his bed - I doubt he'll be back, but he can bunk in with you if he does. You caught me at a good time. I was watching a film because I'm still a bit wired, but it's just finished. I was just about to go to sleep myself. Oh, and before I forget, your laptop is over there. You must've thrown it in my bag when we left Sedona this morning.'

'Good job you told me - I didn't even check if I had it.'

I asked if she was OK regards Michelle and she reiterated that getting it off her chest seemed to have helped a bit. After a few minutes, I could tell she was getting tired. Her answers became muffled and grunted, so I let her nod off when her eyes closed. Typically, I couldn't get back to sleep after being woken up. Things churned over in my mind: Eva, the tour, what next after it, the band, Vegas, Bermuda, how the blogs were being received. The list went on.

I reflected on what I'd experienced so far, trying to make some sense of the trip. My own task started quite simple - write about a band and their gigs. They were becoming less about the gigs themselves and more about life on the road with a band in modern times. There was another layer of depth with the Bobby and Tien aspect, the visit to Sedona, and Ozzie's role. His interview was yet to go live, but he had approved it.

The tour was by no means as glamorous as people presumed, judging by some of the comments on social media. It was exhausting and filled with obstacles. In our own way, we were all lost and trying to find something meaningful, like outlaws searching for our manifest destiny. The only salvation and reason for anything seemed to be onstage. It was where everyone fired on all cylinders and ran at their optimum level.

I gave up the ghost of attempting sleep as what Dee suggested in the car about writing a novel started to play on my mind. So much so that I retrieved my laptop and opened a new Word document. I began to make notes about everything I had experienced in Vegas and set out some sort of plan and structure. I was on autopilot and locked into another realm as words poured out of me onto the page.

CHAPTER 21

Dee making an almighty racket woke me from another night of brief sleep.

I voiced my annoyance, 'Dee! What the fuck are you doing clinking, clanking and clattering about?'

'Wake up, Hot Shot! Big day ahead. I'm packed and ready to get on the road.'

'What time is it?'

'8:30. L.A. beckons. C'mon.'

'8:30? That's way too early,' I argued.

She wandered over to my side and dragged the duvet from my clutches. I lamented her enthusiasm.

'Good job I sleep in my boxers, isn't it?'

'There'd be nothing worth seeing.'

'Always the joker, aren't you?'

She picked the laptop off the floor and inadvertently touched a key to light up the screen. She looked at the open document.

'What's this? she asked.

'Nothing. Put that down.' I was defensive and grabbed it from her.

'Is that what I think it is?'

'What do you think it is?'

In a high-pitched Stewie Griffin voice from Family Guy, she imitated, 'How's that novel you're working on? Gotta big stack of papers there? Gotta nice little story you're working on there?'

I laughed at her impression.

'Not for your eyes. Same philosophy as you and songwriting.'

'Glad you listened and are putting that second brain cell to good use.'

'You're hilarious this morning, aren't you? If you fail as a singer, you could get a job as a comedian... or a clown, more like.'

I got up and headed over to the window. The sun gunned down on another glorious day. I heard a door creak open. A blonde cougar surreptitiously crept out of Kyle's room and walked a little bow-legged down the walkway. Her hair was ragged and makeup smeared. She was devoid of any elegance or class she may have pretended to possess ten hours earlier. I chuckled and told Dee to come over for a peek.

We were both standing at the window like a couple of nosy old bats when Kyle strode past wearing only a pair of black Calvin Klein boxers. I opened the door before he got a chance to knock.

'I'm going to start accusing you two of having an affair soon,' he said.

'*You're* to blame for this,' I claimed.

'Me? What do you mean?' he protested.

'Do you know how thin those walls are? I thought the radiator was going to fly off last night.'

'You could hear me?'

'Hear you? I was practically the third wheel in a ménage à trois.'

He wasn't embarrassed whatsoever. 'Ha. Really? I bet you were pulling yourself silly listening to me.'

'Only once,' I joked.

Dee laughed.

'I had to come in here for some sleep you were *that* loud. Will and Quince weren't there surely?'

'No. They went off to some party.'

Dee butted in, 'Oh great. God knows when they'll be back then. We'll go without them.'

'Why didn't you go back to Cougar Town last night anyway? She looked a bit classy to come back to a cheap motel,' I asked.

'She didn't look classy this morning,' Dee sneered.

'I don't think her husband would've appreciated that, do you? What we've seen of these Yanks, they own guns, so fuck that. I'm not getting a cap in my arse.'

'Just a dildo instead,' Dee quipped again.

'She was married?' I asked.

'They're always married.'

'You dodgy bastard.'

'I'm sure he deserves it. He's probably some seventy-year-old millionaire who can't get it up without a pill. Little does he know that his Mrs hasn't been satisfied for years - until now.'

'Kyle, she's probably been on more hotel pillows than a chocolate mint, so don't flatter yourself,' Dee's wit continued to be cutting.

'Probably. She was pure filth. It was like a hippo's yawn down there. She's consistently stepping out on hubby if you ask me. Unless he has a cock like a can of Stella,' he mused.

'How old was she then?' I asked.

'Forty-eight. Not the oldest I've been with, but certainly one of the fittest.'

'Not the way she looked this morning. She looked like she'd brushed her hair with a toffee apple.'

'Still didn't stop me. Always have to get one in again in the morning.'

'Surprised you had the energy after last night.'

'A bit of beak helped. Powerful stuff the shit they gave us last night.'

'I assumed coke played a part in that energetic hammering. This might be a stupid question, but do you reckon you'll ever get a girlfriend?' I asked.

'You're right, Ricky. Stupid question. What do I want a girlfriend for? I'm in a band that's killing it and I can get laid by fit girls whenever I want. A relationship will only stop that.'

'Forget I asked.'

'Look, men and women aren't meant to live together. We're animals, we're meant to fuck. All this co-habiting, family bollocks is just what society and the powers that be expect from us to keep us under control. Living with someone just leads to stagnation in life, where creativity suffers. I can do without that. I'm in my prime and haven't even begun to peak yet.'

'That's one shallow way of looking at it, I suppose,' I said.

He continued, 'I believe that before you think you fancy someone and fall in love and get your heart broken and mope about, you should first pull yourself off to make sure you're simply not horny or just in lust. Save making a big mistake.'

I pissed myself at the theory. I was just about to add my own thoughts when something caught my eye on the back of Kyle's Calvin's.

'What the fuck is that, Kyle?'

We all shifted our eyes and clocked exactly what it was.

'For God's Sake! That's fuckin' disgusting!' Dee exclaimed.

A used condom was stuck to the arse of his boxers. Kyle laughed as he peeled it off.

'Occupational hazard,' he announced.

'Get out of here with that. That's awful!' I fired back.

He didn't listen and chased me around the room, teasing me with it as I jumped over both beds to get away from him. I sprinted out of the door faster than Usain Bolt to see Quince and Will stagger into the courtyard.

As Kyle saw them, he launched the missile in their direction. It struck Quince's chest and fell to the floor.

'What the fuck's that?' Quince screamed before seeing red when he realised what it was.

'Is that what I think it is? You sick fuck, Kyle,' he barked.

'Pick it up, you sicko,' Will ordered.

Kyle was in stitches.

'Where did that come from?' Quince asked.

'Ricky's arse.'

He adhered to their request and left to dispose of it properly back in his room.

Quince yelled after him, 'And wash your hands, scrubber.'

'What happened to you two?' I asked.

Quince explained, 'We partied with a bunch of college kids on their Spring Break. Things got crazy, and we ended up back at their hotel.'

'I woke up in an empty bathtub in some hotel room,' Will added.

'Where did you end up, Quince?'

'In bed with some big bird. And I don't mean fat. She was proper tall. I needed a Yellow Pages to stand on just to pull her. I'm knackered, but Ozzie messaged us demanding we get back cos we're leaving as soon as.'

Ozzie appeared at this point. He told us that Lynwood had called to say they'd managed to set up an interview with a girl from the reputable Hell-A magazine that evening.

While the lads went to gather their belongings, he turned to me. 'I spoke to Jamie this morning.'

'Oh yeah. Everything OK?'

'Everything's cool. I told him about the tour extension to Vegas and Bermuda. I advised that you should be there, so he should front up the cost.'

'How did he respond to that?'

'I had to talk him round at first, but I put our case forward, and he's agreed.'

'Cheers, Ozzie.'

'Have you decided whether you want to come or not? I think you should.'

'I think I will. I need to, don't I? Aside from helping the band, it's an amazing opportunity.'

'It is. Glad you're on board. Expect Jamie to text you shortly about it to confirm everything.'

We fell back into the groove of travelling and city hopping, leaving a trail of memories in our wake across the land we explored. There was still so much to see and experience as we approached the crucial leg of the tour in a city renowned for being one of the pioneers of modern culture. The next gig at the Whisky a Go Go was *the* big one. It was three days away, which gave us a chance to relax and prepare for what was to be the defining night.

We were back on track, and morale was high. With the Lynwood meeting booked for the following day, there was quiet optimism that everything was coming together.

We left Palm Springs and were back on roads that dissected the desert lands. 'Woodstock', by Matthew Southern Comfort came on from the playlist. The tune and lyrics defined the journey. I started to feel like I was becoming part of something special with the band, like a cog turning in something profound and monumental.

We meandered through the hills and eventually hovered above the colossus entity of Los Angeles. It was gargantuan and intimidating, totally belittling what I was used to in Manchester.

We dropped into the valley, and the Hollywood Sign waved at us from the east, embedded in the foothills. It was a momentous landmark to behold, and I felt like we were watching it on screen.

Our destination was meant to be two hours from Palm Springs, but the robust traffic had clearly not been factored into the journey. I had never seen anything quite like it. The five-lane freeways were gridlocked. Even when we came off one freeway to join another, we hit another army of congestion.

We finally approached Sunset Blvd, famed for so much throughout history: from movie references in Hollywood's cinematic golden age to the sixties riots, to the birth of a counterculture, to the absolute epitome of sex, drugs and rock 'n' roll. The place embodied debauchery, decadence, and devilishness. Under the dazzling lights, dreams could be made in a second, but they could easily be ended the same night in a pit of despair. That was a factor both equally as enticing and fearful for those daring to make something of themselves within the city's erratic clutches.

When we exited the litany of freeways, we grasped a feel for the metropolis. Towering billboards soared every fifty metres or so to advertise the latest films and TV shows due for release, evidencing the importance of the entertainment industry to the region.

The traffic eased, so with clear roads ahead, I fumbled through my iPod to pick a song to capture the spirit of our dart through the heart of Sunset Blvd.

With eight minutes to our destination, I found the perfect track to cement our arrival. I pressed play, wound the windows down, and let 'L.A. Woman' by the Doors steer us through the core of rock 'n' roll paradise. With the sun beating down, the song made the final minutes of the journey so much more upbeat and pulsating, especially when the thumping crescendo hit during the finale. I beat the steering wheel, Ozzie played the drums on the dashboard, and we bellowed out the lyrics as we passed of all places, Tower Records.

We took the following right turn onto Larrabee Street. After a short trundle up a hill, we pulled up outside our abode. What a tremendous location for those corrupted by the allure of the Strip. We were literally a stone's throw from Sunset Blvd, opposite the symbolic Viper Room.

Ozzie knew the apartment owners, Mary and Stephen, from back in the day. Their apartment doubled as an Airbnb, but Ozzie's friendship with them enabled us to get a cheaper deal. They usually didn't let so many people stay at once because they also lived in the house, but they were in Aspen, which meant an extra room was available.

Ozzie gave us a brief insight into them, explaining that they used to be in the music industry but had moved into theatre and art. Mary ran a theatre company called the Last Exit Players, and Stephen was a renowned local artist going under the company name, Dionysus Art. Stephen still played in a low-key band, and Ozzie said he was a gifted guitarist. They sounded like interesting people, and it was a shame we couldn't meet them and let them chaperone us around Hollywood.

The spacious apartment was a typical creative's living environment. It was artsy, with guitars and other instruments propped up in one corner. Several pictures and portraits that Stephen had done were stacked on one side of the room. He created impressive psychedelic portraits of legends within music and film. Ozzie gave strict instructions not to go anywhere near them for fear of damaging any of them. Books relating to entertainment were scattered about and piled up at various points in the living room. Posters of theatre shows covered the walls, all with 'Last Exit Players Presents...'

Dee took the opportunity to light a few of the incense candles provided to develop a relaxing ambience to help us settle in. Ozzie showed us the porch at the back that ran the length of the house. The cool thing about it was that it overlooked the car park to Tower Records. A few weeks earlier, Elton John had hosted his annual Oscar After Party there that saw many A-List celebrities attend. Now that would've been something special if we'd landed in L.A. in time to witness it.

CHAPTER 22

Later that night we were desperate to find what Sunset Blvd had in store for us. Before we could cut loose and take the Strip by storm, the band had to fulfil the pre-arranged interview obligation with a journalist named Anya from Hell-A Magazine. The meeting place was Rock & Reilly's Irish Bar, just a few doors down from the legendary Rainbow Bar & Grill. Just before we set off, Anya messaged Ozzie to say she'd arrived and had secured a booth at the back of the establishment.

The walk down the Strip was a sad and quiet affair. Gone were the days when the youth culture cluttered the streets. It was well-documented that the Strip was not how it used to be and had become more of a place to pay tribute to the hell-raising past. Despite being unable to live in that era, there was a deep yearning to act as though we'd been thrust back in time and relive and recreate the wildness of the Strip's history.

Minutes later, we were in Rock & Reilly's and set about finding Anya. 'The Stroke', by Billy Squier, played and summoned an immoral and sinful atmosphere in the joint. I was struck by the pictures that dominated the walls, especially captivated by the most famous

Jim Morrison image where he's shirtless and his arms are outstretched. For some reason, someone had stuck a makeshift yellow eye patch on him.

I scoped the rest of the décor until my reverie was broken when Kyle blurted out, 'Fuck me!'

I turned to see what the reason was for the outburst. It swiftly became apparent when I saw Anya waving us over to the booth at the end of the bar. She was an absolute knockout! Tall and statuesque with a pristine figure. Her long, wavy, mahogany-coloured hair flowed to just above the small of her back. Her cryptic eyes were as dark as a November night and as sharp as razors. Her bronzed complexion was flawless, and her forthcoming smile and prominent cheekbones made you weak at the knees. She wore a cropped black leather biker jacket that reflected her stylish demeanour. Faded and distressed grey jeans were cuffed at the bottom to show her funky, black strappy shoes with a touch of bling that glimmered when the light struck.

She greeted us warmly with a refulgent smile. Her West Coast accent was as strong as the air of confidence she portrayed. Kyle was the last to shake her hand and I'd never seen him so uncool. The usual Mancunian swagger vanished and was replaced by a goofy and spaced-out expression, like he was lost in another world and oblivious to his surroundings. I sat next to him in the spherical booth and nudged him while Ozzie engaged Anya about the interview.

'Oi! You OK?' I asked.

'Yeah, man…just…I don't know…shit.'

'You never know when that thunderbolt is going to come, my friend,' I taunted.

'What? Don't talk shit. It's nothing like that. Just… she's pretty cool, isn't she…for a journo?'

'What're you trying to say, dick? Like I only have a face fit for journalism, you mean? Thanks a bunch.'

'I was thinking more for radio, but you know what I mean. Stop being soft. Someone like her...you just wouldn't think she'd be a writer. More like a model or an actress or something.'

'We're in L.A., though. Your average admin girl spending all day photocopying is probably model standard.'

'Not like her. She's absolutely beautiful, man.'

'Thunderbolt.'

'Fuck off. You know I'm not like that and don't believe in that shit.'

'Well, maybe you should have a wank to see if you're just horny or if it's lust,' I joked.

'Touché, you bastard.'

Anya spoke louder for us all to hear after chatting with Ozzie. 'I'm psyched to be talking to you guys. I'm a huge fan, and I think you'll do great things here. I want to finish this interview tonight, ready to go live first thing tomorrow to help sell those last remaining tickets.'

'You mean we haven't sold out already?' Dee said, only half-joking.

'Close, but not yet. I'm sure you will by the time it arrives.'

Anya's interview was fluent and professional. She asked seemingly unscripted, insightful questions that got the band to be more talkative than the norm. Kyle had always been standoffish in all the interviews I'd seen on the trip, preferring to let Dee take centre stage. He was at the forefront of the questions on this occasion, but he bumbled his way through awkwardly. It didn't go unnoticed by the rest of us as we glanced at each other. I guessed that in every other interview with a female lead, he didn't give a shit and acted as such. With a girl he fancied, it was a whole new ball game.

After a solid half hour interview that ultimately went well, Anya was done and thanked the band for their time. Will asked her to stay out for a drink, but she declined, citing that she wanted to work on the interview.

As she left, she said, 'I can't wait to see you guys play live. I'll be reviewing the show. Here's my card if you need anything before then.'

She handed it to Ozzie.

We all said bye, and Kyle shouted, 'See you later, alligator.'

I detected her brow furrow at the nerdy comment. After she'd gone, the band ripped into him big time.

'See you later, alligator? What. The. Fuck. Was. That?' Quince said first.

'What? That's a perfectly legitimate way of saying bye.'

'Yeah...if you're Alan Partridge. Did you expect her to reply, "In a while, crocodile"? You sounded a right dick,' Will ridiculed.

'No, I didn't,' he argued.

I stepped in. 'I think Kyle got hit by the thunderbolt.'

'Fuck off, no I didn't.'

'Oh, you did. Why have you gone red?'

'Aww, is the little guitar hero in love with the pretty journalist?' Dee teased further.

'You can all go fuck yourselves. I'm going for a piss.'

We all laughed as he left.

'Can't say I blame him. Jesus!' Quince said.

We left Rock & Reilly's and made the short trip to the Rainbow Bar & Grill, an essential stop for rock 'n' roll fans. My heart skipped a beat as the Whisky a Go Go came into view on the corner, but I refrained from getting on bended knee and worshipping outside one of the temples of rock. There was plenty of time for such tributes at the band's gig.

Seconds later, the notorious sign of the Rainbow peeked out from the side of the building. The vertical writing with the rainbow-coloured background looked tacky and out of place attached to a barn-like building with a deep slanted brown roof, white railings, and worn brickwork around the sides. Yet, it was still mesmerising and mystical somehow and charmed you into its ethereal lair.

This last bastion of a celebrated era was steeped in so much rock folklore that the walls and furnishings could tell more stories than most people in their lifetime. Before he sadly passed away, Motörhead's Lemmy was a frequent fixture at the bar. John Belushi was said to have had his last meal there before his overdose. In the seventies, it was a hangout for the likes of Keith Moon, Alice Cooper, Micky Dolenz, Harry Nilsson, John Lennon, Ringo Starr, Neil Diamond, and Elvis Presley. As time went on it became known as *the* place to be for many of the eighties and early nineties rock stars, like Mötley Crüe and Guns N Roses (who shot part of the video for 'November Rain' in there too).

For a band like the Cutthroats, this was Valhalla. A place to drink with the Gods of Rock and personify the hellish side of the Californian spirit.

I could almost feel the Jack Daniels seep into me as we marched inside. Incredibly, as if the stars aligned, we walked in as the rumbling drumbeat to 'Overkill,' by Motörhead tore through the foyer.

The enigma of the Hollywood Hellraisers could be felt with every step. If you listened closely, you could almost hear them whispering their dirty little secrets from underneath the tables.

The sultry mood was harnessed by the dim lights that bounced off the satanic red leather sofas and booths. Rare pictures and tributes to legends plastered the walls, and the stools by the bar were emblazoned with the Jack Daniels logo.

I absorbed the sleepy history, thinking about how many icons past and present had drunkenly stumbled through the same walkways. I envisaged the Cutthroats being added to the Rainbow's hall of fame, thinking in years to come a bunch of kids would think similarly, wishing they were around to witness the Cutthroats drinking in the same establishment.

The place was busy, awash with the crème de la crème of the cool, the seasoned rockers, and the vagabonds of the rock revolution. Despite the toning down of the Strip over the years, it remained loaded with illustrious characters.

With no seats available inside to house our group, we moved outside. A few tables were free, so we sat and ordered beers and JD chasers. Given the importance of the Lynwood meeting the following day, you'd have assumed drinking would be kept to a minimum. But this was Sunset Blvd, the scene of so much hedonism and self-indulgence, so standard rules and regulations didn't apply.

The music continued to live up to the venue's reputation as 'Superhero' by Jane's Addiction played (the theme song to the show 'Entourage', which was filmed and set in Los Angeles). It was a song that received little airplay in the UK, but I had to remember where we were, and Jane's Addiction was a band cemented into the local scene.

Moments after ordering, a scruffy-looking man wearing a baseball cap poked his head from outside the awning. As he sheltered himself from the wind, he lit a crack pipe just above us, not even apologising for the intrusion. I'd never seen anyone smoke a crack pipe before. The fact that the act occurred on our first night on Sunset Strip made me wonder whether the Rainbow had its own rules, like the Vatican of rock 'n' roll.

Kyle was noticeably a little drunk after tanning the JD faster than the average consumer. He leaned into me and slurred, 'I can't stop thinking about Anya.'

'I knew it.'

'This never happens to me. What do I do?'

'Surely you don't need advice about women from me?'

'Usually, I wouldn't, but this is different.'

'If you feel that strongly then give her a call. Even though it pains me to admit it, you're blessed with enough good looks that she might even be interested.'

'Thanks, but I don't take good look compliments from dudes very well.'

'Relax. I'm not trying to mount you.'

'How do I contact her anyway?'

'She gave her card to Ozzie.'

He clicked his fingers and pointed at me.

'Really? That's interesting. What if she blows me out?'

'Then I'm sure you can find someone else in five minutes to take your mind off her.'

'Not this one. She was something else. Did I really make a prick out of myself?'

'A little, but she might have found it endearing. You weren't horrible...just weren't your usual, "don't give a fuck" self. But she doesn't know you, so she probably didn't even notice.'

'I'm going to get her number from Ozzie and call her.'

'Not a good idea to do that now, Kyle.'

'Why not?'

'Two reasons. One, you're drunk. And two, she's currently writing up the interview. Don't piss her off and disturb her.'

'You're right. Genius, man.'

He slithered off to the bar, and Dee took his place.

'What was all that about?' she asked.

'Boy has it bad for that journalist.'

'He needs to have a word with himself. I'm not having him moping onstage in a few days.'

Kyle returned with two shots each of the finest tequila, and even Ozzie allowed himself a snifter. The buzz of alcohol intensified the feeling of vitality as all thoughts of drinking sensibly were lost. We chose to stay in the Rainbow all night. Why would we move?

Will and Quince had been chatting up a couple of promiscuous-looking girls, who left little to the imagination with their provocative dress sense. They asked Kyle to come over as the girls had asked about him.

He responded, 'I'm not in the mood, mate. Not tonight. Those two don't exactly look classy either.'

We all stopped in our tracks.

'This is serious,' Ozzie remarked in amazement.

Will was pleased. 'Fine by me. Might have a chance with the fittest one if you're out of the picture. Bass player surely trumps drummer,' he joked.

'But being disease-free counts for more than being riddled,' Quince fired back before asking, 'What about you Ricky? You wanna take a shot? Or are you still pining over Eva like *that* lovesick puppy pining over Anya? You don't want to miss out like you did last night.'

'Just take advantage of the fact Kyle is out of the picture and have your pick of them. If I came over, you'd be at a disadvantage again,' I joked.

They brushed off my claim with a mocking laugh and left to flirt some more.

Dee, Ozzie, Kyle, and I were engrossed in drunken conversation while the other two entertained at the bar. The potency of the tequilas, mixed with the copious bottles of Budweiser, had made me fall into a deep ravine of inebriation. Kyle continued to throw them back at a much faster rate than us. It got to the point where Ozzie had to advise him to slow down. He listened, and in his drunken stupor, apologised. 'Sorry, guys. That girl. She got me. She got me good.'

His plight became a source of humour. The once cocksure, 'love them and leave them' attitude had deserted the man, reducing him to a cheap rom-com version of himself.

Later on, I found myself stumbling to the restroom upstairs. I weirdly looked forward to taking a piss in a room where the ghosts of the past indulged in titillation and depravity.

I stepped in, and my mindset immediately shifted as I heard a bang against the closed cubicle door and what seemed like a muffled sound with staggered breathing. At first, I thought it was drug-related, considering it not to be beyond reckoning given what I'd seen before in Manchester.

Slightly concerned, I called, 'Everything OK in there?'

A voice cried out, 'Ricky? Ricky? Is that you?'

I instantly recognised who it was. 'Will?'

'Thank God it's you.'

'You OK?'

'I need help!'

'What's goin' on?'

'Please, just help.'

I tried to push the door, but it only opened a few inches before it wedged.

'No, don't open the door. I'm stuck!' he yelled.

'What do you mean, stuck? What have you done now?' I shouted.

'It's hard to explain.'

Completely confused and a bit worried, I went to the next stall, pegged myself onto the toilet rim, lifted my body up onto the side of the cubicle and peered over. I instantly had to avert my eyes and cringed at what greeted me. To my horror, I looked down on Will standing with his back against the door, arms aloft, both hands handcuffed at the wrists and locked in on a hook above his head. His plain white t-shirt was pulled tightly over his head to cover his face, but bizarrely of all, his jeans and boxers were around his ankles, and his cock and balls swung freely.

'What the actual fuck, Will?!'

'Don't ask!'

'Don't ask? Fuck that! This needs explaining.'

He paused before admitting, 'That fuckin' bitch robbed me.'

'How?'

'Thought I was gonna get a blowjob, proper sweet-talked me into coming in here, whispering all sorts of dirty shit in my ear, but she tricked me. Took my cash out of my pocket when I was trapped. Couldn't do a thing about it.'

'How have you ended up cuffed?' I asked.

'I thought she was being kinky.'

Although I should've been more distressed, the sight of him restrained, talking through his t-shirt, which looked like a gimp mask, with his jeans around his ankles, had me in stitches.

'It's not fuckin' funny! I can hardly fuckin' breathe with this over my head.'

'I'm sorry, mate, but you're not seeing what I'm seeing.'

'Get me out of here!' he demanded.

'How? I don't have a key for those cuffs. I'm going to have to get help.'

'Yeah, involve more people in this!' he barked.

'I'm going to have to. Let me take a picture first and have it as the main photo for the next blog,' I joked.

'I will absolutely murder you if you do.'

The laughter grew louder, and I was creased over the side of the cubicle. To salvage some sort of dignity, I reached down from above and pulled his t-shirt from over his head. His hair was ruffled, and his face was florid with embarrassment.

'Cheers, dude. That's better. I can breathe now.'

He took a few deep gasps.

'I'll get help,' I said.

'No, wait. You're gonna have to pull my jeans up.'

'Bollocks to that.'

'Please, Ricky. I'm begging you. I can't have people coming in here with me like this. I'll get annihilated for the rest of my life.'

I thought for a second, thinking the poor sod had suffered enough, so I agreed to help, but I wasn't ecstatic about what it meant for me in terms of what I had to do.

'You owe me big for this,' I stated.

I climbed on top of the stall, swung my legs over and dropped down onto the toilet seat. It was a cramped space, not meant to house two grown men.

I bent down to help pull his jeans up, but I struggled to keep my head away from his crotch whilst simultaneously not having any part of my body touch the inside of the toilet.

'For fuck's sake!' I yelled. 'I can't do this without getting close to that thing waving about. This is ridiculous.'

'You're gonna have to, mate. I'll buy you a pint.'

'A pint? You owe me more than a pint for this.'

I was trying my best not to face forward, but it was difficult to reach for his jeans and pull them up without turning my head in such a confined space. As I did, Will's flaccid shaft was inches from me, and I caught an eyeful of it.

'For fuck's sake! This is disgusting. This goes beyond my job description.'

'Just pull them up quick like ripping off a plaster.'

'If I pull them up quickly, I might trap your conkers. You don't want that. You *would* have to be wearing fuckin' skinny jeans too, wouldn't you?'

Unable to divert my eyes, I saw that his girth had elevated slightly, and I recoiled as it looked to attack me.

'Are you enjoying this?' I screamed.

'Fuck no!'

'Then why did it move?'

'It hasn't. Stop looking.'

'I can't fuckin' help it!'

In one quick motion, I pulled his jeans up and nearly trapped his right bollock.

'I'm scarred! You can get fucked if you think I'm fastening them for you,' I said,

'That's fine. At least I'm covered.'

'I feel sick.'

'You feel sick? How do you think I feel? Not only have I been robbed of about fifty dollars, but I'm also stuck here like a fuckin' prisoner of war,' he said.

'I need to erase this from my mind, and fast.'

Despite what I'd just witnessed, I couldn't help but laugh. I looked up to see that he wasn't chained to the hook at the door, but the cuffs had been placed over it to lock him in. I lifted him up a few inches so he could raise his arms to release himself. Cuffs still on, he was at least semi-free and could fasten his own jeans.

I jumped back over into the next stall and went straight to the taps, where I vigorously washed my hands, commenting, 'If I could only do this with my mind.'

Will staggered through the stall.

'Cheers, man. You're a lifesaver. I can't believe this happened.'

'Oh, I can. It was only a matter of time before one of you would land yourself in this kind of trouble, given the way you chase it.'

'C'mon, we need to get out of here. I need to get these cuffs off somehow.'

Seconds later, Quince barged in.

He shouted, 'What's going on? I've just seen those two girls do a runner while I was with the others.'

Seeing Will cuffed, he rightly asked, 'What the fuck are you doing with those on?'

Hearing what had happened, Quince erupted with jack-knife laughter and practically fell to the floor in hysterics.

We made our way downstairs. Will told the rest of the crew the story and received a similar reaction.

Ozzie said, 'I don't know how you do it, I really don't. You've outdone yourself this time. How do you get into shit so easily? It just follows you, doesn't it? What the fuck were you thinking?'

'I was thinking how cool it'd be to have sex in the Rainbow.'

'Good answer, to be fair, Boss,' Quince jumped in.

Ozzie tried to remain serious, but when Will's answer sank in and the story hit home, he couldn't contain his laughter, which echoed throughout the bar.

'Imagine Ricky wasn't the one who came in first, and you had to explain how you got into that situation to someone else?'

'They'd have arrested you for sure,' Kyle said.

'He needs arresting,' Dee added.

'She's the one who needs arresting,' Will retorted.

'Good point. I better let the bar know what's happened,' Ozzie said.

'Don't go into too much detail, please Ozzie. Just say I was pick-pocketed,' Will begged.

'Bollocks!' Ozzie said.

Ozzie called Will over, and he gave an account of what happened. Hearing him retell the tale had us in stitches.

Apparently, there had been one or two reports of similar incidents in the West Hollywood area in the past few weeks, but this was the first time the Rainbow was a target. The barman sniggered as if to say that everyone else in the bar would've known better, but not this deviant. He had a point.

The same barman took mercy on Will and brought out a small hacksaw from the back, freeing him in minutes. He rubbed his wrists afterwards, and you could see the inflammation from where the cuffs had dug into him.

We left the Rainbow, and Dee and I stopped at Terner's Liquor Store on the corner of Larrabee St next to The Viper Room. It was somewhat of a landmark with its bright yellow, squared sign and was often seen in the background when filming took place on the streets of Sunset Blvd.

A crate of twenty-four bottles of beer and a bottle of whisky was more than enough to see us through as we churned over the day's events, which inevitably ended in howls of laughter.

It had been one hell of a first night in Los Angeles for so many reasons. The aura of Sunset Strip hadn't failed to live up to its mystical hype.

CHAPTER 23

My first morning in Los Angeles was a bright, smoggy affair, not eased by the Sunset Strip-induced hangover.

As usual, Ozzie was up and working on his laptop at the breakfast bar. The first thing he did was show me Anya's interview for Hell-A Mag that had gone live. It was an engaging piece that painted the band in a glowing light. The picture she used of them sitting in the booth at Rock & Reilly's made the band look right at home in their L.A. surroundings, and she played on that fact. The reputation of Hell-A Mag was evident by the number of likes, comments and shares the article had already received, even though it had only been up for a couple of hours. It reminded me that I needed to write an update for Sonic Bandwagon around Palm Springs.

With a bastard behind the eyes, I persevered with the review. I managed to find some sort of coherence and send it off. When the Cutthroats were as good as they were that night, and Palm Springs was as lively as it was, the words rattled out of me.

Shortly after, I emailed it to Jamie. He responded: *'Will have a read later. Just to let you know, the inter-*

view with Ozzie will go live today. Very good. You put a good spin on it. Don't listen to him though. He's not quite as interesting as you've made out. He's a twat really. Haha.'

I showed Ozzie the text, and he chuckled. 'Cheeky fucker. Reply to him, call him a tight arse and ask him to tell you about the Oasis gig at Wembley in 2000. That'll shut him up.'

I relayed Ozzie's response, and Jamie replied: '*No chance! Tell him to keep schtum! Btw, I've got your flight details for Bermuda and booked you into the same hotel as the band in Vegas in New York New York. Tell Ozzie if I don't see any noticeable return for forking out for this then I'm gonna reveal what he did in 1998 at the Verve gig.*'

Ozzie laughed when I showed him the text, but he refused to be drawn into revealing the hidden meaning when I quizzed him about the two events.

He explained, 'You never know when I might need that story to use for leverage against Jamie, so it stays between us. We have an understanding. He knows I won't tell on him, and I know he won't tell on me.'

I changed the subject and asked him, 'Have you ever met this guy, Lynwood?'

'Not in the flesh. I've heard he's a bit arrogant, but he gets the job done. If he comes up with the goods, I'm happy to take his shit and let him go on with himself.'

'Are CEOs ever nice people?'

'Usually not in this industry, and I've seen my fair share of arseholes.'

The meeting with Charles Lynwood was booked for early afternoon. The offices weren't far from our apartment, located further up the road at the corner of La Cienega and Sunset Blvd, so we decided to walk up and grab a bite to eat on the way.

We dived into a classy institution called State Social House. It was noon when we arrived, and the place was busy, awash with young, conceited yuppies with money to burn. The fact they were sipping champagne midweek spoke volumes. Was this just the Los Angeles way of life? I couldn't tell, but I wouldn't be surprised if it was the standard practice amongst even the low-level office staff.

My addiction to Philly cheesesteaks forced my hand on the menu. It arrived with a side order of sumptuous crispy fries and was animalistically devoured.

We still had time after eating, so we entered a book shop called Book Soup. We were attracted by the substantial array of reading material on music and entertainment displayed outside. It was how a bookstore was supposed to look, crammed to the rafters with a multitude of genres. The music and film sections weren't small like most UK outlets. Instead, it was a couple of large walls dedicated to the history of both genres, with a treasure trove of rare books I never knew existed.

Walking further up Sunset Blvd, we arrived at a flash building with glass panel doors on either side of a revolving entrance. The words 'LYNWOOD MUSIC' gleamed in silver above. We filed through to a contemporary and chicly designed space with marbled columns and spotless tiles that glossed the floors. You wouldn't have thought it was a record label from the number of suits knocking about. We were the only casually dressed dudes in there.

Ozzie approached the front desk to let the young, pretty receptionist know of our arrival. The band looked tense, under pressure and agitated. The realisation that this was their big chance to get a contract that would change their lives weighed heavily.

A well-dressed man appeared from the elevators to the right of us and confidently strode over. He was only small, but he had a stocky frame. His slim-fitted, light pink shirt clung to his chest underneath a silvery, well-cut Hugo Boss suit, complete with a dark pink tie and expensive brown, shiny oxford shoes. It was all a little too flashy for the rock 'n' roll scene for my liking. His polished face had been evidently moisturised and preened, and heavy product helped to coif his hair. His teeth were exceptionally white when he smiled, but his face barely moved an inch due to the amount of Botox underneath his bronzed skin. He was an exaggerated caricature of a briefcase-carrying wanker parading through Spinningfields on his way to order a mojito on a Tuesday evening.

Kyle commented from the side of his mouth, 'Check out fuckin' Wolf of Wall Street here?'

Lynwood spoke when he neared us. 'Ah! Cutthroat Shambles!' His arms were outstretched before he introduced himself grandiloquently. 'Charles Lynwood, CEO of Lynwood Music. A pleasure to finally meet you all.'

He shook hands with Ozzie and the boys, but his eyes noticeably lit up somewhat lecherously when he spotted Dee. He took her hand, adding the word 'enchanted' to the greeting as he clasped it with both of his. It nearly made me vomit.

He moved towards me, and I was struck by the niff of his aftershave that made my eyes sting.

'Who are you?' He pointed at me patronisingly. I had an urge to slap his hand away.

Through gritted teeth, I introduced myself, 'I'm Ricky. Tour blogger and writer for Sonic Bandwagon.'

Ozzie butted in, 'Ricky's day-to-day blogs have been ace and helped generate more interest back in the UK and in the States. He's been doing a great job.'

'Ah yes, I've heard about these blogs. Who do you work for again?'

'Sonic Bandwagon.'

'Never heard of them, but I'm sure they do a job on some level,' he said dismissively.

'We're local but up-and-coming.' My tone was short.

He turned away and adopted a power stance to assert his dominance.

He said articulately, 'I've heard many great things about you from my A&R guys and set up several promos for you. You met Anya from Hell-A last night, didn't you?'

The mere mention of Anya's name grabbed Kyle's attention.

'Yeah. The interview went live this morning and reads well,' Ozzie answered.

'She's a doll, isn't she? Gorgeous. I bet you boys had your tongues out like lap dogs?'

Kyle scowled.

Lynwood continued, 'We've got lots to discuss, so let's head to my office.'

He collared some poor intern and demanded that he bring a couple of bottles of red wine to his office. As we headed back to the elevator, Lynwood turned and stopped me.

'Sorry, this is a meeting for the band and their manager only. No press. You understand, right?'

The guy tested my nerve, but Ozzie nodded to suggest it was fine. The suit was probably right. I had no business being there, but his condescending tone irked me. I'd have loved to have thrown a left, right, goodnight at him to wipe that pompous smirk off his stupid face.

Again, through gritted teeth, I replied, 'No problem,' before saying to Ozzie, 'Let me know when you're out. I'm going exploring.'

I excused myself and left the building.

With L.A. at my disposal and La Cienega Blvd so close, I knew what I wanted to do.

Since I am obsessed with the Doors and Jim Morrison, it was impossible to come to Los Angeles and not seek out significant places in their illustrious history. I'd conducted some research beforehand, courtesy of www.rayandrobby.com, so I knew I was close to many Doors hotspots. Eva messaged me as I began my trek: *'Hi! Are you OK? How was your first night in Los Angeles?'*

Heading straight down La Cienega to my first port of call, I messaged back: *'Hey! I'm great thanks. Last night was brill. I've got a hilarious story to tell you. How's you?'*

She replied quickly: *'I'm great. Just on my break at work. Thought I'd see how you are. What happened?'*

I regurgitated Will's endeavour and several laughing emojis followed. She asked what I was up to.

'The band are in a meeting with the record label who's interested in signing them. I'm not allowed in, so I'm on a Doors trail.'

She replied: *'You and your Doors obsession. You make me laugh.'*

'Imagine you were on a Genesis trail?'

'Oh my God! I would literally die. Anyway, enjoy yourself, break on through. Speak soon.'

Her Doors reference made me smile.

I strolled down La Cienega to visit the Alta Cienega Motel, where Morrison lived for a while. The room he stayed in was a tourist attraction and had become a shrine for zealous fans. I was told that the room was available to stay in overnight. If I'd known beforehand,

I may have been tempted to book in and drop acid in the hope that the man himself would appear to me in my trance. Now that would've been a trippy experience.

I trundled further down La Cienega and came across the old Elektra Records Studios where the Doors recorded 'The Soft Parade' and 'Morrison Hotel' albums.

I then took the short walk onto Santa Monica Blvd, which ran parallel to Sunset Blvd, and was where the official Doors offices used to be from 1968-72. It was perhaps more famed for being where the entire 'L.A. Woman' album was recorded. Both Sunset Blvd and Santa Monica Blvd featured heavily in the Doors' history. By walking those roads, I felt like I followed in their enigmatic shadow.

I ventured further down Santa Monica, where the mood became a hub of liveliness as I hit 'Boystown', the openly gay community highlighted by a cluster of colourful buildings. It literally was 'Boystown' as I couldn't see any females anywhere in the bars and cafes.

After I passed the epicentre of the sparkled pocket, I soon realised the notion that 'nobody walks in L.A.' was very much true. I was on one of the major roads in L.A. with an abundance of cars flying past, and I was one of only five people who walked down the road. It was bizarre.

I came across the famous Troubadour, another iconic venue from the sixties and seventies that helped launch many of the bands from that era, including the likes of Elton John, the Eagles and The Byrds, to name but a few. The place was closed, so I was disappointed that I couldn't stop for a lonesome pint and imagine what it would've looked like back in its heyday.

I circled back on myself towards the apartment and sauntered through the neighbourhoods to soak in the WeHo (West Hollywood) way of life. Everywhere seemed so peaceful, which was not a term usually associated with the city.

I arrived back at the apartment and still hadn't heard from Ozzie. I grabbed the car and headed up into the nearby hills of Laurel Canyon, the scene for so many tales from decades past. Many icons had resided there, including Mama Cass, Joni Mitchell, and David Crosby. They helped mould the reputation of the canyon into being one of the coolest places to live.

Still on the Doors trail, I found where Jim Morrison, and his girlfriend, Pamela Courson, lived on the Rothwell Trail off Laurel Canyon Blvd. The road was immortalised in the song, 'Love Street'. After that, I continued onto Wonderland Avenue, having read the fantastic book of the same name by Danny Sugerman, which was about the Doors and Iggy Pop at different points in time.

As I meandered through Laurel Canyon, I couldn't fail to notice what a nightmare the roads were. How did people drive on them? Apart from the rough condition, they were full of potholes and twisted and turned sharply throughout the hills and often narrowed so only one car could pass at a time.

I pulled up when my phone pinged and saw it was Ozzie.

'Hey! We're done. Where are you?'

'I'm in Laurel Canyon.'

'What are you doing up there?'

'I'm on a rock 'n' roll pilgrimage.'

'Well if you can tear yourself away, we've been invited to a gig tonight through Lynwood so we're going back to the apartment to get ready and we'll be out for 7pm.'

'On my way. How was the meeting?'

'Promising. Tell you when you get here.'

Back at the apartment, Ozzie filled me in on the outcome of the meeting. Lynwood hadn't committed to offering a contract, but he outlined what he *could* offer. He boasted of his contacts in the entertainment industry, saying he could have the Cutthroat's music played in films and TV shows. He had organised an interview the following day with a fabled radio station and DJ. It seemed like the meeting was positive, and the ball was rolling, but the band weren't quite over the line yet.

CHAPTER 24

Dusk fell across the City of Angels as we left the apartment. We ordered an Über to take us to the venue as Ozzie wanted to drink. The gig was in a place called Five Star, located Downtown, about forty-five minutes away.

Back on the freeways, the legend of the infamous L.A. traffic made itself known again. We passed through areas that highlighted the city's contrasting diversity as elements of deprivation and seediness dominated most of the drive. Whenever we drove under a bridge, there was a profusion of homeless people, evident by the wall of tents on the sidewalk. It was sad to see the obviousness of poverty that ransacked the city. I'd never seen it so clearly in one place before. Although the problems had been highlighted in Manchester, L.A. showed worrying levels of destitution, despite being known for its flamboyance.

We arrived at Five Star on the edge of Skid Row. The Über driver told us that the district wasn't the best area for tourists, so he practically threw us out of the moving vehicle on arrival before speeding away. The region was infamous for its high level of homelessness and longstanding history of police raids. I was immediately on guard and didn't feel too comfortable.

A brand new, sparkling white Land Rover Evoque pulled up and parked in a reserved spot by the entrance. Charles Lynwood stepped out and slammed the door shut. He was dressed like he'd come straight from the golf course and was sponsored by Pringle.

Kyle quietly joked, 'What's the difference between a hedgehog and a Land Rover?'

'What?' I replied.

'A hedgehog has pricks on the outside.'

I smirked and asked, 'What did you make of him?'

'He's a bit of a douchebag and a proper know-it-all, but he seems to know his stuff about the industry and has a load of contacts. Or he was just showing off and was full of shit.'

Lynwood strode over. 'Ah! My guys are here. You're on the guest list under my name so follow me.'

He conversed with the doormen, and we were let through. Despite apparently being in a bad neighbourhood, the venue was a cool little dive bar with a bohemian vibe. It resembled Night & Day in Manchester but was more spacious and nowhere near as hot and sweaty. Above the door inside were pictures of famous rock stars, including Jim Morrison, Janis Joplin, and Tom Waits.

Once in, Quince spotted Anya. 'Hey, isn't that the journo girl who interviewed us last night?'

'Yeah, I'm sure it is,' Will confirmed.

'Second chance saloon, Kyle,' Quince teased.

Kyle went white.

'What's up? Why have you gone pale?' Will goaded.

'I haven't... stop winding me up.'

'Proper lovesick.'

'Fuck you.'

'Are you going to talk to her?' I asked.

'Give me a minute.'

'Ha. I never thought I'd see you like this.'

'Shut up, she's coming over here.'

Anya stepped over to us. She looked just as stunning as the previous night.

'How are you doing, guys? Great to see you all again.'

Kyle responded first, 'Yeah, good seeing you too… I read your interview this morning. It was quality. Thanks for that.'

'Don't mention it. It's my job. It's a surprise seeing you all here,' she said.

'We're Lynwood's guests. He invited us down.'

'Ah yes, I forgot it's his bands on tonight.'

'Are they any good?' Kyle asked.

'Yeah, they're pretty cool. You're going to love them all. There isn't a main act tonight, it's a general showcase. He does these quite often. They're usually exclusive affairs for those in the business. Your show is half like that, I believe.'

Kyle blocked everyone off so only he was able to chat directly with Anya. His eyes sparkled after pushing past his awkwardness of the previous night, transforming into the charismatic kid he usually was. I never thought I'd see him so smitten by someone, especially after all the bullshit theories he'd spouted throughout the trip. I guess when the one comes along, all bets are off. I knew all about that from my reaction when I first laid eyes on Eva.

The first band, Electric Parlor, came on. Their brand of bluesy, psychedelic rock created a resounding buzz that harked back to a golden time. The band's dynamic was like the Cutthroats, with three male musicians, a female vocalist, and a tremendous amount of chemistry between them. They prided themselves on being an evolution of sixties and seventies psych rock, using Janis Joplin and Big Brother & The Holding Company as a base to experiment further. They did an excellent job of creating something similar, yet original, to the sounds of that period.

They were followed by Warchief, who were an all guns blazing heavy rock trio. The two guitarists were full throttle and fantastic, but they had a secret weapon in the shape of their enigmatic drummer, Mucho. The way he played was like Satan himself had risen from hell and taken up the drums. He commanded the whole stage and stole the show. My eyes and ears usually gravitated towards singers and guitarists, but Mucho was a focal point difficult to ignore. Quince had also locked onto him and spent the whole set singing his praises.

Dee joked, 'Better raise your game, Quince. I'm going to recruit him.'

'Take him. I'd happily step aside if this dude wanted to join us.'

The intense drummer looked the part too, with long hair, bare chest, tattoos, sunglasses, just a picture of complete coolness. He resembled Carlos Santana and possessed a talent that equalled Santana's genius on guitar. He was so good that he was let loose to deliver an exceptional ten-minute drum solo. I'd never seen a drum solo at that level before in the underground scene. It was stadium worthy. I'd seen live solos by Mick Fleetwood and others like Buddy Rich on TV, but Mucho was up there with the best of them.

The final band to play and round off the night was Winachi, who offered something a little different to the rock 'n' roll onslaught witnessed so far. Six guys of different cultures and ethnicity took to the stage, covering vocals, keys, two guitars, bass, and drums. There was a certain swagger about them that reminded me of bands from the North of England. They were a hybrid of electro, rock, soul, funk, hip hop, and dance, creating something refreshing and exciting.

Full of confidence and with an unassailable stage presence, their following devoured the body-shaking grooves and spent the entire set dancing. It was like an extension of the Hacienda music but modernised for today's audience. Their most notable track was the hip-shaking, 'Funky But Chic' – the clue to the vibe was in the title.

All the bands looked the part and carried a natural rock 'n' roll essence about them that was sometimes lost in the UK. Long hair, tattoos, bare chests, bandanas, beads, beards, cowboy hats, and good-looking individuals. They encapsulated the entire spectrum.

Ozzie was correct in his assessment of the Cutthroats and the British market. The crowds in the States would be more receptive to their songwriting. They were an extension of the music from a celebrated, timeless age. It was no coincidence that the greats were still lauded. Their music was still relevant, so why shouldn't an underground band like Cutthroat Shambles stamp their own authority on it and enjoy similar success?

After the set, Lynwood invited us backstage to meet the bands that had played.

He turned to us. 'Tonight, I'm doing a producer friend of mine a favour and have invited girls from a TV game show to join us backstage.'

'Which show?' Ozzie asked.

'It's called Date Night.'

'Date Night? What's that?'

'It's like a dating game show. One guy has thirty girls to choose from and asks questions till he narrows it down to just one to take on a date.'

'Sounds a little like, "Take Me Out",' I said.

Lynwood continued, 'It's good for business. It's a popular TV show so it's beneficial for the bands to be seen with these girls and create some hype. Photos will probably end up in the media. Never underestimate the importance of what a snap with these girls can do for your career.'

Ozzie leaned into me. 'Told you about these little tricks of the trade, didn't I?'

'I never knew the extent it went to. It just feels too staged.'

'Been happening for years. It's more important now than ever to get noticed.'

'Maybe I'll latch onto a beauty and get my picture taken to promote Sonic Bandwagon,' I mused.

'I think you need to be in a band or on TV for it to work. These girls will be proper media whores and will do whatever's necessary for attention.'

'Like the Kardashians then?' I quipped.

'Yeah, something like that. They'll be like the modern-day groupie but have no clue or care about the music. When fame and fortune are so close, these girls will do anything. I've seen it thousands of times over the years. The one constant you can be sure of is that no matter how times change, certain basic instincts remain the same. A lot of impressionable young girls will always be fanatical about rock stars, fame, or both.'

Normally, Kyle would've been at the forefront of the meet and greet, but with Anya joining us backstage, his attention was firmly elsewhere.

Backstage was a large, darkened room filled with the bands, their entourages, 'Date Night' girls and suits. It was very different to the grime of previous gigs. There was an element of class, which felt wrong.

The Date Night girls were dressed in a way that had no business being at a rock concert: far too chic and fashionable to be backstage at a dive bar.

We were introduced to Electric Parlor and Warchief, who intermingled in the far corner. Both bands were humbled by our assessment of them, and they said they were looking forward to seeing the Cut-throats at the Whisky a Go Go.

The drummer of Warchief, Mucho, was as cool as his playing ability. He spoke passionately about music and drumming. Once Quince got into it with him, their conversation turned to the technical side, which was lost on me, so I left them to it.

I introduced myself to the two main guys and cre-ators from Winachi, who were already talking to Dee, Ozzie and Will. They were both gregarious and friend-ly. They were called Elsie Catflap and Tony California, which I presumed were stage names.

'Have a beer, bro,' Elsie offered.

I shook their hands, and Elsie said, 'I was just tell-ing the guys that we're supporting them at the Whisky.'

'Really? That'd be ace having you play beforehand, really liven the crowd up. I loved your set.'

'Cheers, bro.'

'Are you signed with Lynwood then?' I asked.

'Yeah, moved out here from New York six months ago when we signed.'

'How's it been goin'?'

'Things are moving. Just starting to get some high-profile gigs and our first big tour of the US starts in ten days. Can't wait to get on the road. Tonight's show, the Whisky gig, and one next week at The Mint are like warm-ups.'

Elsie and Tony proved to be great company throughout the night. They were intrigued by the Manchester music scene and revealed that part of the inspiration for their sound had come from the likes of Happy Mondays. Their ambition was to play a gig in Manchester. Ozzie stepped in and offered his services to help them when they wanted to fly across the Atlantic. He also gave them Bobby and Tien's contact details when they said that Tucson was a scheduled date for their upcoming tour.

The Date Night girls were scattered across the room, latching onto those with influence in the industry. It was like watching strippers operate, working the room for the fattest cash cow to milk. Naturally, Quince and Will somersaulted into the Venus flytrap. They were too superficial to not see through it. They encouraged pictures to be taken with the girls by some photographers working the room.

Ozzie had to remind Will to be careful and not fall into a similar dilemma as the previous night. Will brushed off his concerns.

Kyle was nowhere to be seen amongst the attention-grabbing. Usually the focal point, he had sloped off to a sofa at the back, chatting with Anya.

Lynwood had collared Dee while I was talking to the Winachi guys. I kept an eye on them as it hadn't escaped my attention that he had sequestered her away from any prying eyes. There was an element of flirting on his part, but Dee showed no sign of reciprocation. It could've been my dislike for him that clouded my judgement of the situation, but my gut feeling was that he wasn't all he seemed to be. When Dee managed to escape his clutches, she headed straight to us.

'Looks like he's taken a shine to you,' I commented.

'He's an L.A. slimeball.'

'I'm glad you think so too. What was he talking about? Seemed to be getting awfully close to you.'

'He was bragging about what he can do for us... *again*, and who he knows and how he built himself up from nothing. He's full of shit. I'm wary of people who brag about who they are. A lion doesn't have to tell me it's a lion.'

Ozzie argued, 'Just let him flex a bit of muscle, Dee. He's trying to impress you.'

'Yeah, I know what muscle he wanted to flex.'

'Did he try it on?' I asked.

'No, but I've got his cards marked. He's got no shot.'

The night swept by in a flash. Given how far we were from our apartment and the slightly haphazard area of Skid Row, we made the collective decision to leave together and order a taxi while we could. Quince and Will put up a bit of protest, but the thought of having to pay for a taxi themselves swayed their decision.

Before we left, Lynwood told us that he was hosting a party at his home in Laurel Canyon the following night, and we were welcome to attend. It seemed the given thing in Los Angeles was to be at some sort of event every night. It was relentless. Ozzie agreed to the invite, not wanting to cause offence and put any potential deal at risk. Personally, I didn't want to be anywhere near his house party and assumed it'd be packed full of snakes and sharks for sure.

In the taxi, Will was buzzing that he'd manage to have a kiss and a cuddle with one of the dolly girls from Date Night, putting some sort of right to the wrongs of the previous night. He and Quince were both a little worse for wear, having taken it upon themselves to plough through most of the free bottles of beer provided.

Kyle was relatively sober in comparison, obviously not wanting to embarrass himself in front of the delectable Anya. When it came to say his goodbyes to her, we had all kept a beady eye out to see how their evening would end. Incredibly, they parted with nothing more than a friendly hug. Kyle bore the brunt of our communal jibes in the taxi home. Will continuously wound him up, saying he was 'losing his touch' and had 'lost all his pulling power.' Kyle didn't rise to it.

The congestion on the freeways hadn't relented. The taxi driver confirmed that it was a common sight in Los Angeles, even at 2am. There was no way I could consistently stand such jams. I got pissed off in Manchester when a ten-minute drive at rush hour turned into twenty minutes, so my blood pressure would be through the roof if forced to endure this traffic every day.

CHAPTER 25

Not being too drunk from the night before, I was up early and used the quiet time to rattle off an update about landing in Los Angeles and what it meant for the band. I included my Doors trail excursion and a short review of the bands we watched the previous night.

Once it was submitted, I asked Ozzie what the plan was.

'They've got a radio interview at noon, but then we're free until Lynwood's soiree later,' he answered.

I rolled my eyes. 'Oh great. I can't wait for that.'

'You don't like him?'

'Not really. He's a jumped-up, pompous, up-his-own-arse, smarmy prick.'

'Not a fan then?' he jested.

'Hardly. What do you think of him?'

'I'm not a cactus expert, but I know a prick when I see one.'

I spat out my coffee.

Ozzie continued, 'But for how much of a twat he is, he's good at what he does. If we sign with him, then things should take off.'

'I guess that's all that matters,' I surmised.

Once everyone was up, showered and fed, we took the twenty-minute drive to KLOS-FM, a respected and well-loved rock radio station, for an interview and acoustic session.

The radio interviewer was called Jimmy Grace. He was in his mid-fifties, over six-foot tall and looked a rock enthusiast, dressed the part in all black with long, black greasy hair and stylish sunglasses. He bubbled with energy when he greeted the band, stating that not many bands from Manchester had been on his show.

Ozzie and I were not allowed to sit inside the studio, but we observed through the glass window and could hear the interview through the speakers outside. Dee took the lead after Kyle's brief stint. She was super charming and came across exactly like the star she was born to be. She was engaging and humorous, displaying the intelligence and depth that made her a profound songwriter and attractive character. The lads chipped in from time to time, but it was clear where most of the attention was focused.

The two acoustic songs they performed live were 'Lifetime Sunshine' and the heart-rendering, 'Curious Morality'. Jimmy played full versions of 'Rock N Roll Heaven' and 'Two Million Heart Beats' to demonstrate their true prowess. The Whisky gig was heavily promoted, and stories from the road were shared. Jimmy laughed at what he heard. He brought up the arrest as he'd read about it in my blogs, but the band made light of it. I prayed to God that the lads didn't get too eager when pressed for more stories and reveal catching me on the phone back in El Paso, especially as I'd messaged Eva about the interview beforehand and she was listening in (thankfully, they didn't embarrass me).

Dee spoke highly of Ozzie and me in the interview, which made me proud. She promoted the blogs, saying that I'd been documenting the trip and they could be read on the Sonic Bandwagon website. She probably doubled the number of readers in one shout. Some people have a natural flair for making people listen, and Dee had that quality in abundance.

The interview concluded, and Jimmy said he'd loved every minute of the hour and a half. He said he'd continue to play their music and plug the gig for the rest of that day and the next. He was full of praise for the live acoustic performance and adored the recorded songs he played. He also stated his intention of getting himself down to the gig. Ozzie said he'd put his name on the guest list.

There was plenty of time left to enjoy the rest of the day. With a city as vast and culturally diverse as Los Angeles at our disposal, we had our pick of places to visit. We settled on a trip to the famous Venice Beach.

We passed through Beverly Hills, and I couldn't get 'Axel F', the theme tune to 'Beverly Hills Cop', out of my head. We didn't hit the heart of the famous Rodeo Drive, but we caught a glimpse of some of the mansions the area boasted. Will's question about whether 'Pretty Woman' was filmed in those parts was unexpected and met with laughter.

Once we passed Beverly Hills, the areas became a little less affluent, and the disturbing images of homelessness transpired yet again. Underneath every bridge that spanned the freeways, the tents and trolleys of those more unfortunate littered the sidewalks. It was apparent on most streets on that side of the city. It was eye-opening and upsetting to see just how much poverty resided in a city famed for so much wealth and glamour. I don't profess to know the ins and outs of the homeless or the policies of the American government, but surely something more could be done. It isn't one of America's proudest achievements.

I was excited to see Venice Beach, given its reputation. My anticipation invoked images of the summer of love. I expected to see the promenade brimming with cool people dressed in hippie attire who enjoyed nothing more than carrying on the 'good vibrations' left over from a glorious period. I thought the shops and fashion would be quirky and eclectic, like Afflecks Palace, which was an emporium of eclecticism and a totem of indie commerce in Manchester's Northern Quarter.

We parked a couple of blocks from the beach and came across a landmark I desperately wanted to see. It appeared perfectly from where we joined the walkway. The famous Jim Morrison mural, known as 'The Morning Shot', was plastered on the side of one of the buildings on the beachfront. I marvelled at it for a couple of minutes before having an obligatory photo taken in front of it and then sent it to Eva.

Around the other side was the painting of Arnold Schwarzenegger in his younger bodybuilding days. It signified that we were on Muscle Beach, another iconic attraction where the gym was on the beach itself. It was meant to be the place that started the age of bodybuilding and gym fitness. Outside was a poser's paradise as ripped up 'Sted Heads' paraded around the court.

As we hit the promenade, my expectations of Venice Beach exceeded reality. I was left disappointed, and a little unnerved. It was busy but not necessarily full of tourists. It seemed full of unkempt mountebanks and swindlers looking to hustle, manipulate and steal. I was on my guard and walked with my hands in my pockets to stop any smash and grab attempt on my wallet.

The homeless problem that inundated the streets on the way down had flooded the beach itself. You didn't see that in the brochure to promote the place, but it was visible in droves. The grassy areas that linked the beach to the shops were filled with the less fortunate, and it was a sobering slice of truth once again.

It wasn't long before we became targets for the hustle. Three youths, who looked like a cross between the cast of East 17 and House of Pain, menacingly approached us with a walk drenched in purpose and attitude. They wore beanies, white vests and baggy jeans that showed half their boxer shorts.

The taller of the three had a botched attempt at a goatee, and he said, 'Yo! You wanna help out a couple o' homies and listen to our hip hop demo?'

Dee answered, purely to stitch me up, 'You guys are in luck. This guy writes reviews for a music magazine. He'll review your tunes.'

I stared with dagger eyes at Dee. The youths focused on me as Dee and the band turned away, sniggering.

'Yo, fo' real? You can hook me up?'

Panicked, I responded, 'Sorry, it's not my area. I don't review rap.'

'Why? What's wrong wit rap?'

'Nothing. It's just not my area to review.'

'How's abouts you pass dis demo onto your peeps and dey get us a record deal. I wanna get paid mutha fucka!'

'I can take the CD and pass it on when I get to England.'

'En-ger-land. Yo, you's all from En-ger-land? You's know Tim Westwood, man?'

Failing to see why I would, I politely answered, 'No, unfortunately, I don't. Give me a CD, and I'll pass it on.'

'Ah Ah! You gotta pay for dis.'

'I don't have any money on me, just a card.'

Big mistake.

'No problem. There's a ATM up 'ere. We'll waits witchoo while yo gets some dollar.'

Yeah, like fuck, lads.

Sensing that the situation was sharply turning into daylight robbery, Dee spoke up, 'Sorry, guys. Maybe next time. We've got a meeting to get to.'

One of the youths addressed Dee, 'Hey! Yo wanna go on a date later? I'll shows you round Venice.'

Dee politely declined the offer. We walked away, but they followed and continued their astute sales pitch. They eventually gave up the ghost, with one shouting, 'Dat bitch don't work for no music mag.'

We lost them amongst the public, and I confronted Dee. 'For fuck's sake. Why did you say I worked for a music mag?'

'For a laugh. Watching you squirm was so funny.'

'They could've been carrying guns out here.'

'You've seen "Boyz n the Hood" too many times.'

We carried on our stroll down the promenade, where the buildings were decorated with imaginative street art. The walkways were besieged with entertainers, from fortune tellers to buskers, to people in costume and yoga practitioners. Mini stalls selling all kinds of quirky stuff were scattered around. One shop even sold a selection of classy looking crack pipes (if there was such a thing). It was like a zoo, a haven for scammers and schemers.

The odour of marijuana swirled and lingered in the air. It was so strong that we got a little buzz off it just from walking around. A pharmacy called 'The Green Doctors' sold cannabis and was subtly hidden by a bright, green-coloured shop face. Weed had been legalised in Los Angeles, and it was easy to purchase.

Kyle and Will discussed buying some before Quince rightfully pointed out that they hadn't had to pay for it so far this trip, so why start now?

We continued our mosey and constantly came across something bizarre, culminating with the Venice Beach Freakshow. I wasn't even curious to see what was inside.

Venturing off the promenade towards the paths that led to the beach, we joined a gathering at a skate-park rink where teenagers showed off their impressive skills. The beach itself was huge. Miles upon miles of golden white sand extended as far as the eye could see around distant coves and shaped itself around the Pacific coastline.

Dee was sceptical about taking off her flip-flops to feel the sand between her toes. She feared stepping on a needle or something similarly disgusting. It wasn't so far-fetched to think something lurked beneath the sand, given the nature of the people who roamed around. There was obviously a lackadaisical attitude towards narcotics.

The seafront became less bustling further up. A bar advertised food, booze and a 'famous jukebox', so the decision on where to get a drink and a bite was made for us by simple publicity. The familiar smell of classic American food choked the air as the music volume towered above the chatter of the lively customers. 'California Girls' by the Beach Boys played. With plenty of surfer girls with bikini bods flaunting their assets in and around the bar, the song reminded us of the standards the L.A. girls aspired to.

We took a seat and ordered beers and food. After getting over the initial fear and shock of the reality of the busy drag of Venice Beach, my mood calmed, and I began to enjoy the sights. I headed straight for the jukebox, designed in a way where you could flip through

CDs at the press of a button. It featured a wide-ranging eclectic mix of blues, rock, prog, punk, metal, psych, and grunge - from the fifties to the present day. There were a lot of bands listed that I hadn't even heard of, but judging from the album cover shots, they were from the seventies. Even those bands I did know had the obscurer albums and songs listed. I stuck enough money in for ten songs and picked ones rarely heard in Manchester bars.

Looking out onto the stunning ocean view with the company I was in, I was overcome with a wave of emotion. I took stock of where I was and how life had twisted entirely in less than twelve months. I had been a nobody, a man with a distant dream and no plan. I'd been trapped in a relationship I didn't know was doomed, working for an insurance company in customer services and devoid of motivation. Fast forward one year, and I was sitting in a bar on Venice Beach with a band that I'd been writing about. I felt the need to say a few words to mark the occasion.

'I've got to say, I'm having a great time. I know you didn't invite me, but I can't thank you enough for the opportunity. I'll never forget it.'

'Don't be going all soft and mushy, Hot Shot,' Dee mocked.

'It's been great having you here, kid,' Ozzie said. He raised his bottle again and proposed another toast. 'To the journo!'

Everyone repeated and drank again.

Will changed the topic of conversation. 'Did you see some of those girls last night from that game show? They were insatiable. It put me off 'em a bit. I don't mind a groupie, but they were just fame hungry.'

'You still pulled one of them and were chuffed when you did, so don't try and pull the wool over our eyes,' Quince said.

'Yeah, but I was pissed. Now I've had time to think, I'm seeing it differently.'

'Since when did you develop morals and boundaries, Will?' Dee jested.

Ozzie interjected, 'I'm betting since he got robbed in the Rainbow.'

We all laughed.

'Someone took my photo too. I'll probably be in Variety today,' Will revealed.

'Yeah, if anyone knew who the fuck you were. I can see the headline now, "*She* was with *him* last night!"' Dee joked.

'I think I missed all this,' Kyle remarked.

'Yeah, you were too busy trying to get with Anya,' Quince said.

We all giggled as Will stood and wrapped his arms around Kyle's neck. He began smooching his cheek from behind and mocked, 'Oooh Anya, I love you so much. Let me count the ways.'

'Fuck off!' Kyle responded.

But Will wouldn't relent and proceeded to wrestle Kyle off his chair and onto the floor while continuing to kiss his cheek. We keeled over in stitches as most of the bar turned their attention to the ordeal. Even Kyle saw the funny side before eventually pushing Will away.

'He's got a soft spot for her. Have you seen him around her? Smitten kitten this one,' Ozzie goaded.

Quince carried on, 'I don't think she's into him anyway. Never known Kyle to have to wait past one night. If he's not closed the deal already, he's got no shot.'

'Don't be so sure. She was pretty interested in my guitar playing when that lad from Winachi lent me his.'

'What's that? Think I missed that one,' I interrupted.

'Oh, God. I forgot about that. Sickening. He sere-naded her like a poor immigrant gardener who can't have the rich girl,' Will recollected.

'We'll see, won't we,' Kyle casually fired back.

'I'm not sure it's a good idea to start hitting on journalists, Kyle. No good can come from it. Especially when you eventually get bored and piss her off. She's a top writer for Hell-A Magazine. She can make trouble if she wants,' Ozzie warned.

Dee, with her typical poker face agreed, 'Too true. Don't shit where you eat.'

'The forbidden fruit has just become more tempt-ing for him,' Quince joked.

'I'm not going to fuck it up. Trust me, she's not like that. This girl's cool. Did either of you see me make a move last night or get shot down? I didn't do shit.'

'So, you just want to be friends with her then. Oohh, friend...journo friend...L.A. friend,' Will said in his best 'Inbetweeners' tone of voice.

'Fuck off! Whatever will be, will be. Besides, she said she doesn't date musicians.'

Will fired in, 'Ahhh haha! That's it. She blew you out before you even got a chance to make a move. That explains it.'

Kyle blushed but couldn't help snickering at Will's taunts.

'You've finally peaked, Kyle.'

It hit a nerve as Kyle replied with an impassive look, 'Peaked? I haven't even begun to peak, and when I do, I'm gonna peak all over everyone.'

'I don't know what the hell that means,' Will said.

We were having a great time, drinking beer on Venice Beach in Los Angeles, and listening to mood-en-hancing music that added to the upbeat atmosphere. We shared stories, took the piss out of each other, and laughed constantly. It was one of the most enjoyable days we'd had. Sometimes, just being in the moment with friends, having a few drinks, talking about nothing in particular and absorbing the significance of where you are, is what makes something great. *'We were riding the crest of a high and beautiful wave,'* as one famous writer alluded to when expressing monumental feelings of importance and joy.

The desert sunrise was something to be marvelled at, but the same could be said of the Venice Beach sunset. The vision was unworldly as the sun kissed the ocean. The fluorescent rays from the dipped sun sprayed the sky with a translucent orange that lit the Pacific Ocean up in a dark shade of blue. Each dancing wave shimmered in the light to create the effect of a million stars twinkling back. The palm trees slowly morphed into eerie silhouettes as the sun continued its descent. Once the phenomenon was over, Dee stood up and strolled towards the ocean.

'Dee, where are you going?' Ozzie shouted.

'I have an opportunity to carry out one of my bucket list ideas.'

'What's that?'

'To pee in every ocean before I die.'

'Seriously?'

'Deadly. See you in five.'

We watched her as she disappeared, getting smaller until she was swallowed up by distant darkness.

We were settling the bill when she reappeared. Her top half was dry, but her legs were soaked.

'Well, did you?' I asked.

'You bet your sweet ass I did.' She whispered to me, 'That was one of Michelle's weird bucket list ideas.'

'Haha. Really?'

'If you think I'm crazy, she was something else.'

'I know we've not had a chance to talk about Michelle since being in Los Angeles, but are you OK with everything?'

'I'm good, honestly. It felt cathartic to get it off my chest.'

'I hope it's helped. If you ever need to talk, I'm always here.'

'I'll be fine, but thanks.'

We headed back to the car to get ready for Lynwood's gathering later. I was a little wary hanging around Venice Beach in the dead of night when the freaks would really start to come out. Having seen 'The Lost Boys' film too many times, I presumed vampires would be out in force stalking the boardwalk. Without the Frog Brothers around for protection, we'd be too vulnerable and at their mercy.

CHAPTER 26

ack at the apartment, I took the opportunity to call Eva while waiting for everyone to get ready. I stood at the end of the driveway on the sleepy slopes of a Hollywood neighbourhood, looking up and down the street in awe.

She answered just when I thought it was going to voicemail. 'Hey you!'

'Hey. You OK?'

'I'm good. Are you?'

'I'm great. Stood in the heart of the Sunset Strip. It doesn't seem real to be here.'

'Enjoy it. I love the Strip at night. It's paradoxical, so beautiful yet dangerous. It seduces me.'

'I know what you mean.'

'So, what have you been doing all day, cariño?' she asked.

I told her about Venice Beach, and she agreed with my assessment of it as being unsettling and not what was expected.

She said, 'I've read the updated blogs. They keep coming thick and fast. I read the interview with Ozzie. He seems like a nice guy.'

'Yeah, he's great.'

'I listened to the radio show before and heard you got a mention from Dee. She sounds so cool.'

'She's OK when she wants to be. I'm just glad the lads didn't mention our failed phone sex.'

'I think I'd have died if they'd mentioned that and my name.'

'I'd have barged in on them and shut off the show.'

'Haha. Are you happier regards the blogs?'

'I'm feeling more positive. Seems to be flowing better and the attention is growing for the mag and the band, which is the whole point. It's not about me.'

'That's the right attitude to have.'

'I guess I learned some tips from you on remaining grounded.'

'You've always been like that, I'm sure.'

'Maybe. Anyway, I've been given a new idea regards writing.'

'Oh?'

'It's been suggested that I write a book about the six days in Vegas.'

'Wow! That's interesting.'

'What do you think?'

'I think I like the idea and you should go for it. It could be the making of you.'

'You do realise I'd have to talk about you and reveal all the gory details?'

'You'll have to change my name. Who do you think could play me if it got made into a film?'

'Has to be your namesake, Eva Mendes, or Dania Ramirez.'

'Both are hot. I'll take that.'

'Let's not get carried away, shall we? I've only made notes so far. Probably won't ever finish it.'

'When this tour is done, you can focus on writing it.'

When this tour is done? I repeated in my mind, mulling over the loaded statement.

'We'll see,' I said, rather downbeat.

'What's wrong?'

'Nothing. Just, after the tour is done, I'll be in Bermuda and still unsure where that leaves me…or us.'

'We said we wouldn't discuss it till afterwards, so let's not. Until then, you must keep supporting the band and don't think about *us*. Just continue writing from the heart and let your soul shine. You're at your best when you're like that.'

'You have a knack for keeping me focused.'

'Someone has to kick yo ass once in a while.'

'Yeah, yeah, I know.'

'What are you doing tonight?' she asked.

'We've been invited to a house party in Laurel Canyon by the record label.'

'Wow. That sounds very Hollywood. Don't you be getting all A-list on me. I like your…how do you say? "Manchunian" attitude too much.'

'Haha. "Mancunian",' I corrected, 'But yeah, that's right. Not even Hollywood could change a true Manc from being who he is. We're a different breed.'

We spoke for a couple of minutes longer, and I told her my concerns about Lynwood. She advised me to ignore it, saying it was between Ozzie and the band. She was right - I had to let it go. I think he reminded me too much of the power-hungry, arrogant bastards I'd encountered in the past, and I despised that way of thinking. Out in Los Angeles, it came with the territory, and I had to accept that was the way things were.

We said our goodbyes as the band poured out of the apartment, and I promised to call the next day, the biggest and most important day of the whole trip. But first, we had to hobnob with the moguls of Hollywood.

Ozzie opted to drink again, so we booked an Über. It seemed he'd developed a taste for it in Los Angeles, and who could blame him?

After climbing up the winding roads of Laurel Canyon, we found ourselves in an area that belittled any rich area I'd ever seen before. Gargantuan mansions loomed on both sides of the road. Lynwood must've been a real high-flyer to afford such lofty surroundings. Either that, or he was a 'Trust Fund Baby'.

We pulled into a cul-de-sac off Laurel Canyon Blvd. The taxi driver had to ring a buzzer to enter through metallic Spanish-style gates. We exited the cab and gazed at the house in front of us. It represented a whole new level of wealth. The entrance was complemented by stone-tile flooring that led straight to the living room. High vaulted ceilings ran across the space with arched, oversized windows adding to the overall impact.

A waiter approached, offered us a glass of champagne each and informed us to help ourselves to drinks at the bar in the living area. The 'bar' was smothered with bottles of wine, various spirits, and buckets of beer sitting on ice. It was a proper ritzy celebrity style party, exactly how the big screen portrayed the Hollywood lavishness, being far removed from anything I'd ever experienced before. The sizeable living space was consumed by a multitude of people. Attempting not to be star-struck was difficult. Members of mid-level fame bands that I recognised and lesser-known actors from TV roamed about. I had heard that Mila Kunis had a house in West Hollywood and panicked when I envisioned her being present. If she was, then all bets were off.

We ventured to the outside terrace, complete with a large, azure-coloured pool that glistened in the spotlights. Behind the pool was a five-tiered, tiled waterfall fountain and a two-tier sun deck that overlooked the City of Angels, providing a remarkable panoramic view. Handsome men and gorgeous, playboy calibre women strutted about by the pool. The men were dressed in shirts and blazers, and the women wore exclusive, fashionable dresses that sparkled under the lights.

What was happening in the secluded pockets on the decking, amongst the stylish garden furniture, was eye-opening, to say the least. Serving platters filled with powder and pills were haphazardly left about for people to help themselves. Whether I'd lived a sheltered life, or whether it was just L.A., or whether this was what happened in the realms of the rich and famous in general, I couldn't decipher, but I'd never seen anything like it. I knew drugs were rife, but not to this extent.

Given the legalisation of marijuana in California and the shift in how it was taken, several serving platters had different food made from cannabis placed on them. Times had changed, but scoffing a cannabis-ridden hors d'oeuvre didn't look as cool as a good old-fashioned smoky joint.

The guys from Winachi were outside, so we made our way over. They immediately offered us a bump of coke from a nearby platter. Ozzie and I refused, but the others didn't need any encouragement as they lined up, even Dee. Elsie pushed for me to take something, but I politely declined. That was until I saw a familiar bag plonked on another dish.

'What's in that bag?' I asked him.

'That's in case the party turns trippy,' Tony said.

'Is it peyote?'

'How did you know?'

'It's not the first time I've seen peyote buttons,' I said with a glint in my eye.

'Have you had them before?'

'Just once.'

'Fuck, man, what was that like?'

'It's a bit too fucked up and long-winded to tell you now. What about you? Have you had them before?'

'Not peyote, but I've had acid and shrooms? I'm not doing peyote at a house party. Fuck that.'

'I hear you. You gotta go to the desert to experience that,' I advised.

'Is that where you went?'

'Certainly was.'

'Tell me what happened, bro?'

I gave them a brief version of my trip. After telling the story, I was overcome by a strange urge, like the mind-altering drug that helped shape my life was calling out to me.

I leaned into Elsie. 'You know what? Can I take a few of them? You never know when they might come in handy.'

'Help yourself, bro. They ain't mine. They're for everyone.'

I really didn't know where the desire came from, but I stuffed a few of the buttons into my pocket for safekeeping.

I asked, 'What about you and your experiences with acid and shrooms. Anything trippy occur?'

'I've done them five times. Had a blast and tripped my balls off four times, but I had a bad trip once when I stupidly took them and then walked around New York. That was fucked up; trying to keep my head straight amongst the traffic and lights. I thought my head was going to explode as the cars came at me. I was hugging a streetlamp at one point. Then I made the mistake of looking at myself in the mirror when I got home. I could see the ugly side of me. I had this kind of satanic look, and my face was bubbling. It freaked me out, dude.'

I belly laughed at his plight. He then told me that one of his good trips was when he floated to the ceiling of his flat and crawled about in a maze of colour while listening to Beatles records.

Lynwood came over to us then and welcomed us to his home. He was dressed in white, cut-off chinos, a white shirt, and a navy blazer, complete with flip flops. He invited us to help ourselves to any drink or anything on the platters. It seemed so natural to him to offer the vices as if laws didn't exist in the hills.

Taking a hefty snort of coke himself to escalate his ostentatiousness, he gathered us together. 'Friends, I have come to a decision. After hearing your radio show earlier and hearing all the great feedback from my A&R staff, plus reading Anya's interview, I'm offering you a two-album deal to record in L.A.'

The lads couldn't hide their excitement, especially as they were high on coke.

Lynwood continued, 'I will have the contracts drawn up, but you'll find it's a very generous offer. I would love to hold an official signing after the show tomorrow. Ozzie, you'll be taken care of. You've done a fine job, and I'd like to keep you on as manager, but we can discuss those details later over a brandy.'

'Sounds great, Charles.'

They shook hands and congratulated the band, whose faces had lit up like giddy school kids.

Lynwood continued, 'Finish off this tour, play Vegas, go to Bermuda, and have fun. After that, come back to Los Angeles, and we can get started with the recording and set up some mainstream support slots and showcase nights for you.'

'Fuck, yeah. That sounds class,' Kyle said.

'Wonderful. Well, for now, relax and enjoy the amenities. Don't go too crazy. I want to see you at your best tomorrow. I've invited several people down to see you in action. I don't want them disappointed.'

'Don't worry, I'll keep them in line,' Ozzie said.

'Good to know,' he sneered, adding, 'Dee, would you care to join me? Some people have been asking to meet you.'

Dee gave us a fleeting glance as she left. Lynwood took her back into the house as the three lads embraced each other excitedly. The mission had been accomplished ahead of schedule. We poured ourselves glasses of champagne and toasted the success.

Ozzie warned, 'Don't go overboard. We still have this showcase tomorrow night with important industry types there. And you don't want to feel Dee's wrath again, do you?'

'It'll be cool. We won't have a mad one, just a couple of liveners,' Quince said.

Despite the excellent news, something still didn't sit right about Lynwood and the whole charade. He was a creepy little guy who was blinded by arrogance. But then again, something told me that the bigger the dickhead, the better they were at their job when it came to music. The level I was at back home, I just got to hang around with and meet fellow creatives in the same boat, working for a pittance or for the sheer passion of our craft. I didn't know shit about the business side, and my lack of dealings with the money people could've clouded my judgement. Ozzie had already pointed out that he thought Lynwood was a bit of an arrogant show-off, but he got the job done. Maybe that was true of most record label owners, so dealing with those sorts of people to progress a band's career was necessary.

Amid the congratulations, a bubbly L.A. accent came from behind us, 'Hey guys! How's it going?'

It was Anya grinning with an opulent smile that could light up any darkened room. She was dressed in an elegant, gold-coloured fitted dress that flaunted her shapely figure. Kyle was gobsmacked and completely enchanted under her goddess-like spell. He tried to keep his cool and leaned in to kiss her cheek. The rest of us exchanged infantile sniggers.

Kyle revealed Lynwood's news to her, 'You're not going to believe this, but we've been offered a deal!'

'That's fantastic! I had a feeling he would. I told him that you guys rock.'

'We really appreciate it.'

'You're welcome,' she responded before saying, 'Hey, there's some people I want you all to meet.'

Anya led the way, and we followed to the other side of the pool, where she introduced us to other bands. Anya was a well-connected woman, and everyone she introduced us to was charmed by her outgoing character. The celebs and musicians I recognised made the effort to come to her. It wasn't the other way around, emphasising the level of respect held for her. It felt surreal, briefly conversing with people who had starred in shows like 24, Californication and Entourage. They might not have been the main cast members, but they were recognisable to fans like me.

I asked Anya, 'Mila Kunis isn't here, is she?'

'Mila? Unfortunately, not. She's a doll, though.'

'You know her?' I was astounded.

'I've met her a few times. Do you have a crush on her, Ricky?'

'Just a bit.'

'I'd hook you up, but I don't think Ashton would be best pleased.'

I was in disbelief at Anya's nonchalant attitude to knowing people of that calibre of fame. L.A. really was a head fuck for us Manchester folk with simple tastes. I would've been more than happy boozing all day in the Sir Ralph Abercromby pub watching football or sitting in Corbieres hammering the jukebox. But I guessed this was all part of the way of life in Tinseltown.

I went back to Ozzie, who was talking to Elsie and Tony from Winachi. I could hear his slightly drunk Manc accent bellowing above everyone else. As I arrived, Tony turned to me. 'This guy's cool, bro. He knows his stuff.'

'He does. Full of knowledge and stories. I'd listen to what he's telling you.'

Ozzie had found his groove and continued to impart wisdom to the young musicians. 'I don't know if it's similar in the US, but in the UK, the big problem is if you want to get noticed, it costs you. Talent can only get you so far. Marketing is just as important now. Unfortunately, you must treat the band as a business, which sounds ridiculous, I know. You can't just be a good singer or musician anymore, you must have business savvy, and that's an area most bands can't or won't venture into. They've got to invest time and money and be dedicated and passionate. You think how much it costs to set up a business. You're talking £25-30k, and it'll take some time to recoup that. Most bands can't afford it either, so they don't get noticed and just slip away into the unknown. Just another band with potential that falls into the rock graveyard along with their dreams.'

Tony agreed, 'Yeah, bro, it happens here. Unless you get that backing, you're fucked. We've played with and seen some awesome bands, and it's sad to see them split.'

'You need a lot of luck too. I've taken a chance with the Cutthroats. Even though it's costing us, we're managing on quite a strict budget. We don't have a massive tour bus, and we don't stay in fancy hotels. It's all done on a shoestring, but that's the way it is.'

'When we come to the UK, you can hook us up and be our tour manager,' Tony said.

'Of course. I'll sort you boys out. You just make sure you bring a fan base with you tomorrow night for the Cutthroats.'

'Sure thing, bro.'

Ozzie was summoned by Lynwood, so I carried on talking to Elsie and Tony. I agreed to do an interview piece on them when the tour ended. Having had earlier confirmation from Jamie that the new blog was live, which included a write-up of Winachi's show, I showed them the review through my phone. They were made up when they finished reading it.

It was great to have connected with Winachi. They told me some bizarre stories of their time since arriving in Los Angeles, driving home the idea that the city was as crazy as I imagined it would be, and there were no limits to what could be experienced.

They retold a horror story of a time when they were under the influence of PCP. They met a local shape-shifting devil worshipper who looked like she was from the film 'Blade Runner'. High on drugs, they thought it would be a good idea to participate in a séance with her that involved goat horns and pig's blood. They said her face morphed into something beyond this world, something sub-human whilst she chanted an ancient ritual. When she began cutting her own wrists to draw blood for the two lads to drink, they decided enough was enough and scarpered. I was in hysterics as they re-enacted the scene, but I was sure it would give me nightmares for years to come.

That was the tip of the iceberg regards their crazy band stories.

As the horror stories ended, I noticed Ozzie standing alone after he talked to Lynwood. He was looking out contemplatively at the magnificent far-reaching view, nursing a glass of brandy. I excused myself from Tony and Elsie and made my way over.

'You've done it, Ozzie. You've got the band to where you wanted them to be.'

'It doesn't seem real, kid. I'm not counting my chickens until that contract is signed. Charles is coked off his head and giving it the big un' in front of his guests. I'm not sure I can trust anything he says in that mindset.'

'I know what you mean, but I'm sure it'll be OK. I think people are always on something around here. Seems to be part of the industry and just because it's different to our way of life, doesn't mean it isn't going to happen.'

'Yeah, maybe you're right. I've been around a few years but never seen anything like this. It's insane, right?'

'Bonkers. No one would ever believe it. I was introduced to a guy from "The Office", and another from "It's Always Sunny in Philadelphia." Crazy! Wait till I tell my mates at home. I feel like taking a picture and sending it to them, but I can't be *that* guy here.'

'Haha. You can't. You have to be cool.'

I could see that Lynwood was back entertaining Dee. He was beguiling, and his slimy look was perilously close to invading Dee's personal boundaries again. He shovelled more shit up his nose and appeared quite animated. Although Dee had the odd blast, she wasn't as consistent as Lynwood. The more he took, the brasher and rowdier he became. He twitched and gurned more and more, and every so often, his hand brushed the side of Dee's body when he leaned into her.

I turned to Ozzie. 'Lynwood seems a bit enamoured with Dee.'

He looked over. 'What can I say? She's a star. She's always going to be the main attraction.'

'Do you not think he's a bit overzealous, though?'

He looked over again. 'Dee can take care of herself.'

As the night wore on, Kyle, Will and Quince were introduced to practically everyone Anya knew. Although she apparently didn't date musicians, she seemed into Kyle. I'd catch her leaning into him subtly so her thigh or hip would gently rub against his. It was imperceptible to most, but having been in a similar situation with Eva, I clocked those elusive signs of attraction that were well hidden from others.

Dee returned from the clutches of Lynwood and said, 'Ok, I'm ready to go.'

'Everything OK?' Ozzie asked.

'Yeah, fine. We've got the gig tomorrow, and I want to be fresh for it. Plus, it's not really my scene all this. It's fake as fuck.'

She didn't quite look herself, but she had been on the beak.

I agreed, 'I'm with you there. I never knew parties like this went on.'

Ozzie said, 'I think when you come to Los Angeles, especially Laurel Canyon, it'll always be going on. Nice to experience once, but not something I'd want to be part of every night. But I think it's expected every night here – at least until you end up in rehab and sell your story.'

We called a cab and left sometime around two o'clock. We had to wait for Kyle as he stalled and was reluctant to leave Anya. She said she'd see us the following night at the gig.

In the cab, Kyle finally admitted, 'Ok, I'm in trouble.'

Will was the first to rub it in. 'I knew it. Kyle's in love.'

'Can you blame me? Have you seen her? She's stunning,' he argued.

'No, I can't blame you. I just wanted you to admit it.'

'I'm going to have to make a move tomorrow night. Last night in L.A. after all.'

'Don't do anything that'll fuck things up for us,' Quince said.

'Like what?'

'When she blows you out, don't go off on one and get us a shit review and have the music press over here hating us before we've even begun.'

'Don't worry. I'll be discreet.'

'Bullshit. You're about as obvious as an erection in a pair of speedos.'

Kyle turned his attention to Dee. 'What's up with you, Dee? You're quiet. We're getting signed. Reasons to be cheerful, girl.'

'Nothing. I'm just tired.'

'You sure?' Ozzie asked.

'Yeah. Don't worry about me. I'm as happy as a pig in shit.'

I wasn't convinced.

CHAPTER 27

I slept in later than I had all tour. The jet lag and sleep deprivation began to release me from its clutches, and for the first time I was last up in the group.

'Well, well, well. Look who's up. Did you need that, lad?' Ozzie teased.

'Big time. I was knackered.'

Dee handed me a coffee and quietly ordered, 'Get ready.'

'Why? Where are we all going?'

Pointing at me, then herself, she said, '*We're* going out on our own.'

'We are?' I quizzed.

Ozzie echoed, 'You are?'

'Yes. I'm doing the interview for the magazine, and I don't want any of you boneheads around for it.'

I was surprised, especially because she appeared jaded. It had been on my mind that I needed to get the interview done and dusted, and Jamie had asked numerous times for it. Despite our renewed connection, I still thought it would be tough to pin her down so close to the big gig, so the fact she had suggested it was a weight off my shoulders.

I got myself ready, and we headed out in the Chevy.

'Where are we going?' I asked.

'Just follow the Sat Nav. I've put in the destination.'

Dee had remained quiet for most of the drive. The Sat Nav directed us up steep hills into humble residential areas. 'Ventura Highway' by America offered a soothing tone as we drove further away from the hustle and bustle of WeHo. I quickly grasped where we were heading when the famous Hollywood Sign drew closer.

Dee revealed, 'Someone at the party last night told me to take this road rather than the tourist route. Much more scenic, and you can get closer in the car.'

Eventually, we were thwarted in our plan as we hit a private gate.

'Great, what do we do know?'

'Leave it to me.' Dee exited the car and approached a lady in her sixties who was taking out weeds on the other side of the wall of her modest apartment. After a minute or so of conversation, Dee returned.

'What was all that about?' I asked.

'She's going to open the gate for us, so we can take the private road up there.'

'What did you say to her?'

'I was honest.'

'What do you mean?'

'I told her I was the singer of a band and was being interviewed for a magazine, and I wanted to do it with the Hollywood Sign in the backdrop.'

It wasn't the first time on the trip that Dee's natural magnetism charmed people.

After a few minutes of ascending Mount Lee, we stopped on a dirt track and made the short hike to our destination. The path led us above the sign from behind, with the sweeping view of Los Angeles providing an insuperable backdrop. A cloud of dusty smog lingered above the Downtown area, creating a sandy effect to the sun's penetrative waves that made the city glow like it was trapped in a furnace.

Dee sat in silence before I asked, 'Why did you bring me here for this?'

'I need peace and quiet, and I need to speak to someone *not* in the band.'

'Why?'

'I'm not sure about this deal with Lynwood.'

My Spidey sense was correct, although her concerns about the deal were surprising.

'I sensed something was wrong. But this is what you've worked for. Last night should've been the news you've been waiting for your entire life.'

'It should, but it wasn't.'

'There must be a reason and a good one at that.'

'I really don't like Lynwood.'

'Neither do I. He's a smarmy prick, but most people in his position will probably be quite similar.'

'I know that, but he's really sleazy. I get the impression that there's an unwritten clause in the deal if we sign.'

'In what way?'

'C'mon, Ricky. You know what I mean.'

'Like...you have to sleep with him?'

'That's the impression I got.'

'How sure are you? I know he was flirtatious, but you've got to be pretty fuckin' certain you think he was implying *that* given what's at stake.'

'I can't be one hundred per cent sure. He never said as much, but it was the way he flirted and looked at me when talking about the contract. I just had a gut feeling something wasn't right, and there was something more to the deal than he was letting on.'

'What exactly did he say?'

'He made a point of saying that he was the man who was going to make it happen for us and that he hoped his investment would reap the rewards. The way he said it was subtle. On the surface, he meant by doing all I could in the band, but the way he looked at me suggested something more.'

'I'm surprised you didn't say anything and nip it in the bud. It's not like you to remain quiet.'

'I didn't think it was a good idea to make a scene with someone like that in his own house without hard evidence. I might be taking it the wrong way, but if he did mean it, he was clever about it.'

'I don't deny that something about him is off-putting, but I just put it down to being in this crazy part of the world, and that's how people in positions of authority are over here. We ain't in Manchester anymore.'

'Far from it. Has anyone said anything to you?'

'I can't speak for the band, but Ozzie said he thought he was a bit of a twat and is wary of the deal going ahead, but I don't think he saw what you're suggesting. It was more that he was full of shit, giving it the big I am for his guests while coked up.'

'I feel shit that I took a bit of coke last night.'

'Why did you?'

'I don't know, Ricky. Just caught up in the moment. Habit of band life. The man's an enabler, and I was just playing along, but I'm disappointed in myself.'

'Sounds like a typical manipulative cock if you ask me.'

She paused before saying, 'I don't know what to do. If I bring this up, it could spoil everything we've worked for. The band are buzzing about it. I know I'm a hard ass, but it will crush them if I pull the plug hours before the signing.'

'Maybe the contract won't be up to snuff, so Ozzie will reject it?'

'Doubtful. Lynwood told me quietly, and it's good. Ozzie being kept on too and earning what's proposed, there's no way he'll say no to that.'

'Ozzie loves you lot. If you aren't comfortable, he won't be shallow enough to go through with it. He'd probably knock him out if he thought he wanted sex from you in return. And if Quince found out, then forget about it. He'd hospitalise him.'

'Yeah, they would. But Ozzie has been brown-nosing Lynwood a bit.'

'I just think he's playing the game like you were last night. He'd back you up if it came to it. What if Lynwood did make advances, and you said no? What's the worst he's going to do?'

'These people can do a lot to hurt a band. His ego will be more precious than losing a bit of money. He has a lot of power that could fuck us over. It's well documented that some of these moguls don't take rejection lightly and end up fuckin' careers up.'

'Maybe there's another label out there who can come up with an offer.'

'I'm not sure there is. Let's leave it for now. I just needed to tell someone, and it couldn't be any of the other guys.'

We carried on staring out onto the sandy Los Angeles landscape. She pulled out a cig and offered me one. I took it without thinking, joking with her, 'You're an enabler getting me back on these things.'

After a couple of puffs, I said, 'C'mon. Let's do what we initially set out to do up here. You still want to do this interview? We couldn't get a better setting, could we? A nice smoggy view.'

She laughed. 'Let's get this over with, Hot Shot.'

I pulled out my phone to check the pre-written questions that I had chopped and changed several times over the trip as I got to know Dee. I then took the dictaphone out and pressed record.

Before I could ask the first question, she spoke, 'Fuck your questions for now. Just record and let me riff. You can word it however you want when you write it up.'

'The floor's yours,' I said.

'Despite what you've seen when I've been going off with women, the fact of the matter is that I love men, especially men in rock music. Growing up, men were my idols, my first crushes and inspirations. Queen, Led Zep, Eagles, Journey, Sabbath, Stones, Marley...the list is endless. They not only moulded my eardrums, but they also created this beautiful monster inside of me that I endlessly feed but is never satisfied.'

'You're a fan of classic rock then more than anything else?'

'Fuck yeah. Back in the day, rock music ruled all. Anarchy fuelled music that seared your soul and left you bleeding, begging for more. The frontmen and women were more than singers and songwriters. They were made of magic that would one day make them myths and creatures of the night that captured our imaginations and hearts forever.'

'What do you make of it today in how it's changed?'

'In many ways, it's fucked. As a musician, sometimes it feels like I'm chasing a dragon, and that dragon is chasing its tail. We're in the doldrums of music as a generation. I by no means want to re-create the epic times of the past...well, maybe I do, but I wonder why things have changed so much? Where has all the magic gone? When we play live, I know it still exists. We capture it as a band. After all, what is a world without music, and what is a world without magic? Something needs to change, and only the fans can change it.'

The conversation streamed from there, and I saw that she was quite the Dionysian spirit. I tried to steer away from trivial questions asked several times on the tour in the various interviews already conducted.

Dee was an intelligent woman and I wanted to explore that side of her. Because of our new-found trust, I took a risk and chose to take the interview to a deeper level than she'd ever gone on public record. She could only say 'no comment' to any uncomfortable question, but she didn't protest and was openly forthcoming.

I gained an understanding of her upbringing and why she moved to Manchester, and how her love affair with music began. Describing what rock meant to her, she preached, 'Rock 'n' Roll is about saying I'm here and if you don't understand me then fuck you.'

She described her thoughts on why they were in America in just a few short words. 'We were lost in Manchester, so we're touring America,' fully backing Ozzie's idea to bring them over to fulfil a dream.

I asked how she managed to hit it hard most nights, onstage and offstage partying and never seemed to tire. She said, 'I'm used to this life and have learnt to build an impenetrable energy force around me. It's fuelled by music and rock 'n' roll, and it'll never diminish. You need to learn to do the same thing.'

I concurred, given the nomadic lifestyle had left me battered and bruised. She carried on talking and delivered several nuggets that were beauties to highlight in the piece.

When expanding on her love of performing, she revealed, 'They say the two most important days of your life are the day you're born, and the day you find out why. The second of those came very early in life. I knew I was destined to be a performer. There was no other option.'

She turned it around on me. 'How about you? Do you know the day you found out why you were born?'

I thought for a second. 'Until nine months ago, I couldn't answer that question because there was nothing that jumped out. Since then, there's been plenty. Meeting Eva, writing for Sonic Bandwagon, flying to America, being put on this trip, meeting you guys. Maybe it's all connected, but to find out my definitive purpose in life, who knows? Most people may never find out. Meeting Eva stands out. That was the catalyst that opened doors.'

Dee nodded, and I said, 'Anyway, let's get back to the interview. I'm meant to be interviewing you, not the other way around.'

'Shoot.'

'You're from Bermuda, went to university in Vancouver, moved to Manchester. Where do you consider home?'

'Home is a state of mind. Believe it or not, this whole road trip has given me the greatest sense of home I've ever felt. I have a gypsy soul and a deep interest and connection with travel, as you well know. It's where I'm at my most powerful and creative. I believe that travel is of incredible importance in life. Money returns. Time doesn't. Travel while you can. I've felt like Manchester and Bermuda are distant memories of my past. There's no shit job, flat, responsibilities, or possessions to go back to anymore. Just what we have with us. Home has become the road. It feels natural and like I'm fulfilling my destiny out here as if I've found a degree of peace and understanding of life.'

It was an inspiring answer that was classic Dee.

I stopped the recording and turned to her tentatively. 'Listen, Dee, no pressure whatsoever, and I'm not trying to exploit the situation. I'll completely understand if you don't want to mention it, but what do you think about talking about Michelle on record?'

She looked away and fell silent. Her hands nervously played with some smooth pebbled stones she'd found in the dirt.

She turned back to me. 'Yeah, OK.'

'Are you sure? I know it's personal, but maybe it'll help.'

'I've held it in for too long, and it felt like a release when I told you a few days ago. Maybe this is the right moment for it to come out, and today of all days.'

'I think it is. If you want to retract anything you say, that's fine. I'll let you read it beforehand. I won't tell Jamie I've got your interview, so he won't pressure me to send it. We'll keep it under wraps until you're comfortable with it.'

'Thanks, Hot Shot. You're getting quite good at this interview stuff, aren't you? Making the subject trust you.'

'Haha. Maybe I'll be the next Parkinson.'

'You've got a book to write first. Have you done any more on it?'

'I haven't had time, but ideas are percolating.'

'Make sure you write it. I think you may find out why you were born when you do.'

I contemplated that for a second and thought she may have had a point.

Dee opened up about her close friendship with Michelle and their shared love of music. She spoke about how they learnt the guitar together and their singing bond, which she described as 'unrivalled chemistry.'

She pulled out her phone and showed me a video of them harmonising in a small bar in Bermuda. It was just two young, fearless girls with fantastic voices playing and singing 'Piece of My Heart' by Janis Joplin to a few onlookers.

Dee was visibly upset but admitted, 'I watch this often. She's my inspiration. My one true love. You can quote me on that.'

She carried on speaking passionately, describing Michelle's resilient spirit and appetite for life, saying it was 'annoying, but at the same time endearing.' She eventually said, 'We're going to have to stop there.'

'I know. It must be hard for you,' I sympathised.

'No, it's not that. I think you're going to end up with too much to transcribe if I keep going on. But thank you. That helped. Be gentle when writing it up.'

'Of course. Thank you for trusting me with this. Just to give you a head's up. You might want to tell the band about Michelle before the interview goes live. You don't want them finding out by reading about it.'

'When the time is right, I'll tell them.'

'One final question. Give me a quote to sum up this trip.'

She took a second to formulate the right words. Her measured response was, 'It's heightened every sense…physically and spiritually, and some of the experiences have been simply ethereal.'

'Beautiful. I couldn't have put it better myself.'

CHAPTER 28

Early evening had arrived and what we'd all worked so hard for, and looked forward to the most on the trip, was a few hours away. Cutthroat Shambles were playing the famous Whisky a Go Go. I was finally going to set foot inside one of the hubs of rock 'n' roll, where so many of my favourite bands had graced the stage.

After Dee and I returned, I wrote a preview of the gig and transcribed the interview to keep myself busy before the show. I used my adrenaline to help the words carry more weight. I posted the gig preview but held off on submitting the interview until Dee approved it.

Kyle, Will, and Quince returned after taking out the Dodge for a drive around Los Angeles.

'Where have you lot been?' I asked.

Quince replied, 'Compton!'

'You're not serious?' I was stunned.

'Deadly. I love my hip hop music. I wanted to drive around and get a feel for it.'

'Was it as dodgy as it's made out to be?' I asked.

'It was cool. Probably wouldn't want to drive around there at night, though. I had N.W.A on full blast as we cruised through the streets,' Quince said.

'You lot are crazy.'

We set out early so as to have plenty of time to adjust and settle in before the show. Seeing Cutthroat Shambles' name in lights on the board above the Whisky a Go Go was spine-tingling. The white background and blocked capital letters in black made it look like it was from a Broadway theatre of yesteryear. I took a couple of band shots in full view of the sign to mark the occasion.

I felt some sort of transformation as I glided through the doors. I could taste the history, and the atmospheric mystique enveloped me. My immediate focus turned to the stage, which was set up. I was struck by how crisp and cinematic the view was. The lighting was striking. It was like a filter had been held in front of the stage to make it appear in HD. It must've been a photographer's dream to shoot in there.

I raised my head to the balcony opposite the stage, imagining Paul Rothchild watching a Doors performance that blew his mind enough to sign them. My attention turned back to the stage, and I thought of Morrison singing the infamous line in 'The End' that got them banned from the venue (or at least the movie would have you believe it happened that way). Speaking of Morrison, pictures hung on the wall in honour of his status and importance to the venue. Jimi Hendrix was next to him, and in between were three huge bottles, two Jack Daniels and one Southern Comfort. I think Jack Daniels was the official sponsor of Sunset Blvd. The bourbon's presence was everywhere, and why wouldn't it be, in the heart of a rock 'n' roll mecca.

The place was eerily quiet and smaller than I envisaged, with a capacity of around five hundred. But sometimes, the smaller the size, the more historic the venue. It gave an air of exclusivity about each show if you were lucky enough to get a ticket.

After meeting the venue manager and the sound and lighting engineers, we met Lynwood backstage. The sailor outfit from the previous night had been replaced by more formal attire. A few industry types were with him, and he introduced them to the band. I left them to it and went back out front to prepare the merch stand.

After setting up, I sat on my own in an empty booth on a devilishly red leather couch. My mind roamed into the times been and gone that I was not even alive to be privy to. I manifested the ghosts of past giants floating through the auditorium, wondering who had sat where I was and what debauchery had occurred. More recently, I imagined the time when Oasis played there and mistakenly took crystal meth instead of cocaine and completely fucked up their gig. I hoped that the Manchester band following in their footsteps wouldn't suffer a similar fate.

Mötley Crüe's, 'Home Sweet Home' came through the speakers. After the earlier conversation with Dee, I thought about where my own version of home was. She was right enough when she theorised that home was a state of mind and travelling was a feeling close to attaining that. But where did my own version of home lie? Was it with the band? Was it with Eva? Or was it back in Manchester?

Ozzie appeared and signalled for me to join the band backstage while they were getting ready. He handed me a Cutthroats t-shirt, and we both donned them to help with the promotion.

A standard couple of crates of beer were laid on the table in the back, along with bottles of wine, Jack Daniels, Southern Comfort, Gin, and Jose Cuervo tequila. We were told that most of the rider requests had come from Winachi, who were due down shortly.

Dee sat in front of the mirror applying her make-up as the rest of us were oddly quiet and nervous.

'Feels weird being here, doesn't it?' Quince eventually said.

'Yeah. Why are we all so morbid? We never get nervous before a show,' Kyle answered.

'This is a bit different,' Will countered.

Kyle poured us a shot of tequila each. 'Just one to toast the occasion and settle these nerves.'

We stood in a circle with arms raised and shots in our hands. Kyle carried on, 'It's been an honour sharing this ride with you all. To the Whisky a Go Go!'

We threw back the warm spirit, and I recoiled from the strength. With nerves simmering in the camp, it was a necessary edge shaver.

The stillness remained palpable, but the atmosphere lifted as soon as Winachi arrived. They were their usual energetic and outlandish selves, which stemmed the tension shrouding the room. Having gotten to know Elsie and Tony over the past couple of days, it was good that Winachi were entrusted with the support slot. Dressed in sportswear and sunglasses, they looked as cool as their funky sound suggested. Elsie ripped open one of the crates and dished the beers out, bemused as to why no one had done it already.

'What's the matter with you guys? This crate should be half empty by now,' he asserted.

'I think they're just a little focused,' Ozzie offered.

'Ah, they'll be fine. This is rock 'n' roll. Just blow their fuckin' minds.'

'Fuck it, he's right. What the hell are we so quiet about? Let's loosen up,' Quince exclaimed.

'No more than three bottles each,' Ozzie warned.

'Fine. But afterwards?'

'Oh, go nuts. But don't forget we've got Vegas tomorrow.'

'We'll be fine for that,' Quince assured.

We enjoyed a couple of beers with Winachi before they went to soundcheck and left the six of us to our own devices.

Dee went back to the mirror, and I sat next to her.

'How was Lynwood when you met him?' I whispered.

'He didn't say anything to me like he did last night, but I didn't like the way he looked at me.'

'What are you thinking?'

'I'm not spoiling tonight. Just going to have to get on with it and do our business.'

'But if you feel uncomfortable…'

'Ricky, it's fine. Drop it.' She was stern. 'What will be, will be. I can handle anything that comes my way. Do *not* say a word to anyone.'

'Ok. You want me to get you anything?'

'Just grab me a beer.'

The band were called for soundcheck, and I took the opportunity to give Eva a call whilst backstage on my own. I told her that the band were on the verge of being signed, and good things were happening. I said I'd call her afterwards, and she told me to wish the band good luck and congratulate them. Until the document was signed, I held off on the latter part of her request.

I stayed backstage while the band continued to soundcheck. Elsie and Tony returned, and they made it difficult to *not* get annihilated on booze with their constant barrage of peer pressure. I had to remain level-headed, so I could do the review justice and remember every detail, so I limited my alcohol intake.

Elsie sat next to me. 'They sound fantastic,' he declared.

'Wait till you hear them in full flow,' I said.

'I can't wait. And they're getting signed after the show. Maybe we'll see more of each other in future if we're on the same label.'

'Yeah, that'd be cool.'

My enthusiasm waned, so I took the opportunity to sound Elsie out.

'How have you found being signed to Lynwood?'

'It's been great, bro. You asked me this the other night, didn't you?'

'Yeah. I just want to be sure. What do you think of him as a person?'

'Oh, he's a total dick, but he's done alright by us.'

'Have you heard anything about him... abusing his power in any way?'

'What do you mean?'

'I don't know. You hear these stories about Hollywood moguls. I was just wondering if he was part of that club?'

'What have you heard?'

'Nothing. Forget I said anything.'

'Can you keep a secret?' he said.

'Of course.'

'This didn't come from me, and if you drop my name, I'll deny till I die.'

'Trust me, whatever you tell me, your name will be left out of it.'

'I know he's bedded a few women in the bands on his roster and who work for him. And although uncon- firmed, one member of an all-girl group refused him, and they were off his books pretty quickly...so the ru- mour goes.'

'What do you think? Any truth to it?'

'Who knows, bro? This is fuckin' Hollywood. Any- thing's possible. It's all rumour mill, and it's not like anything will happen if it's true. He's too protected and has money to burn. If there's any truth to it, I'm guessing people have remained silent or been paid off. Why do you ask?'

'I don't know. Just being overly cautious, I suppose.'

'Relax, bro. Enjoy the night. It's all good.'

We clinked bottles, and I took a hefty quaff. The conversation with Elsie played on my mind. It confirmed my suspicions that Lynwood wasn't all he seemed to be, and Dee was in his crosshairs. I feared once those papers were signed, it would be too late. Even if she resisted Lynwood's advances, it could prove fatal for the band's future, given the power he held. With a contract signed, they'd be under his control, and if Dee didn't yield to his desires, they could be sat on the back burner for years, which is what Ozzie dreaded would happen with some UK labels.

The band returned with Anya and two photographers in tow. Anya was unsurprisingly escorted in by Kyle. Elsie and Tony tried to lighten the mood by taking control of the sound system, playing a song related to their own band's style - Grandmaster Flash, 'The Message'. It wasn't long before heads bobbed, and hips grooved to the funky beat.

Time crept on, and Lynwood eventually appeared to give us a brief lowdown, announcing that Winachi were due on. The Cutthroats would follow at 9pm, and the signing would take place onstage after the show.

It was time for Winachi's slot. The band couldn't watch them due to press that had arrived for interviews and photos, but that didn't stop me from seeing how a show at the Whisky would play out.

The place had become a lot busier since we first arrived, so I opened the merch stand during the performance. A few people came over to purchase t-shirts, including Mucho, his band, and Electric Parlor, who had played a couple of nights earlier at Five Star. It was terrific to see them and great that they came down to offer their support for a fellow up-and-coming band. Jimmy Grace, the radio interviewer, also arrived with his wife, Roxy, who looked like she should've been in Sons of Anarchy judging by her biker attire dress sense and glut of tattoos.

A simmering hysteria swept through the crowd, made up of industry types and fans, who were the disciples and seekers of rock. Winachi's fan-appeasing set offered an insight into the sound quality of the Whisky. It was crystal clear, with no feedback whatsoever, and it sounded unreal as it echoed through the auditorium.

Their set ended with a nod to the main act. 'Stick around for a fuckin' brilliant band coming up after us. Our friends from England, Cutthroat Shambles!'

As they exited, I went behind the scenes in the lull that followed to offer my support, leaving one of the bar staff to look after the stand in my absence.

Shortly after, the stage manager popped his head around the door to call the band. Dee appeared from the side room she'd been holed up in, and I was the first person she saw.

She asked, 'How do I look?'

'Wow! You're gonna knock 'em dead!'

She was every bit the rock 'n' roller. Her make-up was applied to perfection, and strikingly dark eye shadow amplified her menacing attraction. She wore a sleeveless, black top that revealed the tattoos that smothered her arms and shoulders, a tight, dark purple skirt that revealed the flesh of her lower thighs, and shin-high black boots. It was a look that exemplified Sunset Blvd.

'I cleared it with Ozzie and the venue, but I have a little surprise for you,' she said.

I looked bemused.

'I know how much *this* venue and *that* stage means to you, so why don't you get on there and announce us?'

'Seriously?' I was flabbergasted.

'Sure. Why not? You've earnt it. Just don't fluff your lines.'

I moved to hug her, but she resisted. 'Whoa! Don't smudge my make-up before I go on.'

'Sorry, but thanks for this.'

She smiled before turning to her bandmates and said, 'You know the drill. Bring it in fuckers.'

They huddled together for their harmonious rendition of 'With a Little Help from My Friends.' Now that I knew why Dee insisted on singing this before shows, I felt like welling up. They clasped each other's palms as a knowing, empathic look shimmered between them.

Ozzie gave final words of encouragement, 'You don't need me to get you up for this. Just do what you do best and rock the fuck out of these L.A. fuckers.'

He and the guys filed out. As Dee was about to join them, I pulled her back when I noticed she'd left something behind.

'Hey, rock star!'

She turned. 'What?'

'You're gonna need this.'

I handed her the burgundy cowboy hat that had been her main staple of the tour.

She rolled her eyes. 'How could I forget?'

The lights flicked off, and the theme song to 'The Good, The Bad, and The Ugly' ripped through the hall.

I asked Dee, 'Whose idea was it to play this song?'

'Mine. Always been the plan to come out to this for the Whisky gig.'

'I love it.'

'C'mon. You're gonna miss your cue.'

We left the room and waited as the song played out.

I made my way to the front of the band and waited by the curtain as nerves rumbled. The idea that I was about to step out onto the same stage as my heroes left me dizzy but excited. I was signalled to go on by the stage manager, and I strode out first with the lads following, blinded by the spotlights that fired upon me. Everything plunged into complete darkness beyond the stage, so I couldn't see shit, but I heard the clapping of a packed crowd somewhere in front. The band headed for their instruments, and I swaggered up to the mic, Mancunian style, trying to keep cool and soak up every moment of my thirty seconds of fame. My mind raced with what to say. I was tempted to go all Jim Morrison and scream, '*You're all a bunch of fuckin' slaves*', just to incite a riot and revolution for the hell of it. It was hardly the time. Instead, I borrowed a line from a Manchester legend to highlight our beloved city.

'Manchester in the area, we're international we're continental, hello!' The words were a nod to Ian Brown and the immortalised words he shouted when he landed onstage at the famous Blackpool Empress Ballroom gig in 1989.

The onlookers hollered back, and goose pimples swarmed all over me. I smiled back, half-thinking I was about to go into full karaoke mode and hog the mic, giving an exemplary rendition of Neil Diamond's, 'America'.

I bellowed like a ring announcer at a world title fight, 'Ladies and Gentlemen...for your listening pleasure this evening...please welcome...from Manchessstterrr, Englllaaannnddd! Cuttthhhroooaattt Shammmmbbblllesss!'

The roar reverbed back at me once more, and I felt that euphoric rush swarm all over me again. The stage lights switched off for a moment and I saw hundreds of faces staring back at me in a packed-out venue.

As the lads hurled into their opening crowd-pleaser, 'Rock N Roll Heaven', I gave a peace sign and walked back off the way I came. The guitar opening was faultless, and it sounded epic under the guidance of the Whisky a Go Go's illustrious sound crew.

A pumped-up Dee waited alone behind the curtain as the instrumentals stoked the fires. She grinned and said, 'Great job, Hot Shot. Didn't think you were ever gonna leave the stage.'

'That was mint!'

'You mind if I go and do my show now?'

'No, let me go on instead,' I joked.

I grabbed her attention again after we took a step away from each other.

'Hey!' I shouted. 'For Michelle, yeah.'

She smiled, proclaiming, 'Always for her!'

I watched from the side for a moment as Dee strutted out to tremendous adulation. She took charge of the mic, and I hadn't even noticed it was draped in a purple scarf. She sounded electrifying, belting out the opening lyrics with such passion. The early nailing of the song heightened the band's confidence and settled any lingering nerves. Dee's stage antics during the instrumentals were born out of the fires of where we were. Her usual fluid headbanging, and swashbuckling flexibility, wowed the fans. Kyle found his groove too. Inspired by Anya's presence, he constantly played up to where he knew she would be.

After the song finished, the crowd erupted with applause and whistles. I ran back down the walkway that led out to the hall, where I stood with Ozzie and Anya by the merch stand. Anya turned to me and mouthed, 'Kyle's awesome.' It was almost like seeing him play had stirred something up inside her, and she'd succumbed to the unique power a guitarist held.

Dee spoke confidently, thanking the audience for attending and namechecking me, Ozzie, and Lynwood (it must've hurt her to mention him).

The high-octane 'Oblivion' followed, delivered with force to keep the crowd pumped up. They kept the intensity high with 'On Your Knees', maintaining the pulsating, foot-stomping tempo in the opening few tracks. It was only on the fifth song that they allowed the spectators an opportunity to breathe, with the wonderfully crafted ballad, 'Curious Morality'. Dee gave it her absolute everything. The zeal in her voice hypnotised the crowd. Many were awestruck by the emotiveness of the song's underbelly. As the final notes frittered out, the volume of the shouts and claps was deafening. Dee thanked them with both hands cupped to her heart.

There was no time for another sentimental song as they propelled back into the rocking rhythms. 'Eyes Wide Shut' followed 'Even' to keep the Sunset Strip vibe at an optimum level. I may have been biased given my connection, but the performance was, without doubt, the best I'd ever seen from them. They were advancing to a different level, a level that could end up in the same bracket as the greats. Lynwood *had* to be impressed and must've rubbed his hands in glee at the new cash cow soon to be at his disposal.

Sandwiched between the high-tempo tracks that continued to attack like bombs was the slower, 'Ready to Love', reminding us that they were far from one-trick ponies. The final track to close out the show was a token cover that befitted Sunset Blvd. Pandemonium swept through the masses when the opening notes to 'Highway to Hell' sent the fans into a screaming frenzy that continued throughout the song and when they left the stage.

The pulling power of the fans chanting, 'We want more! We want more! We want more!' brought them back on for a two-song encore, ending as usual with 'Lifetime Sunshine'. The Whisky exploded as they concluded. The ovation continued, signifying the band's bludgeoning first impact on the Los Angeles rock scene.

A collection of industry types made a beeline for Lynwood afterwards. All sorts of offers could be on the table on the back of those conversations: studio time, gigs, photo shoots, guest spots, song use, and interviews with well-known media. The world was at the Cutthroats' feet.

The merch stand went crazy afterwards, and I struggled to cope with the demand. Ozzie talked to all sorts of people who were directed to him, and I did my best to keep the queue flowing as merch flew off the shelves, so to speak.

It felt like ages before it calmed down, and I could grab a minute. When it did, I took the opportunity to quickly run to the toilet before the signing ceremony.

As I came out of the restroom, something caught my attention. I heard two people talking around the corner in the opposite direction to the stage area. I recognised Dee's voice, so delicately tip-toed towards where it came from.

'...what do you think's going to happen? I'm just going to turn up and fuck you. Who the fuck do you think I am?'

Lynwood's voice then said, 'Dee, you've got to play the game. This is how it works out here.'

'I'd rather not be signed than be forced to do this shit!'

'Don't disappoint your bandmates. You've seen how much they want this.'

'I don't give a fuck. I'd rather busk on street corners than sign to this shit!'

'You don't want to go against me, Dee. I'll pull the plug on this, and you'll be nothing.'

'Then we'll be nothing. Fuck you and fuck this industry!'

'You walk away now, and there's no coming back.'

I made my presence known. 'What the fuck's going on here?'

'This fuckin' dirty, rotten sleazeball has told me his room number at the Chateau Marmont and expects me to drop by later.'

My blood boiled. 'What? You're lucky I don't knock you the fuck out, right here, right now.'

'Go for it. I'll sue the shit out of you,' Lynwood sneered.

'He's not worth it, Ricky. Leave it,' Dee pleaded.

Just then, Quince appeared, 'What's all the shouting?'

'Quince, get Ozzie and the others,' I said.

'Ozzie's behind me. What the fuck's going on?'

'Tell him, Dee,' I said.

'This fucker has been trying to get into my knickers ever since we landed in Hollywood. He's invited me back to his room later to become his personal fuckin' sex slave.'

'That's a preposterous allegation. She's misunderstood me,' Lynwood lied.

Ozzie heard every word. 'Are you serious?' he fumed.

'Ozzie, she's got it wrong. It was purely for a celebratory drink.'

'I don't think she has, Charles. You fuck with one of my bands, you fuck with me.'

'And what are you going to do about it? You're a nobod...'

Before he even finished speaking, Ozzie threw his head sharply at Lynwood's. The force he connected with almost knocked me sick as he crumpled to the floor. Blood spattered across his face as he cried, 'My nose! You broke my nose!'

The commotion attracted attention, and before we knew it, bouncers and security were on us, with Kyle, Will and even Winachi jumping in to attempt to calm the situation down.

Some of Lynwood's cronies moved to intervene as arguments and allegations were hurled back and forth. The turmoil escalated with shoves and punches thrown by both sides. Quince, the beast, started to clean house, dropping anyone who got in his way. Dee was stuck in the middle, screaming at Lynwood, who had remained on the floor. I moved to drag her away from the melee, but not before she kicked out into his midriff.

Dee begged me, 'Come with me! I need to get out of here!'

Her eyes were filled with tears, so I followed her and exited the unmanned door.

Outside, Dee gasped for breath and became hysterical.

'I don't fuckin' believe this! I don't fuckin' believe this! What have I done? What have I done?'

'Hey, hey, hey! You haven't done anything wrong. You can't be expected to sleep with a guy for a contract.'

'I've fucked it all! I've fucked everything!' She was hyperventilating.

'Oi!' I screamed. 'You haven't fucked anything. This is just one of those bumps in the road. It's gonna be OK.'

She was inconsolable, pacing around in circles with her head in her hands. She kept repeating, 'What do I do? What do I do? I need to get out of here!'

'Where? You want to go back to the apartment or get a drink?'

'No. I need to leave. I need to leave Los Angeles.'

'Dee, it's the middle of the night.'

'I don't care. Just take me away from here,' she implored.

'Ok. Calm down. I've got a key. Let's get our stuff and just drive, yeah? Just drive away.'

Her heavy breathing continued as I waited patiently for her answer.

'Ok. Let's get our stuff and just drive.'

CHAPTER 29

We rounded up our stuff and got back on the road. Dee had cried herself out and was sat in silence, staring pensively out of the window. She was always so tough, but the pressure of the situation had broken her.

'Are you OK?' I asked.

'No. I'm pretty fuckin' far from OK.'

With L.A. in the rear-view mirror and the desert looming ahead, the slow, soothing opening guitar strum to 'Moonlight Mile' by The Rolling Stones began to reverberate within the car. The song fitted the trials and tribulations of life on the road, with philosophical lyrics that were a noticeable reflection of our arduous trip.

My phone buzzed, and I saw it was Ozzie calling.

Dee pleaded, 'Don't answer it.'

'I have to. Hello, mate.'

'Ricky, where are you both?'

'We bailed. Dee's upset, and she wanted to leave. I thought it was best I went with her. What's goin' on there?'

'Not pretty. Few scuffles and that, nothing we couldn't handle but it all eventually calmed down. We've packed up and left.'

'What happened to Lynwood?'

'Fuck all. These people know what he is, but they'll protect him cos that's just the way it is out here. How's Dee?'

She stared vacantly through the window. 'Not great.'

'Tell her I'm sorry.'

'I don't think you've got anything to be sorry about, Ozzie. She doesn't blame you. She blames herself. You couldn't have known this would happen.'

'That's ridiculous. Tell her not to blame herself. I'm the one who should feel like shit for putting this deal together. I didn't listen to what my heart and gut were telling me. Where are you heading, anyway?'

'We're almost out of Los Angeles.'

'You're what?' he screeched.

'Dee wanted to leave town.'

'I thought you'd just gone for a drive to cool your heads. I didn't think you'd fucked off again. You know we've got a gig in Vegas tomorrow night?'

'I'm not too sure about that now, Ozzie. She's hit hard by this.'

'Let me speak to her.'

I moved to hand over the phone. 'Dee, Ozzie wants you.'

Without flinching, she said, 'I don't want to speak to anyone.'

I brought the phone back to my ear. 'Ozzie, she said…'

'I heard. I'll let her cool off. Look after her but get her to that show tomorrow. We can still get this tour back on track. Tell her not to worry about that. Have you got all your stuff?'

'I think so, but just have a check and make sure we haven't left anything.'

'Will do. I'll catch up with you later. Take it easy.'

'You too.'

I hung up and told Dee what Ozzie said. She ignored it.

After about five minutes' silence, she spoke, 'Everything's fucked. I don't know what I'm doing.'

'What do you mean?'

'I don't know whether I want this anymore. It's too hard. If our best shot was with a sexual predator, I'm done.'

'You can't think like that. Ozzie's still hopeful.'

'I'm not. I've been busting my ass for years. It's too much of an emotional rollercoaster. I can't do it.'

'You're a fighter. Of course, you can.'

'There's only so much fight I have in me. This shit wears you down. It's draining me. I don't want it anymore.'

'And what about Michelle?'

'Do *not* bring her into it!' She shot me an enraged glare.

'You're too emotional now. You can't throw it all away... and yes, for Michelle. She would be so disappointed to see you go out like this.'

Her face screwed up again as more tears flowed, and she cried, 'I need a sign. I need to find answers.'

Memories of nine months earlier instantly sparked an idea. After a bit of deliberation on whether to bring it up, I eventually fumbled with the Sat Nav.

'What are you doing?' she asked.

'Setting a new course.'

'Where?'

'Do you really want to find answers to all this and have a clear direction mapped out for you?'

'Yeah.'

'Then trust me. There is a way.'

'What do you mean?'

'I told you what happened to me in Vegas, didn't I?'

'So?'

'Well, at that knobhead's party the other night, I noticed some peyote buttons on a platter. I don't know why, but I felt obligated to take some. Seems like I now know the reason. What do you think?'

'Take peyote? Now?'

'Definitely not now and not in the dark. But this may be something you have to do when the sun rises. People don't know that there are angels out there.'

'Angels?'

'Guardian angels!'

'Sounds trippy, but I'm game.'

Soon after, somewhere outside of Los Angeles beyond the city's beady eye, we pulled up into a remote rest area.

'I say we bunk here for the night. It's warm enough, for now, and we'll save some money. You have the whole of the back seat, and I'll crash in the front,' I suggested.

'You've spent too much time with me, Hot Shot. Your ideas are getting crazier than mine. Stay out here? I can't believe we're doing this.'

'It'll be one for the memories. Get that pad out and write a song about it.'

'I'm not in the mood.'

'You want to talk instead?'

'Not really. I've nothing to say.'

'How about a drink? I swiped a bottle of wine from the apartment.'

'No. I'm not in the mood.'

'Shit, this *is* serious,' I joked.

'I'm not an alcoholic, you know.'

'I know. Sorry, just trying to lighten the mood.'

'Pick your timing, Hot Shot. I just want to sleep.'

'Ok. Well, I'm going to catch up on some writing if you don't mind - gonna write the shit out of that performance tonight. Maybe add a piece about Hollywood sexual deviancy.'

'There's no need to. Don't mention the aftermath.'

'Ok.'

'I feel I let Michelle down tonight.'

'You didn't let her down. You'll only let her down if you quit. Look at tonight like she's a guardian angel on your shoulder and she protected you by stopping that signing going ahead. She'd have been proud that you didn't sell your soul.'

She smiled at the concept.

'This is just a small blip on the road to rock stardom. I told you in Sedona - the road is never meant to be smooth.'

'I can't think about anything right now. I just want to sleep.'

'Ok. Everything's gonna be alright you know, rock star. I won't allow you to fail.'

I let her drift off in the back as I typed away on my laptop. I was far too wired to sleep, to the point that I opened the wine and drank it all myself straight from the bottle. Maybe it was me who had the alcohol problem. California's finest was rather moreish with a sweet kick that created a buzz and helped the words flow.

After I'd finished scribing, the laptop started to blur as the wine kicked in, and exhaustion seized me. With a bottle of wine sank deep into the gullet, I churned over the night's events. Aside from losing out on a deal, we were left in limbo. I didn't share Ozzie's optimism, but what did I know? I had to present positivity for Dee's sake. Her mindset put the remaining two gigs in jeopardy. Even if she turned up, I was sceptical of her performance level as she appeared devoid of any drive, like a candle on the cusp of burning out. She had deep-lying issues that made her as vulnerable as a wounded bird. Those issues needed resolving, and she needed to find peace and balance whilst also retaining the edge within her that made her shine. She was a firecracker, a femme fatale, but an intelligent and highly spiritual human being.

We were so different, yet somehow in perfect synergy with each other. She had my heart as a fan of her words and music and through her charming but unpredictable personality. Somehow, I felt irrefutably connected to her, like our paths crossing had some sort of fateful meaning.

CHAPTER 30

I jumped out of my skin when the voluminous blast from the Chevy car horn woke me from my awkward, upright sleeping position. My back and neck were as stiff as a credit controller. Dee sat in the passenger seat chuckling her head off at my reaction.

'Sorry, I couldn't resist. You've got saliva on your, chin by the way,' she pointed out.

Wiping my face, I reacted, 'I shit myself then.'

'I know. Funny, wasn't it?'

'Hilarious. What time is it?'

'Gone seven.'

'Seven! You couldn't let me sleep?'

'Not if you want to take peyote.'

'At this time in the morning? You're joking, aren't you?'

'No, but once we've eaten and found a suitable spot, we'll be ready.'

I couldn't believe I'd slept completely exposed to whatever psycho prowled the desert - a very real fear in America. Thankfully, all my limbs were intact, and I'd not been drugged, dragged into a field, and sodomised during the night. It did feel kind of cool that we'd slept in the car in the wilderness, like a proper sixties thing to do. In different circumstances, we could've listened to a 'Summer of Love' playlist, smoked weed, contemplated life, love, and music, deciphered the meaning of the universe, and offered unconventional mind-altering answers to questions that floated around our expanded psyches. But the previous night was far too scrambled and raw to make any sense of anything.

'How are you feeling?' I asked.

'Shit. Feels like a bad dream.'

'Dee, it's not your fault. Fuck him and his deal. You're still a great band with so much to offer. Your fate isn't sewn up on this tour. There's plenty of time.'

'It just feels like we had the Whisky gig built up to be this galactic moment where it would all come together.'

'You know life doesn't work like that. It will happen when you least expect it.'

'It's our own fault for putting too much emphasis and hype on it. I don't know what I'm thinking, which is why your idea, although ridiculous, is actually quite appealing.'

'Ridiculous and appealing is *exactly* how I'd describe it.'

'If we're doing this, then there's one rule.'

'What's that?'

'No phones. There can't be any phones if we're doing this. I don't want any disturbances,' she insisted.

'You got it. It's going on silent as soon as we find somewhere suitable. I need to ask you something in return?'

'What is it?'

'Your interview is pending to be sent. If you're happy with it, I'll send it, and it'll be published, but you can read it first if you prefer?'

She thought for a second. 'Send it.'

'You don't want to read it first?'

'No. I trust you.'

That was a big admission for Dee.

We found a McDonald's nearby, where I smashed through a token brekkie. More importantly, I connected to the Wi-Fi to send the interview and the L.A. review.

Dee asked, 'Where are we going anyway?'

'Joshua Tree. I've heard it's a place to find answers. The Tree has powers apparently, much like the desert in Nevada.'

'I've always wanted to go to Joshua Tree,' she revealed.

'Yeah, me too. It looks beautiful.'

In my best Alan Partridge voice, I mimicked, 'Do you know the album, The Joshua Tree? Well, he wrote half of it over there...and the other half...over there.'

She looked at me blankly. 'What the hell are you going on about?'

'Have you ever seen Alan Partridge?'

'What the fuck is Alan Partridge?'

'I forget you're from Bermuda sometimes. Never mind.'

'You're weird.'

We'd driven quite far the night before, so it wasn't long before we entered the confines of the National Park. We were met by powerful, resplendent topography and awe-inspiring landscapes that were truly nature's porn. The region's bristled Joshua trees scattered the terrain amongst cactus, rock piles, and monolithic boulder formations. We were on the brink of the Colorado Desert and the Mojave Desert, where two different ecosystems met. The road weaved and carved its way through the hazardous territory, sculpted by elements that created a showcase of geologic wonderments.

'Going to California' by Led Zeppelin came on, and the tone brought a melancholic vibe to the car. The reflectiveness of the lyrics embodied the mood, and from Dee's perspective, she was *'going to California with an aching in [her] heart.'*

I didn't expect to be back on another search for answers so soon after Vegas. This time, the tables had turned, and it wasn't me in need of salvation. It was the broken, bewildered girl who sat beside me. I looked at her and empathised with her delicate frame of mind. The confident, tenacious star who could cut you into shreds with an icy stare or with the edge of her callous tongue had become a shadow of herself.

Once we were lost in the Park's peaceful riches, I pulled up on the side of a gravel clearing that led nowhere.

'This is it. This is where you'll find answers,' I announced.

I took plenty of bottled water in my backpack, ready for the expectant regurgitation after Dee swallowed the buttons.

The zephyr provided respite from the intense sun as we exited the car.

'Are you sure you want to do this? You don't have to,' I asked.

She looked at me. 'I think I need to, don't you? I'm confused right now, and I need answers.'

'You have to be sure. It's no joke taking this stuff. It's powerful as fuck, and you have to be prepared to see some shit. I felt out of options, but just because it worked for me, doesn't mean it'll work for you. I still think you have options, and your situation is different to mine. Ultimately, it's your call from here.'

She thought for a moment as the desert crosswind howled between the boulder mountains. She broke the wind's clean whistle, 'Fuck it. Why not? I've always wanted to do this anyway. There's no better setting and circumstance for it. Are you dropping with me?'

'Not this time, rock star. I've been there, done that, and worn the t-shirt. Although I have my own answers to find, I don't feel I need to delve into what peyote brings to find them. Besides, someone needs to look out for you and be sober enough to drive later.'

'Fair enough...pussy.' Her snappy joke-filled tone resurfaced.

'You just can't help yourself, can you?'

'You should know why I do it by now, and not take offence.'

'You'd think so, wouldn't you? But you have an uncanny ability to piss me off, and you...'

She stopped me short, 'Shut up moaning, and give me the peyote, will you?'

I gave her one of those looks that had no effect and blasted, 'God, you're annoying. You know, we're in the desert, and no one knows we're here, and no one is around for miles. I could bury you here, and no one would ever know. Don't tempt me, Dee.'

'You could try and get your ass kicked in the process.'

For such a petite girl, she was strong and had a lot of rage inside her. There was no way I would take her on.

I asked, 'How many missed calls do you have? I've got five from a combination of those four. They're going to be royally pissed at me.'

'I've got nine, so what?'

'So what? She says. So what? Driving band members into the desert is above my pay grade. Especially when you've got a big gig tonight, and everyone is hammering my phone to get in touch.'

'I said no phones. Do *not* respond. I've just started to grow fond of you these last few days, don't spoil it. Now give me the peyote, will you.'

'Fine.'

I rummaged through my backpack for a plastic bag that contained the buttons I'd snagged from Lynwood's. I handed them over, and she snatched at them.

'So, how do I take these then, expert?'

'Just eat one and take some water...and try to hold it down because they taste vile.'

She ripped the bag and emptied the contents into one hand, taking the bottle of water with the other. She was about to shove one into her mouth but stopped short. She closed her palm to make a fist and looked meditatively into the harsh moonscape.

'What's wrong?' I asked.

'Just give me a minute. I need some music on. What did you listen to when you dropped?'

'Loads because I had my earphones and walked about. But 'The End' by the Doors was the main track that inspired answers.

'Good choice, but I'm not emulating you. Put 'Atmosphere' on by Joy Division. I love that track.'

I nodded my approval, played the song through my phone, and left her to her own thoughts. I savoured the rare, quiet moment where I had space to reflect on the past few weeks without interruption. Joshua Tree was a beautiful and striking setting. The barren, ruthless land stretched for miles and weaved in and out of rocky mountain ranges, canyons, and ridges. Nothing was around whatsoever, which was a tranquil yet scary proposition in the same breath. I was somewhat envious that my search for answers hadn't happened there.

Dee broke my trance, 'Hot Shot?'

'Yep?'

'I don't need this.'

'Don't need what?'

'I don't need peyote to find answers.' She put the buttons back in the bag and handed them back to me. 'This is ridiculous. I'm not letting some scumbag drive me to this. I'm in a great band, and we *are* going places. We've come this far, and we'll carry on till we fuckin' make it. Fuck him!'

'Yes, Dee! Fuck him!'

'Who cares if we don't get signed? It doesn't matter. We've done a tour of the States, and it's been epic. We're about to support the Red Hot Chili Peppers too. Whatever happens, or doesn't happen, fuck it. It's been an amazing ride.'

'You're right. It's been amazing!' I roared.

'Now get me to the show. Hop to it, Hot Shot.'

We darted back to the car. I started the engine and searched the playlist.

'What are you doing?' she asked.

'We need a song for this moment.'

I pressed play and the opening riff to 'It's a Long Way to the Top (If You Wanna Rock 'n' Roll)' by AC/DC penetrated the speakers.

'Love it,' she laughed.

'Lyrically suitable, I think.'

I swung a one-eighty in the Chevy and careered out of Joshua Tree, leaving a trail of dust in our wake.

The drive would take three hours or so, and we let the song repeat ten times over to sustain the euphoria. That was until it wore thin, and we let the 'shuffle' function soundtrack the rest of the journey. 'Solsbury Hill' by Peter Gabriel played next and plunged me into thoughts of Eva.

I commented on the track to Dee, 'This song! It's one of Eva's favourites.'

Dee turned sharply and looked flustered. 'Shit!' she exclaimed.

'What? What's wrong?'

'Oh. Nothing.'

'Doesn't sound like nothing.'

She dug out her phone.

'Hang on. You said no phones.'

'That was while we were in Joshua Tree. It doesn't apply now.'

'What's wrong?' I asked again.

Her response was cagey, 'I just…thought, that I… should let Ozzie know we're OK. I remembered that he doesn't know we're on our way. I'm up to twenty missed calls now.'

She typed away for a minute or so and then made a call. I turned the music down.

Ozzie's voice could be heard clearly on the other end. 'Where the fuck have you been?' he shouted.

'Ozzie, relax. We're OK and on our way.'

'You two can't keep pulling this shit.'

'Where are you?' Dee asked.

'We're nearly in Vegas. What time are you gonna be here?'

'Couple of hours yet.'

'Well, get your arses over to New York New York, check-in and then get over to Count's Vamp'd. We're gonna have to meet you there cos I need to get there early to sort shit out.'

'Ok, cool. Speak soon. Love you, love you, Ozzie.'

'You're driving me insane!'

He hung up, and Dee joked, 'He's in a calm mood.'

By the time the music came back on, 'Solsbury Hill' had finished, and we'd moved on with the conversation.

We were on one of the more exciting drives in the world, from Los Angeles to Las Vegas, via Joshua Tree.

It was a drive that had been immortalised in many movies over the years. It still baffled me how the entertainment capital of the world was in such a remote area. I'd only ever arrived in Vegas by plane before, so to do so by road from Los Angeles was something special.

We finally entered Nevada as our five eventful days in California ended. Although we were still in the desert, the outer rims of the mountainous scenery appeared smoother, and the conditions less brazen. It amazed me how topographies changed almost immediately after crossing State lines.

We were thirty minutes away, and civilisation appeared on the distant horizon. What we thought was Vegas turned out to be a false alarm as we passed through the small resort, Primm. The same distant mirage could be seen again a little further down the road, but it turned out to be Jean, another hamlet of a resort plonked in the middle of the desert. Fifteen minutes out, we curved to the left and passed a small boulder-filled mountain close to the side of the road. We rounded the bend, and the colossal, enigmatic empire bathed the horizon. Vegas was in sight. Part of me was returning home...again.

CHAPTER 31

Ozzie and the band were already at the venue when we arrived in New York New York. I let the nostalgia wash over me as I strolled through the grand foyer of a place that meant so much.

Sensing that I was in the realm of memories, Dee asked, 'When did you last speak to Eva?'

'I messaged her before the gig last night. She doesn't know what's happened since. I've not exactly had time to make a call, and I have no clue how to explain everything.'

'Call her later when we get to the venue. You'll have time before we're on.'

'Yeah, I will do.'

After a short taxi ride, we arrived at Count's Vamp'd Rock Bar & Grill, in a part of town far removed from the areas I'd experienced nine months earlier. It was a truer representation of Vegas away from the glitz and glamour of the Strip - more illicit and sinful.

The venue was a clear homage to the classic era of rock - dark and dirty with a penchant for immorality - our sort of establishment. Ironically, there was a very Sunset Strip theme to the joint. The place attempted to replicate the aura of bars like the Rainbow and Rock

& Reilly's. Count's Vamp'd had a bubbling reputation for live music, having played host to many bands that went onto bigger and better things. The stage, sound and lighting system were impressive, providing the ultimate live music experience.

The place was already quite busy, with loud, seasoned boozers making up most of the clientele. We asked the barman to show us backstage after we identified Dee as the lead singer of Cutthroat Shambles. He accompanied us through the double doors behind the stage until we saw Ozzie in the corridor.

'Fuckin' finally. They're here!' he snapped.

He hugged Dee and asked, 'Are you OK, kid?'

'I am now. Let's put it behind us. I'm ready to rock out with my cock out tonight.'

'Just keep doing what you've been doing on that stage, and it'll happen, I'm sure. Fuck Lynwood. Do *not* blame yourself for this.'

'I'm over that now. I can't believe you butted him. I didn't know you had it in you,' she said.

'No one fucks with my bands.'

'Has there been any fallout from it?' I asked.

'Nah. I'm sure it'll be left at that. Only you guys saw me butt him, so he can't prove shit.'

We were about to enter the room when Ozzie blocked my path.

'Whoa, just hang on there, Ricky.'

'What's up?'

'There's a surprise package for you in there.'

'What do you mean? Have you bought me a bunch of flowers? Chocolates? Signed Cutthroats CD? Speedboat, like on Bullseye? You didn't need to do anything for me.'

'I didn't do anything. Maybe it's just best you see for yourself.'

I was bemused. Ozzie moved to let me open the door. I stepped in, and my heart wrenched as I gazed upon a familiar face sitting on a stool on the far side of the room, being accosted by three male band members I knew well.

The figure turned her head and locked into a split-second, intense stare with me. She smiled with a grace that melted me and said, 'Hey you!'

'Eva! What the...? How the...?'

'I wanted to surprise you.'

'I'm gobsmacked!'

Dee poked her head in and confessed, 'I arranged for her to come to the show a couple of nights ago. Thought we'd surprise you and keep it a secret.'

Eva hopped off the stool, and I almost ran toward her.

'I can't believe you're here,' I whispered as I swallowed her up in my arms.

Will spoke up, 'I'll tell you what I can't believe. How someone as fine as her is with you?'

'Told you,' I said before turning to Dee. 'You did this? Why?'

'I wanted to return the favour for what you did for me in Sedona...and Flagstaff. And you needed a little push to do the right thing and bring this girl out here with us.' Turning to Eva, she said, 'He's been constantly talking about you by the way.'

'And jacking off to you too,' Kyle interrupted, bringing belly laughter around the room.

My face turned tomato red, and Eva turned a similar shade at the comment.

'Now you know why I said "shit" in the car. I'd totally forgotten she was coming, given what happened last night, so I had to make other arrangements,' Dee revealed.

'You sneaky fucker.'

Dee said to Eva, 'Sorry for the rushed plan, chick. I've been a bit preoccupied the last twenty-four hours, and we had a no phone pact for a while.'

'It's OK. I got here fine. Thank you for inviting me.'

'You're welcome. Oh, and Ricky?'

'Yeah?'

'Good work. She's hot.'

Eva blushed, and I smiled. Dee added, 'You don't swing the other way, do you?'

Eva shied away again. I guess she had to get used to Dee's lack of filter.

Dee whispered close to me, 'Listen, I'm going to take the boys out of here and tell them about Michelle before they read the interview.'

'You want me there with you?'

'No, it's cool. Stay with your girl. I got this.'

'If you need me, you know where I am. Good luck.'

She turned to everyone else. 'Right, we need to soundcheck and leave these two to catch up. And there's something I need to talk to you about.'

The band filtered out, leaving Eva and me alone. Her undulating autumn brown hair reached down the small of her back and was wavier than I remembered. I moved towards her to stroke the side of her cheek with the back of my fingers and became lost in her glittering eyes. I softly kissed her luscious lips. She tasted delicious, and the familiar ambrosial scent of fruit and patchouli in her fragrance propelled me back to nine months earlier.

'I can't believe you're here. How did you get here? Surely you didn't drive?' I asked.

'No, I got a plane. It only takes an hour. It was worth it to see you. I've missed you so much.'

'I can't tell you how much I've missed you. This lot are crazy. I'm a broken man and need some normality back in my life.'

I stepped back to fully admire her. 'You look sensational by the way.'

She was dressed in a stylish, navy blue, skinny fit blazer, a pair of tight-fitted, sky blue coloured jeans that showed her snake embossed ankle boots, and a cream frill front shirt. The top few buttons were unfastened, exposing a subtle snippet of her smooth, tanned flesh. A pair of large rimmed dark brown sunglasses rested on her head to complete her fashionable look.

'You look tired,' she said with empathy, adding, 'Good, but tired nonetheless.'

'Tired? I'm a wreck and probably look a right state. I slept in the car last night and got about two hours sleep. I've been driving all day and dealing with the pressures of the last couple of weeks. But it's all worth it for this moment.'

'Still the same Casanova. Such a smooth talker.'

'I think you're the only woman to ever call me smooth.'

Her hand rested against my cheek. 'Your beard has grown. Look at all this hair.'

She grabbed it with her fingers and playfully tugged at it.

'I know. You forget to shave on the road.'

'I like it. Very sexy and manly.'

'Where are you staying?' I asked.

'Dee told me you were staying in New York New York, so I booked a room there. How fitting, yeah?'

'I know, right. Of all the hotels they could choose, Ozzie picked that one. I'm meant to be sharing with Dee. I'm sure she'll appreciate being on her own now I can get in your room.'

'Oh, you think it's that easy, do you?' she teased.

'You going to make me work for it?'

'Oh yeah. Just like our first night.'

'If memory serves, I don't think I had to work that hard for it,' I joked.

She nudged me mockingly. 'You're so cheeky, Mr Englishman.'

'How about I start with a drink?'

'You're on.'

'Vodka and soda, on the rocks? Filled to the top in a large glass?'

'Well remembered.'

The selection of drinks on the table was enough to accommodate a small army.

The door swung open. To my astonishment, Anya walked in.

'What are you doing here?' I asked.

'I came down with the boys, but I've been on my phone doing an interview. How are you, Ricky?'

'I'm great, thanks.'

Where is everyone?'

'They're having a band meeting before sound-check.'

'Cool. I'll wait by the bar till they're done.'

'Hang on. Are you here in a journalistic capacity?' I asked, still confused by her presence.

'Hmmm. Not exactly. I'm here as a fan and a friend of the band.'

'Oh yeah. Any particular member you're a *friend* of?' I delved.

She looked coy and held her hands out as if she knew nothing.

'You don't fool me, Anya. You and Kyle?' I guessed.

She just flicked her eyebrows at me, 'I don't know. Maybe.'

'That boy never fails to surprise me,' I countered. 'By the way, this is Eva, a good friend of mine.'

'We met before you arrived, and they told me the situation. Were you surprised?'

'Just a bit.'

'Aww. Bless you, hon. I'll leave you both to catch up.'

She closed the door on her way out.

'Good friend?' Eva quizzed.

'Well, we don't have a label, do we?'

'I guess we don't.'

Rather than stay on the subject, I relayed everything that had happened since we last spoke, especially about the previous night, but I found myself talking about the whole trip. It dawned on me just how much had happened. The anecdotes gushed out of me like a waterfall as she listened intently.

The band returned, and I made a point of catching Dee's eyes. I mimed, 'Are you OK?' She looked upbeat and gave me a thumbs-up, which was a weight off my mind.

Kyle headed straight for Anya, and as he sat down, she planted herself down on his lap. He wrapped his arms firmly around her waist while she draped hers around his shoulders. I wondered what had happened after the show the previous night that led to them hooking up.

Shortly after, Dee shouted to the rest of the band, 'Right, you fuckers. Bring it in.'

They huddled together for their usual ritual, but Dee stopped short and turned to the rest of us.

'C'mon everyone, bring it in. All of you are invited for this one.'

Anya and Eva looked confused, but all of us circled together, shoulder to shoulder, arms interlocked with our heads bowed. Dee began serenading, 'With a Little Help from My Friends', and the band joined in, followed by the rest of us. Within seconds, we were in perfect harmony and howled the lyrics out to fill the room, much to the bemusement of the main band due on afterwards. It was a pivotal moment, and never a truer word was said to describe the people I was lucky enough to be in the presence of.

The Cutthroats were filling in for a band that had to cancel. Because of that, they were the first band on before the main act, The Blinders. It was a chance to play to a new audience that had filled the bar to the brim and bustled with anticipation, curious to see what the late stand-ins could offer.

Eva, Ozzie, Anya, and I watched from behind the merch stand as the Cutthroats shook Vegas to its very core, leaving a lasting impression on Sin City. They blitzed through a forty-minute set of their best songs. Dee, burgundy cowboy hat in tow, was the typical star of the performance, completely indomitable and unfazed by the previous night. I didn't know where she found the motivation and energy or how she could completely upturn her mood within hours. It was an enviable strength.

Eva was blown away. I spent the entire show standing behind her with my arms wrapped around her slender waist and my fingers interlaced in hers. I kissed her on the cheek and neck intermittently between songs, and when my lips touched her soft flesh, her eyes closed as she dissolved into me.

It was the first gig the Cutthroats had performed where I didn't need to make any notes on my phone. I knew their set all too well, and there was no way I was releasing Eva from my grasp. I was too caught up in the emotion of the surprise after being apart for so long.

When the band delivered the slow and sentimental ballad, 'Ready to Love', I heard it in a different light. I hadn't noticed before, but the lyrics were a little closer to home and illustrated what I was feeling. *'I don't know where I'm goin', or who I'm gonna be, All I know is I need you, I need you here with me, Are you ready to love me? I don't know.'*

Ozzie was approached by a couple of guys early in the show and engaged in conversation with them throughout. They were both dressed in smart shirts and jeans but didn't look like the average gig-goer. They spent the entire show gesturing toward the band, looking like they were impressed by what they saw.

The show ended, and the band lapped up the plaudits from new-found fans, who incessantly applauded the performance.

Backstage, Eva told Dee how fabulous she was and praised the band, which encouraged Will to try and wind me up. 'Told you she'd fancy us once she saw us play.'

'You've got no chance. All I have to do is tell her the Warticon and Rainbow stories.'

Everyone sniggered as Will's face dropped.

Eva asked, 'What's Warticon?'

'Never mind. It'll just make you throw up.'

Ozzie entered with the two men he'd been talking to throughout the show.

He grabbed our attention. 'Guys, I want you to meet James Quinn and Conor Gregory from Purple Universe Records.'

James was first to introduce himself, 'It's a pleasure to meet you all.'

Handshakes and introductions followed before Conor took the lead, speaking in a heavy New York accent, 'I'll cut to the chase. We've been monitoring you for some time now. Word on the street was that Lynwood had the monopoly on you, so we backed off, but we kept an eye out to see how that developed.'

'Oh yeah. That went swimmingly,' Dee said, rolling her eyes.

'Yeah, we heard about the Whisky gig last night. It's why we came down here.'

James came in again, 'For the record, we never liked Charles Lynwood, so I'm glad he got a smack however that came about.'

'Don't know what happened there. All very strange,' Dee joked.

Conor continued, 'Like I said, we've known about you for some time now, and we've been keeping up with the blogs that your man from Sonic Bandwagon has been writing.'

'That's Ricky. Come say hello, Ricky,' Dee exhorted, shifting me into the limelight.

I shook hands with them both.

Conor turned back to the band. 'Look, I won't beat around the bush. You guys have got something, something perfect for Purple Universe. We want you to be part of the family and get you into a studio as soon as possible in New York.'

'You're shitting me?' Will yelled. The rest of the band echoed his reaction.

James intervened, 'We're not like Lynwood. We don't have hidden agendas. I can imagine you're sceptical after last night, but I can assure you we don't bullshit or fuck around. We're fair with our bands, and we just want to make great music.'

'That's all we ever wanted. No bullshit. Just about the music,' Dee affirmed.

'You don't have to make any decisions now. We'll get the paperwork sent over tomorrow morning. Mull it over while you're in Bermuda. If it's all good, it's an easy flight to New York from there, and it'll be on our dime. We'll arrange to pick you up and show you the offices and the city.'

Ozzie said, 'Sounds good, fellas. We'll discuss it and get back to you, I'm sure.'

'Thanks, guys. No pressure to give us an answer immediately. We wanted to meet you in person to show we're serious and act fast after last night. If you want to grab a drink after, we'll be out by the bar,' Conor said.

Conor pulled me to one side before they left. 'Ricky, I don't know how this arrangement works with the band, Sonic Bandwagon, and your future involvement, but I'd like you to come to New York too if the band take us up on the offer.'

'Really? Why?'

'I want you to continue writing about them and bring in the process of recording an album. Maybe you could extend the piece to be about the record label and how it works in modern times. I like the angle you've portrayed in the blogs about the comparisons between today and yesteryear. Have a think, speak to the band, and your editor, and we'll talk soon.'

He gave me his card.

'I don't know what to say. I'm a bit shocked, to be honest. That's some offer, and of course, I'm interested, but I'll see what the band decide and go from there if that's OK?'

'Of course. Hopefully, we'll see you out front for a drink.'

Conor and James left, and the excitement erupted at the prospect of working with a reputable label. It was a relief, and at that moment, it really felt like the band had finally completed the mission, with no apprehension about the deal this time.

Ozzie was visibly more excited. 'This time, I know it's gonna be the real deal. It never felt right with that prick in Los Angeles, but my fault for allowing it to play out.'

'Put it all down to experience,' I said.

'I was too desperate and should've known better. That's not how it should be. I have a good feeling about this one, though.'

Dee came over, and I whispered in her ear, 'You finally did it. And without taking peyote.'

'It helped bring clarity out in Joshua Tree, even if I didn't drop anything.'

'It's what this part of the world does. It provides answers.'

Quince picked Dee up from behind and bounced her up and down enthusiastically. Dee laughed and ordered him to put her down.

Eva and I were alone again as the band talked about their collective good news.

She said, 'I heard what that man from Purple Universe said to you. You are *so* going to New York and carrying this on.'

I looked forlornly at her. 'You know what that might mean for us, don't you?'

'Don't even think like that. We've had plenty of setbacks, so another isn't going to make any difference, is it? But I get to see you tonight, and that's all that matters.'

'You know what? You're here for one night only, and I'm not going to spoil it by talking beyond the tour like we agreed.'

'I'll drink to that.'

We went out front to watch the main band, The Blinders. They hurled themselves into the menacing opener, 'Gotta Get Through'. It was possibly one of the most explosive ways to open a show that I'd ever witnessed. I was immediately hooked as their tracks unnerved and pulverized the audience. The performance unleashed fire and fury that created a spate of hedonistic rage down by the front. Their avant-garde and edgy approach to psych-orientated rock 'n' roll enthralled the crowd, and I made a mental note to give them a plug in the next blog review.

After the show, the night carried on in the same celebratory, relief-filled manner. The band and Ozzie spoke with Purple Universe and conveyed their hopes and dreams. James and Conor understood their vision and were eager to facilitate. Conor expressed to Dee his desire to keep me on in a writing capacity. She agreed it was a good idea which made me feel like an important cog in the Cutthroats' wheel.

We eventually left the Purple Universe guys with the agreement that the band would look over the proposal and confirm the deal with them. It was safe to assume there would be no issues - James and Conor seemed trustworthy and genuine music men. Their roster of globally based bands highlighted their reputation and spoke volumes about where their allegiances lay.

CHAPTER 32

The eight of us ended up drinking back in New York New York. We sat in a familiar part of the bar on the outskirts of the gaming area. I told the story of how Eva and I met and how she returned to Vegas to see me on my final night. Naturally, I embellished my importance and self-worth in the tale, joking that 'she couldn't live without me.'

Everyone turned the tables. They accused me of not being able to live without her, pointing out that she had only travelled a couple of hundred miles to see me, but I had travelled thousands of miles halfway across the world to see her. My argument that she had done the surprise visit *twice* fell flat on its arse. Not that it mattered, it was blatantly obvious to even the most visually impaired individual how besotted with each other we were.

I'd nipped up to my room and grabbed the gifts I'd bought for Eva on the Indian Reservation - the authentic Indian bracelet and chakra stones. She loved the gesture and put the bracelet on straight away.

It was a cherished time sitting inside the casino bar. All of us were relaxed, high on life and looking forward to the future, wherever it took each of us. 'Heroes' by David Bowie played somewhere in the background, just to add an element of sweetness to the setting.

What we'd experienced together on the road meant something more than being bandmates, a manager, a journalist, or friends. We were family! Dee had revealed in her interview that 'home was a state of mind'. I began to understand what she meant and couldn't agree with her more. I felt at home, bound by the music, the vision, the thirst for adventure with people I loved, and a flat-out refusal to succumb to a version of normality that I felt uncomfortable being part of.

Kyle, Will, and Quince happily took up the reins of the conversation. They relentlessly took the piss out of each other in the typical Mancunian way, which left Anya and Eva puzzled at times. Dee had at least been subject to Manc humour for a couple of years and had an understanding. Eva and Anya asked what certain words and phrases meant that were unheard of beyond the realms of Manchester and England.

Ozzie had approached me and admitted that seeing Eva and me together reminded him of Mia, the love of his life from many years earlier. I asked whether he was still in contact with her, and he said that they were just Facebook friends and limited to wishing each other Happy Birthday. I asked if he had ever wanted to take it any further than that. He replied, 'I couldn't put her through any more shit again. She's probably too much of a high-flyer for this life now.'

'But if there's something still there after all this time, then maybe it's worth pursuing,' I suggested.

'I have enough rejection in life from this music shit. I'm not prepared to go through it in my personal life too,' he responded.

'You can't go through life like that. You know as well as I do the importance of taking chances and that you'll never know until you try.'

'Different when it comes to Mia.'

'If you say so, but I believe it's all the same ball-park.'

He shrugged and ordered another drink from the passing barmaid.

It didn't take long for Quince and Will to become restless and express their desire to experience the hedonistic side of the city. Dee stated her intentions to go with them. Ozzie surprised us all by saying he was going too, citing that he deserved a blowout after the crap the band had put him through in the past couple of weeks. I thought it was a way for him to forget about Mia, who was clearly on his mind.

Kyle said he was going to hang back in the hotel with Anya, which brought about wolf whistles and persistent teasing about how Kyle had changed and was now under the thumb. Anya assured us that it was Kyle's decision and had nothing to do with her as she wanted to 'party with the Mancs.'

The thrill seekers eventually left the hotel in search of a debauched night. Kyle and Anya retired to their room soon after, and Eva and I bought another drink.

She said, 'You know what? I've not seen you in so long, but I don't want to go upstairs with you. Is that weird?'

'Oh, thanks. Are you that repulsed by my heavy stubble or something?'

'No, that's not what I meant. I just love being with you and talking, and sometimes that's more important. Like it's more intimate.'

'I understand completely.'

She looked at the ground sheepishly and then said out of the blue, 'I need to ask you something, and I want you to be honest. Whatever you say, I won't get upset. I probably don't have any right to ask.'

'What is it?' I interrupted, concerned.

'Have you slept with anyone on this tour?'

I was caught off guard by the question.

'I've seen how girls flaunt themselves at the band. You must have had the opportunity, and I wouldn't blame you if you did,' she added.

I looked deep into the well of her eyes. A twinge of guilt sat inside my stomach about the night with Lucy.

'I'm not going to lie, Eva. Yes, there have been opportunities, but I resisted most of the time.'

'Most of the time?'

'There was one time in Phoenix at a party where I was blind drunk. It's not an excuse but ask anyone how bad I was. I drank from a keg whilst being held upside down and then took a hit from a bong. Add to that plenty of shots and near enough a bottle of JD, and I'm surprised I didn't end up in hospital. Anyway, I barely remember it, but I ended up kissing someone. That was all that happened. I woke up in the same bed as her, don't ask me how because I don't remember that, but she assured me that I passed out, and she was only there to make sure I didn't choke on my own vomit. The fact she was *that* concerned shows how drunk I was. I felt so bad afterwards. I could've lied, but I'm telling you now,' I pleaded.

She laughed at me, which wasn't the expected reaction. 'You *only* kissed someone? Is that all?'

'Yeah. I'm so sorry.'

'That's no big deal.'

'Oh yeah. Does that mean you've been with someone else?'

'Not recently. I kissed one guy about five months ago and went on a date with another guy three months ago, but that was all.'

'I think I can live with that without knowing the details.'

'This is the twenty-first century, Ricky. I didn't expect you to put your life on hold and not meet someone else when you live so far away.'

'But I wasn't looking for anyone. I was too busy trying to get my life in order, but I'm amazed you haven't dated more. Have you seen yourself? You must have men throwing themselves at you? We live thousands of miles away, and we've never defined what we are. Why didn't you move on?'

'Why didn't you?' she returned.

'I was focused on sorting my future out and got engrossed with the music writing. You?'

'I just didn't want anyone else. I kissed someone at a party after my friends practically forced me, to help get over you because they convinced me you would be out doing the same. I felt terrible afterwards.'

'I can honestly say I wasn't out doing that at all.'

She smiled. 'You're sweet. I expected you to say you've slept with many girls, and I was prepared to accept that.'

'I guess I know I've got something not worth ruining, whatever *this* is. But I don't think I could find *this* in Manchester.'

She leaned into me, and I clasped my arm around her.

She asked, 'Are we going to have the same conversation as last time we were in New York New York together?'

'Things are different now. This isn't going to be the long goodbye. I don't know what's going to happen, but I need to see what the band's plans are after Bermuda, what this contract means, and then what New York entails and how long it could last. You could come to Bermuda?' I suggested.

'I can't. I have work, and I don't want to encroach.'

'You won't be encroaching. Kyle will probably ask Anya.'

'Thank you for the offer, but I have to be back at work in three days.'

'I don't want this night to end. You know we've never spent more than twenty-four hours together and have only been together physically for three days in total.'

'How scary is it that we have this connection having seen so little of each other?'

'Crazy!'

'I want you to know... that Vegas trip meant everything to me, cariño,' she revealed.

'It did to me too.'

'Whatever happens between us, I'll always have those nights.'

I kissed her again, but she quickly pulled away and asked, 'Speaking of Vegas. Tell me about this book you're writing?'

'I've not written much.'

'I think it'll be the making of you. Go for it.'

'You have a knack for galvanising me.'

Somewhere around 4am, we made a move to Eva's room. We kissed passionately when privacy prevailed. She pushed me onto the bed and started to seductively strip for me. I wasn't as graceful, yanking off my t-shirt, jeans, and trainers. I lay there in my boxers and admired her perfect, tight body. Her clothes fell to the floor one by one. Her legs were luscious, and her butt was peachy, but those fuckin' spellbinding snake hips were dynamite. The way they shook was beyond exotic.

Her bra fell to the floor, but she covered her breasts teasingly by crossing her elbows and resting her palms on her shoulders. She stared at me with those beautiful brown eyes, lips pouted enticingly. Her arms fell to her sides before she pushed me onto my back. The animal-like, insatiable look on her face had me. She peeled off my boxers, flashing an amorous grin when she unleashed what lay beneath. She manoeuvred her way down to work it with her mouth and make sure I stood fully to attention, which took no time at all. My body shuddered as her lips worked my shaft. Satisfied that I was more than ready, she climbed up my body and kissed me. I cupped and stroked her fleshy, silken thighs as she positioned herself on top of me. Her eyes glittered, and her skin flushed. The familiarity of be-ing inside her was tantric, intense and mind-blowing. Just like our first time, I knew there was something far more meaningful to our relationship than what hap-pened in the secrecy of the bedroom.

CHAPTER 33

The next morning, I awoke flat on my back with Eva firmly enveloped in my arms. Her head rested on my chest, and we were as naked as the day we were born. I contemplated how a regular lad from Manchester had ended up with a gorgeous girl from Puerto Rico. I was so far removed from my own normality and upbringing, yet I felt about as close to how normal should feel when I was with her.

My phone buzzed to stop me from analysing further. It was a message from Jamie: *'Dee's interview is phenomenal. How did you get her to reveal so much? Great work. Los Angeles reviews are spot on. Minimal edits needed. Well done. You're really improving your technique and style.'*

I was delighted at Jamie's praise. When I first started writing about the tour, I constantly checked social media for some sort of blank approval from the readers. By that point, I didn't care anymore. All that mattered was whether I was happy with it and had done the band justice. I was proud that I had managed to keep pace with what was required and delivered under testing circumstances. It had been an incredible challenge that served as a test of character as well as a test of my writing ability. My determination to succeed and grasp the opportunity presented was probably the biggest accomplishment of my life. I had never put as much effort into anything 'work-related' ever. I smiled to myself at that realisation. I had finally found my niche, something that made me shine.

Jamie followed up his message: *'I spoke to Ozzie and looks like the band will be in New York. I believe Purple Universe invited you too. I think it's a great idea for you to cover that. Following them through the process of recording would make a brilliant piece and be great for the mag to have that connection with a top label.'*

I was grateful for his support and thanked him. The downside was another delay to my intent to travel and spend more time with Eva. I had no idea how long I was expected to stay in New York. I knew I couldn't say no to the opportunity, but something uncomfortable tugged at me when I thought of prolonging the time spent on tour.

I cast my phone aside and lay in perfect bliss with the girl of my dreams. Eva stirred, and her eyes blinked open. Even bleary-eyed, she melted me. She pulled my head towards hers and kissed me with those succulent, soft lips.

'Good morning, Mr Englishman.'

'Morning. Did you sleep well?'

She purred, 'Mmmm. I sure did.'

My phone rang. It was Dee, and I answered with sarcasm, 'What do the hell do you want?'

'Don't be acting tough in front of Eva,' she fired back.

'What's up?'

'Leave that poor girl alone and stop trying to get laid with your two-inch pecker. I'm just letting you know that I'm drunk and have only just come back to my room.'

'Are you kidding?'

'Nope.'

'What time is it?'

'Erm... nine o'clock.'

'You disappoint me, Dee. On my first night in Vegas, I went to sleep at about 10:30 in the morning.'

'There was a reason for that,' Eva interjected.

Dee shot back, 'I heard that. There's no way you were having sex till 10:30. That's the most disgusting image I've ever had.'

'The abuse I have to take from you. Where are the others?'

'Oh, they went to bed. I drank them under the table as usual. Showed them who's boss.'

'What about Ozzie? Did he last the distance?'

'Ozzie is a sly one. He brought some girl back.'

'No way!'

'It was so funny. He was hammered, but she was well into him. She was about twenty-five. I think she had daddy issues.'

I laughed before Dee pointed out, 'I've just realised something. If you two get married, Eva will be known as Eva Lever. That's funny.'

'Bye, Dee.'

I hung up.

We stayed in bed for a few hours until Ozzie messaged to say everyone was meeting in the lobby. We had a long drive to LAX airport in Los Angeles for a direct flight to Bermuda. The flight wasn't till midnight, so we had plenty of time to get there.

We all convened downstairs. Ozzie had received the contracts from Purple Universe, and there were no problems. It was a generous offer that could support them as full-time musicians for the contract duration if they fulfilled their obligations.

He was then grilled about bringing a girl back to his room, and boasted, 'Still got it, haven't I, boys? Good to flex a little muscle from time to time.'

Will said, 'It'll be good to have another person with us on the pull now Kyle's off the market.'

Ozzie answered, 'Careful Will. Once I drop a charm bomb or two, you're gonna be shit outta luck.'

'Bring it on, Romeo,' he countered.

Kyle, as predicted, had asked Anya to come to Bermuda. She had wanted to join us, but she had responsibilities to fulfil with gigs to attend and interviews to be conducted for the magazine. She was hitching a ride back to Los Angeles, so the pair would at least have a few hours to say goodbye. Who knew what was next for them? I had some understanding of the difficulties they were about to face if it was blossoming into something more serious.

Eva had to hang around for a couple of hours at the hotel after we'd left due to her later flight back to San Diego. After everyone had said bye to her, they picked up the Dodge from the valet. Dee said she'd ride with me and took the keys to the Chevy so she could pick it up for when I was through with my pending, painful goodbye.

Alone, Eva and I stood face to face, eye to eye.

I spoke first, 'Here we are again then. Saying goodbye in a Vegas hotel, unsure of when we'll see each other next. It's becoming a habit and not a nice one.'

'Let's not make a big deal out of it, yeah? I don't think I can handle another tearful goodbye. Let's just kid ourselves into thinking we'll meet up real soon.'

The tear she fought to hold back broke through to the corner of her eye. I reacted similarly and fought extra hard to swallow the weakness devouring me inside.

I muttered, 'I can do that. It's been the best moment of the trip seeing you again.'

'I've loved it. I love being with you, Ricky. I...I...' she was hesitant.

'What?'

Her eyes pierced through me and flicked to the side. She was unsure where and what to fix upon.

'What is it?' I gently asked.

She regained her composure and plucked up the courage to search deep into my soul and whispered, 'I think I love you! No...I don't think...I *know* I'm in love with you.'

I was stunned by her admission.

'I know it's crazy, but I am. I know you have to go to Bermuda and New York, and the last thing I wanted to do was make this harder, but I have to tell you how I really feel to your face and get this off my chest.'

She looked so vulnerable, and her trembling demeanour cried out for me to hug her. Without saying a word, I clutched her in my arms. She sniffled on my shoulder, still trying to hold back the emotion engulfing her.

Before I could answer to offer her comfort, she said, 'You need to go. Don't say anything. Whatever you say will make me hurt more, and I can't handle it either way. There's no win for me here, is there? I told you how I feel, so let's just leave it there. Don't say anything,' she repeated.

I didn't know what to say, even if I could find the right words. I was lost and couldn't identify the feelings that raced around my heart and mind. Through tear-soaked cheeks, head tilted to one side, she sighed, 'Fucking Vegas!'

I laughed to break the tension and repeated those same words she'd spoken on our first night. They were becoming the two simple words that defined us.

'Everyone's waiting for you. You need to go,' she said.

Reluctantly, I agreed and eventually tried to speak, 'Eva, look...I...'

'You don't need to, Ricky. I'll call you later, yeah?'

She smiled so sweetly.

'You just look after yourself, yeah?' I said. It was a pathetic, cop out response.

I kissed her tenderly before trudging to the lift. I took one last look at her seraphic face as I entered. In the distance, 'Make it With You' by Bread floated through the air and wrenched at my heart to make the scene more painful.

Once the doors closed, the magnitude of the situation hit me, and I broke down, desperately trying to fight back the tsunami of grief that attacked me.

By the time the doors reopened, I'd composed myself somewhat and found Dee waiting in the Chevy. I got into the driver's side, slammed the door, and sped off.

'Whoa! Slow down, Knight Rider.'

I dismissed her comment.

'Are you OK?' she asked.

'Not really. This fuckin' girl, Dee. I feel like I'm in a Lana Del Rey ballad.'

'You wanna talk about it?' she asked.

'Not really, but thanks.'

'Well, you better speak at some point. I'm not putting up with your mopey ass face for the next three or four hours.'

Quietness descended as we exited the bustling cauldron of Las Vegas. It wasn't long before we were back amongst the natural beauty that gave the States its secret, magical essence.

Half an hour into the drive, the mesmeric opening to 'Turn! Turn! Turn!' by The Byrds began. I fell head-first into some sort of abyss with Eva at the forefront of my mind.

Dee broke the silence, 'What is it about this chick?'

I paused to find the right words. 'She gives me hope, and she makes sense. We fit somehow. I don't know why because of how different we are, but we do.'

'If it feels like silk and moves like water, you're done for,' she theorised.

I laughed. 'I just want to be with her constantly. I can't stop gazing into her eyes when I'm with her. It's intense.'

'You'll see her again. It's all going to be OK. The same way you assured me it was going to be OK.'

'Who knows when that will be? We'll be in Bermuda for five days, then fly to New York. God knows how long that'll last. Then I've got to get a flight back to this side of the country. I initially wanted an adventure on my own, but I don't know now. I don't know what I want. In fact, I know fuck all.'

'That's not true. You *know* you love her. Maybe that's all you need, as the Beatles said.'

'You think I love her?' It was a statement and a question rolled into one.

'Oh, c'mon, Ricky. Isn't it obvious? You *know* it! I could've told you that back in Sedona. You're not that dumb, surely?'

'Why didn't you say anything?'

'Because I didn't think someone would be so stupid not to realise his true feelings and run away from them just because of his past.'

'Psychologist now, are you?'

'That was my major at college.'

'Now you tell me. So, what are you saying?'

'From what you told me, you were so hurt by your ex that you kept Eva at a distance, emotionally and logistically. Self-preservation after what your ex put you through.'

Something jolted inside me as if Dee's words summoned a revelation sent by some higher power. Everything suddenly became clear.

'Why the fuck didn't you tell me? I didn't know,' I yelled.

'Maybe *you* should've dropped peyote.'

'I can't believe how right you are. What have I done?'

'Why? What did you tell her before you left?'

'She told me she loved me and not to say anything because I sort of hesitated, so I didn't.'

'You really are a useless shit, aren't you, Hot Shot?'

'I was too stunned. I didn't expect her to say she loved me.'

'Far be it from me to be all emotional and rom-com about it, which I know you love, but you should've told her the same. She was begging you to, you absolute idiot.'

'She didn't. She said she didn't want me to talk.'

'And you believed that? Trust me, she did. How you got this girl in the first place blows my mind. Luckily for you, you have me to rectify the situation.'

Dee plucked out her phone and made a call.

'Kyle... tell Ozzie to pull over at the next stop, even if it's by the side of the road...just do it. Don't argue with me.'

She hung up.

'What are you doing?' I asked.

'I'm relieving you of your duties.'

'What do you mean?'

'I mean, I'm getting out of this car, and you're driving back to Vegas, and you're going to be with your girl.'

'I can't. What about Bermuda and New York?'

'You don't need to come. We've got the deal. You've done your job for us and your magazine. You don't belong on this Bermuda trip. What did I tell you in our interview in L.A.? Home is a state of mind. I know where mine is. You need to realise where yours is. Eva's your home. Out here is where you belong.'

I tried to get to grips with her statement. 'I don't know, Dee. Isn't this a bit extreme?'

'She's at the centre of everything you've done the last nine months. Think about it. You found peace after your ex because of her. You found music writing because of her. Initially, you flew over here to see her before we kidnapped you. She's the central theme to this Vegas book that you damn well better write. She's your life, Hot Shot.'

It suddenly became clear. 'Fuck! I've never looked at it like that.'

'You're a dick if you don't go. Trust me, you're not going to do better than that one. She won't be leaving the hotel for a while. Turn this car around, go back to Vegas and be with her. You know deep down that's what you really want.'

The thought of Dee's dreamy scenario hit home and spurred me on.

'It is what I want! I proclaimed.

'Finally!'

'Are you sure you don't need me in Bermuda?'

'Honey, I didn't even need you in America,' she shot back.

'Jamie will be pissed at me.'

'So, he'll be pissed. He'll get over it. There's nothing more you can do. I'm sure Purple Universe will have plenty of writers if they really want someone covering their side of things. I'll square it with Ozzie to smooth it over with Jamie for you.'

'What if Eva doesn't want me to go back with her?'

'Trust me...she does. She came out to see you as soon as someone offered her the chance. It should've been you making the offer, but as usual, I had to step in.'

My mind raced at a hundred miles per hour. 'Fuck. I can't believe I'm doing this.'

Ozzie pulled off into the next lay-by, and I followed.

He got out of the car and approached us. 'What's going on? Everything OK?' he questioned.

Dee pulled her bag from the boot and said, 'Ricky's going home.'

'What do you mean?' he asked.

'I've told him he's not invited to Bermuda any-more, and he needs to get his ass back to Vegas to be with Eva.'

Ozzie looked astounded. 'Are you serious?'

'Deadly,' she answered for me.

'Wow. Are you sure about that?' he asked me.

'Yeah, I am. Dee put up a good case.'

'Good for you. You're doing what I didn't with Mia.'

'Who's Mia?' Dee asked.

'Never mind,' Ozzie said.

He moved to shake my hand and said, 'We'll miss you, kid. It's been an experience, hasn't it?'

'That's one word for it, but it's not over for you guys. There's plenty more life left in the tour and then New York. It'll be the classic cliché of world domination next.'

The lads and Anya filed out of the Dodge to find out what was going on. Despite ripping into me for putting the girl before the band, they were ultimately happy for me. I hugged them all as they expressed their gratitude, declaring that it had been one hell of a ride.

They all returned to the Dodge, apart from Dee.

She divulged, 'I know I was a hard ass on you, for your own good cos you needed toughening up, Hot Shot. But I just want to say… thanks. You've been a good friend this tour, and I never expected that at all.'

'Me neither, you crazy rock star.'

She brought me close to her. 'Let's hug it out, bitch.'

I laughed.

After a couple of seconds, she said, 'C'mon, you need to get a move on.'

I pointed at her. 'You just make sure you keep in touch, yeah?'

In typical Dee fashion, she held her hands out and shrugged her shoulders nonchalantly without saying a word. She got into the Dodge. As it pulled away, Ozzie threw his arm out of the window to wave. Dee appeared at the back of the vehicle and knocked on the window to grab my attention. She grinned, blew a kiss at me, and signalled a peace sign as the van dashed off onto the freeway until she became invisible to the naked eye.

The dusty sand spiralled up from the tyre tracks, and I stood alone in the eerie quietness of the desert terrain. I'd just taken myself away from a rock tour, a trip to Bermuda and a stint in New York, and a part of me felt I was foolish. I took a deep breath and for a split second questioned my decision to leave. But my fears were dispelled when I caught sight of something out of the corner of my eye. Basking on a rock, a lizard stared right at me. Without giving my decision another thought, I got back into the car, swung a one-eighty, and pelted back down the freeway to Vegas…to Eva… to home.

EPILOGUE

Eighteen months had passed since I toured America with Cutthroat Shambles. The experience lurked somewhere in my subconscious, serving as a constant reminder of the enormity of that pivotal point in our lives.

The band stayed in touch following my departure from the tour, but that was the last time we'd seen each other. Life became hectic for them in the aftermath. We mostly communicated via the WhatsApp group that was set up by Will, aptly named 'G.N.R.E.N.', which stood for *Guns N Roaches and Eviction Notices* in reference to the craziness of Flagstaff. They often posted pictures in the studio or from their various travels.

After they returned from Bermuda, where they received the accolade of 'Best Unsigned Band', they were straight into the studio at Purple Universe to record their first full album. It mainly featured re-recordings of the best of the three EPs, with three new tunes thrown in. There was a little more production quality on the self-titled twelve-track album.

In America, the album charted in the Billboard 100 at number 32. It was quite an achievement for a debut rock act, but positions in alternative charts that focused more on rock were much higher. They hit the top five on iTunes and penetrated the British and European markets on the back of their US success. Things were rolling along great for them.

As for myself, I caught up with Eva back in New York New York. She was shocked beyond belief when she saw me return to the bar. I revealed my true feelings, telling her that I loved her too and that being with her was more important than the tour. Eva, being Eva, told me I was 'loco' for leaving, but she was secretly ecstatic at my romantic gesture.

I went back to San Diego to stay with her, and shortly after, she booked some time off work. Together we took a few weeks touring the length and breadth of the West Coast of America as per my initial plan.

We spent a few days in Sedona and Tucson on a separate occasion, where we stayed with Bobby and Tien. We were able to explore more of Sedona, and Eva fell in love with the place. She got on famously with our esteemed hosts in Tucson, who pampered us more than any 5-star hotel could.

My decision to stay in the States, coupled with the writing success I enjoyed documenting the Cutthroats' journey, led to doors opening. Anya had recommended me to her editor at Hell-A magazine when she heard I was hanging around. I became a frequent contributor for them, bringing a different cultural perspective to the West Coast music scene.

Jamie got over his initial disappointment of me bailing, leaving the Bermuda and New York part of the story a secretive, undocumented mystery. His first reaction was to send a replacement journalist, but Dee outright refused. This time, Ozzie didn't argue with her.

I still wrote for Sonic Bandwagon, and my status had been elevated off the back of the tour. I was inundated with emails from aspiring bands asking me to review their music for the site, and I was only too happy to help.

As well as reviewing albums, I had become a liaison over the pond to write articles and features on bands playing in the States. I tried to seek out the British ones in my area to give them a lift.

What I hadn't counted on when I began the journey into music was moving into radio. The contacts I'd made led to an offer from a local San Diego station, Pure FM. I'd never considered being a broadcaster before being offered the role. They had asked if I would be interested in hosting a weekly two-hour show that played all the best up-and-coming music. I jumped at the chance and called the show, 'The Roadhouse' after one of my favourite Doors songs.

I gained a modest stream of listeners, and it served as another string to the bow. I loved broadcasting and putting together playlists. Cutthroat Shambles were probably my most played band, despite trying not to be biased.

Music writing and the radio only took up so much time. There was one outstanding dream left to accomplish that I became obsessed with after the Cutthroats tour. It was an idea born out of a night in Sedona from a girl ploughing through a bottle of whisky.

I threw myself deeper into writing the Vegas story as a book. It proved to be an intense but rewarding experience. After several edits, drunken nights searching for inspiration, rewrites, and frustrations, I eventually found my way to a completed version that I (and Eva) was happy with. She had the honour of naming the book – 'Found in Vegas'. Her first suggestion, 'Fucking Vegas', may not have been quite as marketable.

Via the contacts I'd made in the industry and with the help of Anya, I was able to release the book through an independent publisher in California.

It was the greatest accomplishment of my life. Regardless of the level of sales, I learned that success was measured simply by doing and trying. I didn't want to die wondering without at least giving it a go. That was all that mattered. I was more than content with what I had and where I was.

Life with Eva had been everything I'd hoped for and more. My reason for prematurely leaving the tour was justified because of how happy I was. Dee was right. Home was a state of mind, and I really had found mine. The mantra I lived by after the Vegas trip over two years earlier was still a factor today: 'Reasons, Seasons, Lifetime'. Eva was a testimony to that. She was my fate, my destiny, and the light that was my whole reason for being.

I found myself striding through a lively city centre. The bitter cold and paralysing wind was a sensation I'd not experienced for so long.

Hearing the chatter of the people we passed, Eva commented, 'Everyone here sounds like you. They all look quite intimidating and walk funny.'

'This is Manchester, we do things differently here.' The quote from Tony Wilson suited the occasion.

'I like it. I love this city's vibe.'

'There's nowhere like it in the world.'

It was great to be back in Manchester and heading to a venue I loved - the Ritz. The trip was only a fleeting visit before we returned to San Diego. There was no way I could pass up the opportunity to see the Cutthroats play on home soil. It was also a chance to catch up with family and good friends I'd not seen in so long, some of whom had bought tickets to the show intending to meet up afterwards.

We reached the venue and picked up our VIP passes, flashing them to the security guard to enter the back of the stage.

We could hear the raucous ramblings of familiar voices booming through the door as we walked down the corridor.

I knocked.

'Come in,' a voice shouted.

I knocked again.

'Enter,' they said.

I knocked again, loudly.

The agitated voice came nearer the door. 'Come in! What the fuck's wrong...'

The door swung open, and Will stood with a can of beer. His face transformed. 'Ricky! Eva!' He launched at both of us and nearly knocked us over as a bit of his beer spilt to the floor. Kyle, Quince and Ozzie jumped up and offered us the same welcome.

Anya lurked behind the boys, and I joked, 'Shouldn't you be at the Greta Van Fleet gig at the Troubadour at the moment?'

'I've got someone else covering it for me. It's good to see you, Ricky. Loved the book by the way.'

'Thanks. I saw your review. Much appreciated. When did you get here?'

'I flew to Paris to catch that show five days ago and have been with the band ever since.'

'You and Kyle getting all serious then, I take it?'

She scratched her eye with her fourth finger on her left hand to reveal a rock the size of an iceberg.

'He proposed to me the night I arrived the sly romantic,' she revealed.

'You've got to be kidding! Congratulations!'

I shouted over to Kyle to congratulate him too. He lifted his beer in my direction.

I searched the room for Dee. She had remained seated, unperturbed by my arrival. Her devilish eyes rested upon me from a distance. She looked spectacular, every bit the famous superstar she now was. I weaved my way through to her.

'You think I'm gonna get up just for you, Hot Shot Writer? You're mistaken,' she said with a serious face.

'You never change, do you?'

She leapt up, approached Eva, and embraced her warmly. 'Come here, girl! How the fuck are you?'

'Oh, that's right. Go to her first,' I protested.

'Of course. Why wouldn't I?'

She released Eva and turned to me. 'I see you wrote that book finally,' she said.

'What did you think?'

'Meh. I'd have done better,' she smirked.

I moved to hug her and said, 'I'd only take that sort of feedback from you.'

'Hey. It's what I do. Don't want you getting a big head now.'

Eva stepped in, 'Oh, I won't allow that. Not while he's living with me.'

'Good to know he's in good hands.'

'In all seriousness, Hot Shot. I enjoyed it. Good job. I knew you could do it.'

'Thanks, Dee. It means a lot. It was your idea after all.'

'Does that mean I get a commission?'

'I think you do alright without that royalty check.'

'Do better if I fired these assholes,' she joked.

'Annoying you again, are they?'

'You try spending every waking moment of a huge tour with them. I need a Sedona to escape too.'

'I hear you.'

Ozzie grabbed my attention, 'Ricky, I want you to meet someone. This is Mia.'

'Nice to meet you, Mia.' It then dawned on me. 'Mia? As in, your old flame, Mia?'

'That's right,' Ozzie confirmed.

'Well, that's a surprise. What happened?'

'I was inspired by what you did in the States.'

'I thought you couldn't go down that road?'

'Well, someone told me to get a grip, so I went for it. Took me a few months like.'

'I'm made up for you, Ozzie.'

He brought me up to speed. Ozzie had decided to risk it and messaged Mia. She had been single for four years after the breakdown of a long-term relationship. She had never stopped loving Ozzie but was too scared to contact him and find out if he was in a relationship and happy. I guess the lesson was to take that step and find out. Although she still lived in London, and he was based in Manchester/New York/touring, they were taking it slow and giving the long-distance relationship a chance.

We headed out for food over the road to Gorilla, where the band's fame became more noticeable as fans recognised them and requested pictures.

Dee asked me whether I'd heard about Lynwood. Working closely within the Los Angeles scene, I *had* heard. It turned out that the #MeToo campaign caught up with him, and he was facing charges. The label was in disarray too, so it looked like the band had dodged a bullet. Fortunately, Ozzie had advised Purple Universe to look at Winachi, and they had duly signed them up.

I had seen Elsie and Tony once, when they played Los Angeles and invited me up to cover the show and spend a long weekend with them. Meeting up with them was one of the wildest experiences of my life, which made me wince every time I was reminded of it. I had threatened to reveal the details of that fateful weekend if I was ever asked to write their biography.

Back at the Ritz, The Cutthroats took to the stage and ripped into their overdue homecoming show after what had been an extensive European tour and stint in the US. The place was brimming with bloodthirsty lovers of unadulterated rock 'n' roll, paying homage to the new heroes of the Manchester music scene.

Dee, burgundy cowboy hat still in tow, said that it was a homecoming for the musicians, but Manchester was her adopted home. Her declaration of love for our city was well-received.

The band raced through and rocked their hits, throwing in a couple of newer ones that were going to feature on the second album. These included 'Sedona Paradise', 'Deserve', which sounded like it was aimed at Lynwood, judging by the lyrics, and 'Michelle', an incredibly moving tribute to Dee's late friend. She never explained the song's meaning to the crowd.

The gig was phenomenal. Afterwards, we celebrated our reunion properly at the after-party. We sat in the Lions Den on Deansgate Mews. I spent much of the night catching up with the good friends I'd been to Vegas with: Turner, Ian, and Johnny. They had attended the show with other friends, and it was great to see them all again after so long.

Later, I found myself sitting with Eva and Dee in the far corner, away from everyone else. I nursed a glass of Woodford as we spoke about the future.

Dee revealed that the Cutthroats were finishing off the European tour with the remaining few UK dates. Then they had a couple of weeks off before they were due to record the second album in New York. Eva invited her to stay with us while she was off, but Dee didn't commit to an answer. They were being lined up for an extensive coast to coast US tour, so I promised to see them when they headed west.

'These Are the Days of Our Lives' by Queen played through the sound system, providing the perfect tonic for us to reflect on our shared past. Dee asked me, 'What now for you, Hot Shot? You got the girl. The book's selling well. You still write your reviews and blogs, and your radio show is growing. So, what's next?'

'Are you going to tell her, or shall I?' Eva said.

'Tell me what?' Dee leant forward inquisitively.

'I've been working on something that I've only told Eva about.'

Eva excitedly intervened, 'It's fabulous so far. I've read a snippet.'

'What is it then?' Dee asked.

'Do you remember in Sedona when you gave me the idea of writing about my Vegas trip?'

'Yeah.'

'And then afterwards, you said I should write a second book about the US tour with you guys.'

'Yeah...'

'And... you also promised that, if I wrote it, you'd play at the book launch?'

'Yeah...'

'Well... do you do mates rates for gigs?'

A MESSAGE
FROM N.J. CARTNER

Thank you for reading *Lost in Manchester, Tourin' America*. I truly hope you enjoyed it. Reviews are incredibly important to self-published authors. I would be extremely grateful if you took the time to post a short review on Amazon or Goodreads etc. to help spread the word.

Your review can help the book get noticed.

ABOUT THE AUTHOR

Born and raised in Manchester and heavily influenced by music, film and literature, I've aspired to work in and around the creative arts since my teenage years. When I hit my late twenties, life took a fortunate turn and allowed me to fulfil those dreams. I was invited to write for a local online music fanzine, naturally jumping at the chance to review and interview underground bands on the rock music scene. Over the years, my involvement with music continued to progress, and I co-hosted and co-ran the Sonic Bandwagon radio show on Stockport radio station, Pure 107.8FM.

I've always been drawn to novels that explore coming of age as part of the theme. The likes of Rex Pickett and Nick Hornby are personal favourites. They capture the idea of ordinary people thrust into dark times, who eventually come through adversity improved by the experience. But I'm also attracted to the extremities and intrigue of writers such as Hunter S Thompson and Charles Bukowski and their use of brutal honesty and pushing boundaries into the darker side of life. It's their ingenuity, coupled with their depravity and rebelliousness which hooks me.

My involvement in music and radio led me to meet Mohawk Radio, who I became great friends with. That friendship eventually resulted in being asked to tour with them when they travelled to America for a mini tour. 'Lost in Manchester, Tourin' America' is the book born out of that adventure, although most of the events in this book never happened.

ACKNOWLEDGEMENTS

Completing my second novel has been another thoroughly enjoyable journey, and there are several people I'd like to thank for helping make this dream possible.

First of all, I'd like to take the opportunity to thank everyone who attended the book launch for my debut novel and everyone who purchased a copy. It's made this whole adventure worthwhile.

I'd like to thank my family for always supporting me and indirectly influencing the soundtrack to the book through their tastes in music that have inspired me over the years.

To Sheridana! Again, thanks for being so instrumental in inspiring the spiritual nature of the book, influencing some of the characters, and providing parts of the dialogue and in-jokes. You have been an inspiration from the start and the true embodiment of 'Reasons, Seasons, Lifetime'.

Thank you to my close friends. Without our history and warped humour, many of the more comical elements of the book would never have come to mind.

Thanks to Stret from Purple Universe for helping to provide more insight into the business side of the music industry and for reading through in the early days. Similar thanks to Maddy Hunter and Kim Hawes for advice around the business side of music.

Thanks to Gemma Gervis for reading through a later draft and giving extensive feedback and suggestions.

Thank you, once again, to Stacey Knowles for designing the artwork for the front and back cover and subsequent tickets and posters. I'm overwhelmed by the time and effort you've put into it, and the quality of the work is nothing short of genius – just as it was for the first book. To Matt Johnston, a huge thanks for helping with the website, for being my photographer at gigs over the years, and for providing the photo in the About the Author section.

Thank you to Michael Knaggs for the invaluable advice around book signings. If it wasn't for you, the debut novel would've sold to fewer people, and I may have lost heart to write the sequel.

A special thanks to Mohawk Radio for inviting me on the trip to America that gave birth to this story. I'm forever in your debt as it was the greatest adventure of my life. Thanks for allowing me to attribute your music to Cutthroat Shambles. The same goes for all the bands who've allowed me to use their music in the book – Winachi, Jess Kemp, Gorilla Riot, Twisted Wheel, The Blinders and Matt Fryers.

Regards Mohawk Radio and Winachi, I would like to clarify that the events of this trip and the characters involved do not represent the band and what actually happened. Apart from the scenery and the places we visited, this is mostly a work of fiction.

To Judy Forrister, who I've put through the paces again editing this love child of mine. I cannot express my gratitude in words for the help, advice, encouragement and support you've given me. Your huge contribution will never be forgotten. Hopefully, the editing this time wasn't as strenuous as the first book.

Also, a huge thank you to those people I met in the States. However small or large a role our meeting played in the overall story, it served as inspiration one way or another. Special thanks to Mickey and Noomie in Tucson and Mucho and Electric Parlor in Los Angeles. Fantastic people.

I'd also like to thank Hammad and the team at Book Printing UK for helping with the self-publish process.

To Mary O'Meara – an amazing writer. I wish you were still here. The world needed to read more of your work.

And just a huge thank you in general to everyone involved - I'm overwhelmed by people's feedback, reviews, and support in helping me achieve a lifelong ambition...again.

And finally, I'd like to pay tribute to Anya Grace Robbie Ottley for her bravery and incredible attitude in the face of adversity. She is an inspiration to all of us!

LOST IN MANCHESTER, TOURIN' AMERICA SOUNDTRACK

Fleetwood Mac - *The Chain*
Neil Young - *Heart of Gold*
Bruce Springsteen - *Born to Run*
The Coasters - *Down in Mexico*
Jess Kemp - *Camden*
Rod Stewart - *Hot Legs*
Velvet Underground - *Venus in Furs*
AC/DC - *Givin' the Dog a Bone*
Creedence Clearwater Revival - *Green River*
Thunderclap Newman - *Something in the Air*
Aerosmith - *Sweet Emotion*
The Beatles - *With a Little Help from My Friends*
Twisted Wheel - *You Stole the Sun*
Seahorses - *Love is the Law*
Slade - *Everyday*
The Undertones - *Teenage Kicks*
Rival Sons - *Pressure and Time*
Chris Stapleton - *Traveller*
Chris Stapleton - *Parachute*
Israel Nash - *Rain Plans*
The Last Internationale - *Wanted Man*
Black Mountain - *Space to Bakersfield*
Dope Lemon - *Honey Bones*
Joe Walsh - *Turn to Stone*

The Charlatans - *Opportunity Three*
The Pretenders - *Brass in Pocket*
Elvis Presley - *Polk Salad Annie (Live)*
Oasis - *Talk Tonight*
Black Rebel Motorcycle Club - *Beat the Devil's Tattoo*
Curtis Stigers - *This Life*
Curtis Stigers - *John the Revelator*
Matt Fryers - *Last Words*
Matt Fryers - *Searching For Answers*
Frankie Goes to Hollywood - *Relax*
Tears for Fears - *Everybody Wants to Rule the World*
Simple Minds - *Don't You Forget About Me*
Michael Jackson - *Beat It*
Bronski Beat - *Smalltown Boy*
Kenny Loggins - *Danger Zone*
REO Speedwagon - *Keep on Loving You*
Visage - *Fade to Grey*
Gerard McMahon - *Cry Little Sister*
Richard Ashcroft - *They Don't Own Me*
Echo & The Bunnymen - *The Killing Moon*
Wanda Jackson - *Funnel of Love*
Black Sabbath - *War Pigs*
Electric Light Orchestra - *Evil Woman*
Stevie Nicks - *I Can't Wait*
Alanis Morissette - *Thank You*
Pink Floyd - *Shine on You Crazy Diamond*
America - *A Horse with No Name*
Elton John - *Tiny Dancer*
Houndmouth - *Sedona*
Muddy Waters - *Champagne and Reefer*
Elton John - *Rocket Man*
Howlin Wolf - *Smokestack Lightnin*
Simon & Garfunkel - *El Condor Pasa*
Carole King - *It's Too Late*
Mamas and Papas - *California Dreaming*
Beth Hart - *My California*

Albert Hammond - *It Never Rains in California*
Robert Plant - *29 Palms*
Led Zeppelin - *When the Levee Breaks*
ZZ Top - *Gimme All Your Lovin*
Josh Turner - *I'm Your Man*
Foo Fighters - *Best of You*
Journey - *Don't Stop Believin'*
The Sex Pistols - *God Save the Queen*
Matthew Southern Comfort - *Woodstock*
Doors - *L.A. Woman*
Billy Squier - *The Stroke*
Motörhead - *Overkill*
Guns N Roses - *November Rain*
Jane's Addiction - *Superhero*
Doors - *Love Street*
Winachi - *Funky But Chic*
Harold Faltermeyer - *Axel F*
Beach Boys - *California Girls*
America - *Ventura Highway*
Janis Joplin - *Piece of My Heart*
Mötley Crüe - *Home Sweet Home*
Grandmaster Flash - *The Message*
Ennio Morricone - *The Good, The Bad, and The Ugly*
Neil Diamond - *America*
Rolling Stones - *Moonlight Mile*
Led Zeppelin - *Going to California*
Doors - *The End*
Joy Division - *Atmosphere*
AC/DC - *It's a Long Way to the Top (If You Wanna Rock 'n' Roll)*
Peter Gabriel - *Solsbury Hill*
The Blinders - *Gotta Get Through*
David Bowie - *Heroes*
Bread - *Make it With You*
The Byrds - *Turn! Turn! Turn!*
Queen - *These Are the Days of Our Lives*

CUTTHROAT SHAMBLES
TRACKS INC COVERS

Mohawk Radio - *Rock N Roll Heaven*
Mohawk Radio - *Oblivion*
Mohawk Radio - *Two Million Heart Beats*
Mohawk Radio - *Curious Morality*
Metallica - *Enter Sandman*
Mohawk Radio - *Lifetime Sunshine*
Mohawk Radio - *On Your Knees*
Mohawk Radio - *Even*
Fleetwood Mac - *Gold Dust Woman*
Mohawk Radio - *Million Lights*
Mohawk Radio - *Ready to Love*
The Eagles - *Hotel California*
The Cranberries - *Zombie*
Bon Jovi - *Blaze of Glory*
Mohawk Radio - *Eyes Wide Shut*
AC/DC - *Highway to Hell*
Mohawk Radio - *Deserve*
Mohawk Radio - *Michelle*

LOST IN MANCHESTER, FOUND IN VEGAS SYNOPSIS

If you enjoyed 'Lost in Manchester, Tourin' America' but haven't had the chance to read the preceding novel, 'Lost in Manchester, Found in Vegas', to see how the story began, then you can read a brief synopsis below. It is available at all usual outlets.

Ricky Lever's life is thrown into despair following the break up of his long-term relationship, and with it comes the realisation that life is in danger of passing him by.

Desperate for answers, he embarks on a soul-searching trip to Las Vegas with three of his oldest friends, hoping that a new direction in life will be revealed to him.

In the midst of the excitement, madness and ecstasy of the city's atmosphere, life changing revelations prove to be a little harder to come by than Ricky hoped, and he is pushed to take the ultimate gamble.

Bringing the city of Las Vegas to life with a killer soundtrack running throughout, this uniquely told coming of age story twists and turns through euphoric highs and emotive lows.

From excessive gambling to heavy drinking, strip clubs to the desert, the biggest hotels to the lowliest bars, ride along for the trip of a lifetime as these four ordinary lads from Manchester make the most of the extraordinary world of Las Vegas.

Seen through the eyes of Ricky, 'Lost in Manchester, Found in Vegas' is a hilarious, honest, and emotional journey showing how six nights in Sin City can influence a man at a crossroads in life.

A SELECTION OF AMAZON REVIEWS FOR 'LOST IN MANCHESTER, FOUND IN VEGAS'

Brilliantly well-written and makes compelling reading as we follow the hero's journey to exorcise his demons.

What a book! Drags you in and you feel as though you are there! One of the best books I have read in a long while!

You will laugh, cry, fist pump and be in absolute awe as this incredible adventure unfolds

Brilliantly well written, hard to put down, and I now find myself impatiently waiting for the second book... a fantastic read.

A really well written book. The story was funny, sad, interesting and had me hooked by the end of chapter one.

Once I started reading this book I couldn't put it down, really enjoyed It. It has a great storyline and a brilliant soundtrack.

It's endearing, entertaining & funny. Having not had the opportunity to go to Vegas, it was a great insight.

A great read, I loved the music and Manchester references both of which I could relate to.

What a book, what a read! I haven't been able to put it down since I bought it about 10 days back.

What a great book! Well written! I was laughing out loud!

Loved this book!!! Brought out all sorts of emotions. Kept me enthralled and intrigued all the way through.

A saucy, rampaging tale of drunkenness, desperation and ultimately hope. It's Vegas with a Manchester chaser.